Beautiful at All Seasons

Beautiful at All Seasons

Southern Gardening and Beyond

with Elizabeth Lawrence

ELIZABETH LAWRENCE

EDITED BY ANN L. ARMSTRONG
AND LINDIE WILSON

Duke University Press
Durham and London
2007

Printed in the United States
of America on acid-free paper ∞
Designed by Amy Ruth Buchanan
Typeset in Fournier by Keystone
Typesetting, Inc.
Library of Congress Cataloging-in-
Publication Data appear on the last
printed page of this book.

To Bev Armstrong,

and our beloved cats

Paku and Beau,

who helped

every keystroke

of the way

Contents

Illustrations follow page 120

xiii *Acknowledgments*

xv *Introduction*

xxi *Note to the Reader*

ONE *Seasonal Flowers*

1 Garden Resolutions

3 Flowers for Christmas Time

5 Flowers Greet the New Year

7 Winter Flowers

8 The Green Winter

9 A Hard Winter

11 Bamboo

13 Storm Damage

14 The Merry Month of May

16 Tender Perennials for Hot-Weather Gardens

18 Flowers in the Fall Border

19 Fragrance in the Garden

21 Fall Additions to the Border

22 Sow Hardy Annual Seeds During September

24 Planting Annuals in Autumn

25 Late-Blooming Flowers

27 The Gardening Year Is Just Beginning

TWO *Perennials and Annuals*

29 Planting in Relays
31 Badge of Gardening Includes Black Knees
33 Gardening Surprises
34 The Law of Supply and Demand
36 Variegated Foliage
38 Selections for the Rock Garden
39 Tropical Plants
41 Annuals
43 Sweet Peas
45 Peony
46 Tree Peonies and Others
48 Clematis also Flowers in Shade
49 Beautiful Lilies
51 *Asteromoea mongolica—Kalimeris pinnatifida*
53 Hellebores
54 The Christmas Rose and Other Hellebores
56 Giridlian . . . A Master of Plants
58 Night-Blooming Cereus
59 The Dividends of Fall Planting
61 Savannah Lands of East Carolina
62 Petasites

THREE *Bulbs, Corms, and Tubers*

65 Planting Bulbs, Corms, and Tubers
66 Bulbs Through the Seasons
68 Some Early Spring Bulbs
70 Daffodils Need Early Start
72 Specialty Bulbs
73 Crown Imperials
75 *Lycoris radiata*
77 Amaryllis Family
78 The Surprise Lily
79 Lilies Grow Where None Were
81 Garden Casualties

FOUR *Trees and Shrubs*

83 Planting for Ice Storms
85 Plants for Parking Strips
86 Flowering Trees for the City
88 Street Trees
90 Trees with Colored Bark
92 Witch Hazels
93 Flowering Cherries
95 Serviceberries and Sloes
97 Dogwoods
98 Buckeyes
100 Eucalyptus
102 Honey Locust
103 Osmanthus
105 Hollies
106 Conifers
108 Firs and Cedars
110 Flowering Shrubs
111 March-Flowering Shrubs
113 Viburnums and Other Flowering Shrubs
114 June-Flowering Shrubs
116 Viburnums
118 Pyracanthas
119 Nandinas
121 Hydrangeas
122 Sasanquas
124 *Camellia saluenensis*
125 E. A. Bowles's Lunatics

FIVE *Vegetables and Herbs, Climbers and Creepers*

129 Fall Vegetables
130 Two Vegetable Gardens
132 Mrs. Hobbs and Her Herbs
134 Sweet Woodruff
136 Dandelions

137 Vines Are Useful Tools
139 Smilax
140 Clematis Hybrids
142 Akebia and *Rosa banksiae*
144 Ground Covers
146 Ground Covers Pose Problems
148 Tiny Creepers

SIX *Gardeners and Gardens*

151 Wing Haven
152 Importance of Garden Details
154 Steps in Your Garden
156 Walks and Paths
158 Terraces and Patios
159 Water in the Garden
161 Mr. Krippendorf's Garden
162 Physic Garden at the Country Doctor Museum
164 Mr. Busbee's Garden
166 A Visit to Italy's Oldest Botanic Garden
167 Colette's Mother's Garden
169 The Splendor of Royal Gardens
171 Gotelli's Collection of Dwarf Conifers
172 The Scented Garden
174 The Gardens of a Soldier's Wife
176 Pioneer Seedsmen
177 Young Belgian Guided Southern Horticulture
179 Meet Caroline Dormon
181 She Talks to the Birds
182 The Hunt Arboretum

SEVEN *Gods, Legends, and Rituals*

185 The Gods of the Garden
187 The Ash, a Symbol in History
189 The Tale of the Magical Hawthorn Tree
190 The Holy Thorn Blooms for Royalty

192 The Christian Year Parallels the Garden Year
194 Holiday Wreaths
196 The Advent Wreath
197 Legend and Lore of the Christmas Tree
199 International Christmas Trees
201 The Flowers of the Trinity
203 The Flowers of Passiontide
205 The Story of the Passion Flower
206 Rituals of the Palms
208 Rogation Days—The Blessing of the Crops

EIGHT *Bits and Pieces*

211 Asafetida
213 Feeding the Birds
214 Honey
216 Organic Gardening
218 Pruning
219 Pruning Should Be Done Every Day
221 Historic Flower Arrangements
223 Bouquet Carried Messages
224 Pomanders
226 Creatures Add to a Garden

229 *Index*

Acknowledgments

We are deeply indebted to Emily Wilson, Roy Dicks, Ken Druse, Nancy Goodwin, Peter Loewer, Judy Goldman, and Allen Lacy for their counsel and support. Allan Armitage, Larry Mellichamp, Bobby Ward, and Doug Ruhren were invaluable for their help with nomenclature and general assistance. We are indebted to Warren Way III and his sister Elizabeth Rogers, literary executors of the Elizabeth Lawrence estate, for enabling us to republish Elizabeth Lawrence's columns, and to the librarians in the Carolina Room of the Charlotte Public Library, whose patience we tested with endless questions about the microfilm machines. Finally, we are grateful to Reynolds Smith, the executive editor for Duke University Press, whose encouragement, wit, and enthusiasm greatly facilitated the completion of this work, and to Katharine Baker, assistant managing editor, whose patience and skilled editing expedited the publishing of this collection.

Introduction

When I purchased the house and garden of Elizabeth Lawrence on February 11, 1986, I did not have the slightest inkling of what lay ahead for me. I knew of Elizabeth Lawrence, of course, but the garden had been neglected for two years by another owner, and on that cold and dismal winter day it was covered with invasive vines and weeds. Recently, there had been a record freeze of minus five degrees. Scores of plants had succumbed to the frost and now littered the garden. I had been told that very few of her treasures remained, and it certainly seemed unlikely that many could have survived.

However, having an intractable passion for gardening, and inspired by the appearance of the golden flowers of the *Adonis amurensis* shimmering in the shadow of the pines at the back of the garden, I set about the daunting task of gardening in this "new" garden. Soon many other horticultural surprises struggled out from underneath the thick mat of ivy and periwinkle. Winter aconite and snowdrops smiled at me along with Elizabeth Lawrence's beloved Algerian iris, *Crocus tomasinianus*, and daffodils. As the work of pruning and the removal of vines and weeds progressed, even more treasures appeared. Among these was a gorgeous violet-blue Japanese iris, *Iris ensata*, that bloomed with Miss Lawrence's many yellow daylilies. It is a wonder that this moisture-loving iris continues to flourish in this dry garden.

Visitors from both near and far also began to appear, and I soon realized that my garden was not to be just for my pleasure. This responsibility began to weigh heavily. However, loving gardening as I do, I have not let this responsibility diminish the joy I feel when in the garden.

The opening of Elizabeth Lawrence's garden gate has led me to a world of gardening friends and acquainted me with many new and exciting plants.

I have met many of these plants both in her garden and in her books. During her lifetime, four of her books were published. They were *A Southern Garden*, *Lob's Wood*, *The Little Bulbs*, and *Gardens in Winter*, of which the latter three were written in Charlotte. *The Little Bulbs* and *Gardens in Winter* were filled with direct references to existing plants in the garden. They became my constant companions. Four more Lawrence books were published after her death in 1985, and with their publication many more garden mysteries were solved for me. *Through the Garden Gate*, edited by Bill Neal and published in 1990, was a collection of some of her garden columns written for the *Charlotte Observer*. This book was a rich source of information, and caused me to realize that many more tidbits of horticultural information must certainly be in the remaining columns. Thus it was with great excitement and anticipation that I began the project of the editing of this book with Ann Armstrong. I learned even more about my garden during the course of our research.

A healthy stand of bamboo grows outside my living room window. In the article "Bamboo," Miss Lawrence identifies it as *Phyllostachy* × *aurea*, the golden bamboo, and she goes on to write, "Dearly as I love this bamboo, it is more trouble than anything else in the garden." I definitely concur! After years of struggling with it, I have finally succeeded in containing it with a barrier sunk two feet into the earth. Troublesome as it has been, I would not give it up, as it is a joy in the garden. In *Gardens in Winter*, Miss Lawrence writes, "All winter the green leaves rustle outside my window, and the low winter sun sends slender shadows into the room." The cardinals still sleep in the bamboo in the winter, and in spring, it is their favorite place to nest.

Reading the article about planting the parking strip in front of the house in Charlotte was fascinating. It made me very sad to learn of Miss Lawrence's love of the pear, *Pyrus calleryana*, planted next to the driveway, because a few years ago it had to be taken down. It had become a dangerous tree, regularly shedding large limbs across my driveway entrance. I still miss its lovely and profuse display of white flowers in early March. Of the trees she described in the article, ironically only the *Malus* × *miromalus*, the midget crabapple, remains in the parking strip. She writes, "The small round yellow fruits are borne very freely and are rather a nuisance. I think I may replace this when I find something I like better." Evidently she never found a suitable replacement. The handsome quince, *Cydonia oblonga*, with its beautiful exfoliating bark, also grows in the parking strip but strangely is not mentioned in this article.

In another article, Miss Lawrence writes of her *Camellia saluenensis*. With its early bloom, beginning in October, and lasting for many months, it has always been a favorite of mine. It has reached treelike proportions, and continues to bloom through the worst of winter weather. She writes that the blossoms are "single, and delicately modeled with a slender column of pale yellow stamens. The petals are ivory with a flush of wine." According to Miss Lawrence, it was planted in 1965, more than four decades ago.

I was thrilled to find many wonderful bulbs planted by Elizabeth Lawrence growing in the garden. In the article "Green Winter," I discovered that in February 1962, she found "two violet flowers of *Crocus imperati* in the melting snow." These same lovely bulbs continue to delight me with their radiant blossoms each winter. The identity of the summer snowflakes in the garden has been a puzzle for me because their bloom period seemed to go on for many months. In the chapter "Bulbs," that species is discussed in detail, and I am now delighted to know that it is *Leucojum* var. *pulchellum*, which begins its early bloom in January. She wrote that this variety blooms with crocus and daffodils as well as the tulips, and that she once found a flower on New Year's Day. How remarkable it is that these bulbs have survived since at least 1960 when this article was written! After living in the house for twelve years, I was surprised with the discovery of the lady tulip, *Tulipa clusiana*, blooming in one of the sunny borders. And recently, in autumn, charming pale white crocus, their identity as yet unknown, have appeared.

One of the most glorious sights in the garden occurs in late winter or early spring when three magnolias, *Magnolia denudata*, *Magnolia* × *veitchii* and *Magnolia* × *soulangiana* 'Lennei', bloom in unison. The magnolias are planted in a row at the back of the garden behind the pool. They are very clever about eluding the grip of frost, most often waiting until it is safe to display sweet-scented, deep pink and white flowers. The air is filled with their perfume, and then they drop their petals, creating a beautiful, pink path of fragrant blossoms under the pines.

In the article "Walks and Paths" Miss Lawrence writes, "In my garden a width of six feet seemed right for the main path which is over a hundred feet long. It is slightly tapered, with the beginning widened to six feet six inches, and the end narrowed to five feet six inches. This is supposed to make the vista seem longer than it really is." While the garden is small (70 feet by 225 feet), its center path seems quite long and grand, and it is her excellent design that makes it seem so.

In the small study of the house in Charlotte, I work at a long desk in front of a large picture window with a full view of the garden. While working late at night, editing Elizabeth Lawrence's garden articles in the room where so many of them were written, I frequently felt her presence peering over my shoulder.

Lindie Wilson

This book collects a number of essays written by Elizabeth Lawrence for the *Charlotte Observer*. Leaving her well-known and loved garden in Raleigh, Elizabeth Lawrence and her mother moved to Charlotte in 1948, where Elizabeth designed the house and garden where they were to live. On August 11, 1957, when Elizabeth was fifty-three, her Sunday gardening column, *Through the Garden Gate*, appeared in the *Charlotte Observer* for the first time. She wrote 720 columns, the last of which was published June 20, 1971.

Bill Neal, a friend and fellow gardener, edited 142 of her columns, publishing them in 1990 as the book *Through the Garden Gate*. Lindie Wilson and I realized that some fascinating columns remained unavailable to most readers. We spent long afternoons peering over microfilms in the Charlotte Public Library. They were pleasure-filled hours reading Elizabeth Lawrence's work. Even after we eliminated the columns that pertained to flower shows, plant laundry lists and the like, many captivating and insightful articles remained. We gathered 132 articles for this book, choosing to organize them by subject matter rather than chronologically. We have used brackets to change plant names to conform to present nomenclature.

Long before I met her and her garden, and while I was building my own garden, I had fallen under the spell of Elizabeth Lawrence's writing when I read the 1942 edition of *A Southern Garden*. Reading these articles renewed that spell. Elizabeth Lawrence shared her ideas, knowledge, opinions, and her garden with her friends, visitors, and the world at large through her books and articles, correspondence, and garden columns. Her well-furnished mind ranged over a vast number of interests, as you will find in these essays.

Her garden was her laboratory, where she tested the hardiness, beauty, and suitability of a plant. "Dates given in catalogues and magazines seldom apply to our part of the country," she wrote. We were constantly amazed that many of the plants Elizabeth grew and wrote about have only recently become available in our nurseries.

Many of her friends helped her make her garden through their correspondence and advice. In these essays you will meet many of them, for they frequently populated her newspaper column. Among them were Eddie and Elizabeth Clarkson, close neighbors and owners of Wing Haven; Hannah Withers, a knowledgeable gardener and traveling companion; Linda Lamm, a great friend and driving force in the North Carolina Wild Flower Society (recently renamed the North Carolina Native Plant Society) and the Herb Society; Lamm's sister Laura Braswell; Dr. Walter and Helen Mayer, good friends and fellow gardeners; and Dr. Herbert Hechenbleikner, a distinguished horticulturalist. Soon after she began her columns, she published *The Little Bulbs*, in which she introduced her readers to Mr. Carl Krippendorf and his Ohio garden. *Gardens in Winter* was published in 1961 and illustrated by another close friend, Caroline Dormon. After Mr. Krippendorf's death she wrote *Lob's Wood*, a tribute to her dear friend and his garden.

Her passion and strong opinions for plants and gardens are evident in much of her writing. She wrote unblinkingly about some: "Getting rid of poor plants is as important as seeking out the best. Nearly every garden in the South has a large ungainly Christmas honeysuckle, *Lonicera fragrantissima*, that is dull at its best, shabby at its worst, and never the least bit beautiful, even when in full bloom. . . . This, I hasten to say, is not the fault of the nurserymen. It is the fault of gardeners, who should learn to know good plants and to demand them."

Her writings revealed a deep knowledge of centuries of literature, mythology, the church, gardens, and gardeners. Elizabeth's library was exceptional. She was a prodigious reader and an inveterate correspondent with an immense number of gardeners, nurserymen, farm wives (who often had plants and seeds for sale), and writers. She kept vast cardboard files of three-by-five-inch file cards, on which all manner of information was stored. Readers of these essays cannot help but be impressed with her vast knowledge on so many subjects, and realize that these essays were written long before the existence of personal computers, the internet, and search engines.

Her strong personal voice, warmth, and enthusiasm for her various subjects emanated from her weekly columns as an increasingly devoted and enthusiastic audience reached for the Sunday paper to share some time with Elizabeth Lawrence. We sincerely hope you enjoy these articles and find them as delightful, fascinating, and informative as we have.

Ann L. Armstrong

Note to the Reader

The scientific names of some plants have changed since these essays were first published. In such cases we have included the present nomenclature in brackets immediately following the plant name. Our sources of reference were *The Royal Horticultural Society Dictionary of Gardening*, *Royal Horticultural Society Plant Finder*, *Manual of Woody Landscape Plants* by Michael A. Dirr, and *Herbaceous Perennial Plants* by Allan M. Armitage.

ONE

Seasonal Flowers

GARDEN RESOLUTIONS

On New Year's Day I always make good garden resolutions. First, I resolve to catch the weeds as they appear, for as John Evelyn warned in the *Kalendarium Hortense* (1729), "Neglecting it til they are ready to sow themselves, you do but stir and prepare for a more numerous crop of these Garden-Sins." During a mild January, the weeds come up very fast, and unless they are got rid of they crowd out the seedlings of fall-sown or self-sown annuals.

Then I promise myself that I will prune at the proper time; that I will cut back the firethorn before, not after, it flowers; that I will cut some limbs from *Magnolia* × *soulangiana* 'Lennei' before it ruins *Cotoneaster lacteus*; and I make up my mind to cut back the wild grape before it grows into the double-flowering English bird cherry, and to paint the stumps with that stuff that is supposed to kill woody plants. Each summer I let the grape get ahead of me. Then, when it is pulled out of the tree, it breaks the delicate and brittle branches.

This year I mean to start in January to order the things I have had on my list for several years. One is the *Crinum* 'Herald' which Mr. Giridlian says is the first to bloom, and the finest he has ever grown. It might be the finest, for it is by far the most expensive. Another plant on my list is *cenizo* [*Leucophyllum frutescens*]. Dr. Solomosy sent me the name of a Texas nursery, Flowerland, that grows it in cans so I want to give it another trial. This nursery also has (in gallon cans) *Eucalyptus rostrata* [*E. camaldulensis*], which is considered one of the hardiest species. Last March it was killed to the ground in my garden, but came up again in the late spring. I have it on the northern side of the house and I am sure it would do even better with a southern exposure.

Flowerland also lists *Tecoma stans*, a tropical shrub, called the yellow elder. As it has proved root hardy at the Hodges Gardens in Louisiana, I think it might be given a trial here. When I wrote to the nursery to inquire about it, the manager, Mr. Ishmael, answered that he would be pleased to send it this way if I wished, but added, "We would be guilty of negligence if we failed to tell you that this plant will freeze in your area." I shall tell Mr. Ishmael that he will not be blamed if it does freeze, for at least I shall have had the pleasure of seeing it and growing it for a summer.

Plants whose hardiness is unproved should not go out until April, but I find that time slips up on me if I don't order them at the beginning of the year. It is better to leave the nurseryman to do the remembering, unless the nurseryman is Wyndham Hayward, and then you had better not order until you are ready for the plants. I mean to try to get some rare amaryllis out of him in the spring.

This January, I have added a new resolution to the old promises to get behind my garden sins; the new one is to take time to enjoy my garden. It has been a long time since I sat in it with a book that I didn't read, and never gave a thought to weeds or watering or plants overgrown by other plants. I have always found it hard to reconcile a resolution to do nothing with one to do everything and do it ahead of time, but I used to find it easy to put my sins and negligences out of my mind. This year I am going to try to recover the talent for leaving things undone. I shall remember the "merry credulous days" and remind myself that

> in this dourest, sorest
> Age man's eye has looked upon,
> Death to fauns and death to fays,
> Still the dogwood dares to raise—
> Healthy tree, with trunk and root—
> Ivory bowls that bear no fruit,
> (Though I always did wonder what Edna St. Vincent Millay meant by saying that dogwood bears no fruit; what does she think the berries are?)
> And the starlings and the jays—
> Birds that cannot even sing—
> Dare to come again in spring!

January 1, 1961

FLOWERS FOR CHRISTMAS TIME

> Some say that ever 'gainst that season comes
> Wherein our Saviour's birth is celebrated,
> The bird of dawning singeth all night long. (Hamlet)

Stories of singing birds and bursting buds on the night of the Nativity scarcely seem miraculous when we have one of our warm winters. As I write this, on the third Sunday in Advent, there is more bloom than usual in my garden and the neighborhood.

The winter flowers are early and the spring flowers way ahead of themselves. In my garden there is more than a sprinkling of tiny flowers on *Spirea angustifolia* [*Sorbaria tomentosa* var. *angustifolia*], on the way home from church I saw the yellow bells of forsythia and, for a while, I was afraid buds of the oriental magnolias were going to burst their fur coats.

Samuel Cooke, in an old English garden book, writes, "When October and November are warm and rainy, January and February are frosty and cold but if October and November be snow and frost, then January and February are open and mild." In general I have found it true that warm weather before Christmas is followed by cold weather afterward and vice versa.

This is the earliest date I have known for *Prunus mume* and I have kept records for more than twenty years. The few times it has flowered before the New Year, it has come late in December but this year Elizabeth Clarkson called to say that the first flower of the white mume was open, and as she said it, I looked out the window and saw scraps of pink on my mume.

Viburnum fragrans [*V. farreri*] also bloomed earlier than ever before. Since the fourteenth of November, there have been small, light, corymbs of creamy, fragrant pink-tipped flowers. The flowers are said to smell of heliotrope, and they really do. Next to *V. fragrans* is *Osmanthus fragrans*. Both of these went on blooming even when the temperature dropped to eighteen degrees. But the camellias have never been the same since the morning I found ice on the pool. Even the flowers of *Camellia* 'Berenice Boddy' are yellow in the center. However, the little wine-tinted flowers of *Camellia saluenensis* are still pretty, though not as large as they were when they came into bloom in mid-November. They are cup-shaped or, perhaps I should say, chalice-shaped, and about the size of California poppies. They are delicately but definitely fragrant. A nice little shrub that came in a gallon can from Mr. Coleman has bloomed well its second season, in spite of the fact that it is in poor dry soil, and in full shade in summer. Mr. Coleman said he didn't see what I wanted with it since the flowers are so small but I think it is going to be one of my favorite evergreens. It comes from southern China where it makes a large shrub to fifteen feet tall.

I have not noticed any flowering quinces about town (but would be glad to hear of any and anything else I have neglected to mention, for I haven't space to tell of all of the season's flowers), but in my garden the variety 'Pink Lady' has been blooming freely for some time, and the flowers are unusually large. Always, at this time of year, they are paler and prettier than they are in spring. I planted this variety because of a promise of winter bloom, but I don't always get it, perhaps because the bush is not in a warm or sunny spot.

Two asters are in bloom, and the frail lilac flowers of the Algerian iris open even on mornings when there is ice on the birdbath. *Sternbergia fischeriana*, like a highly polished yellow crocus, was battered by the rain; but the first white hoop-petticoat daffodil is still upstanding and more buds are crowding up.

Yesterday I picked a little white violet, *Viola striata*. From time to time I hear of violas in bloom in December in various parts of the country, even as far north as Woodstock, New York. Last week I had a letter from Alexandria, Virginia, offering me a plant of the sweet violet 'Prince of Wales'. "You say you have no source for it," she wrote, "but I ran across it on the 'one-cent sale' pages of the Spring Hill Nursery's catalogue. I ordered three in April. Of course they did not bloom last spring but they did begin blooming in the fall. I picked four, protected by mulch, between heavy frosts on the sixth of December."

December 27, 1964

FLOWERS GREET THE NEW YEAR

As the New Year comes around I always wonder what flowers will be here to greet it. The winter heath [*Erica carnea*], really the spring heath as it blooms in March in the mountains of Europe, is sure to produce a few flowers no matter what the weather, and I have hopes for the Chinese witch hazel.

The witch hazel [*Hamamelia mollis*] has been in bloom for the New Year only once since I have had it, but now, in mid-December, it is full of swollen buds tipped with glints of gold. Last year, Mrs. Booley's Christmas honeysuckle began to bloom in December, and so did her mahonia which is on the south side of the house and always blooming before those in my garden. The fragrance of both of them came over the fence to me whenever the air was warm.

Beverley Nichols, who was one of the first to write about winter flowers, and seldom (if ever) writes a book without a chapter on gardens in winter, tells in *Down the Garden Path* how he came home one dreary and bitter afternoon in February, just as it was getting dark, thinking that it was really not worthwhile to make his usual tour of the garden, and certainly not to the farthest corner of the orchard to see if the witch hazel had come out. But he thought better of it and went, and there "in the gathering darkness, with the high, strange wind roaring through the great elm branches above me, I saw that the twigs of the witch hazel had broken into golden stars."

Mr. Nichols puts flowers in his detective stories, too. One of my detective-story-reading friends sent me a passage from *Murder on Request*, in which one of the characters, returning to his garden in Surrey, long after dark on an evening in January, pokes about the dead leaves to see what has happened since he left. "For the home-coming gardener," Mr. Nichols writes, "it is never too dark or too cold to 'make the tour' and nearly half an hour had elapsed before Charlotte could persuade her uncle to put away his torch and come indoors. In the meantime he had discovered signs of pink in the winter heather, several yellow stars of jasmine, some rather forlorn Christmas roses and, greatest triumph of all, a bud of the first iris to pluck, very gently, in order that he might set it in a wine glass on the chimney piece where, in due course, it would open its petals as flamboyantly as an orchid." And, he might have added, would smell as sweet as a bunch of violets. "Do not forget the importance of picking many winter flowers in bud," Mr. Nichols writes in *Down the Garden Path*. "It is a secret which brings astonishing rewards."

In my garden the paperwhite narcissus bloomed before Christmas, the first flowers I have had for a number of years. I expect the buds that are still coming will be caught before the end of the year. I know there will still be little white hoop-skirt daffodils in January and I think one of the hybrid hellebores, the Lenten roses, will be out by New Year's. The early one is pure white. Two years ago it bloomed in December for the first time in all the years I have had it, and now, in mid-December, the buds are plump and white.

Mr. W. F. Parker has just called to say he had a double-flowered Carolina jessamine [*Gelsemium sempervirens* 'Pride of Augusta'] in bloom, with more buds to come. He says it has been in bloom almost continuously since spring. The plant came from Hastings and was bought for the typical *Gelsemium sempervirens*. None of the botanies or plant dictionaries at hand mentions a double form, but I remember having seen it somewhere and finally found it listed in an old Fruitland catalogue.

The Chinese say the pine, the bamboo, and the flowering plum are the three friends of winter. One of my friends, the *Prunus mume* (called flowering plum but it is really an apricot), will not bloom for the New Year. It was killed by borers. I have two small seedlings, but I am afraid it will be some time before they begin to bloom, though two seedlings of my tree have reached the blooming stage in other gardens.

Louisa Anne Twamley, one of the early Victorian flower painters, wrote a poem about the friends of winter: the crocus, the snowdrop, and robin redbreast. In my garden winter has another friend, the squirrel, and he is spending this one digging up the newly planted tulips and hyacinths. He had already devoured the crocuses. I doubt whether there will be one for the New Year.

January 2, 1966

WINTER FLOWERS

Barbara Harding asked me why no one knows about the winter daphne, *Daphne odora*. I thought everyone knew about it, but she says no. When she asks people why they don't plant it, they say they never heard of it. One reason it is not more common in gardens is that it has a name for being difficult. I tried it four times before I managed to get it established. Now it has been in the garden for five years, and I think the reason for this final success is that the plant came in a gallon can. Also, I have learned to leave it alone. It should not be fertilized or pruned or cultivated, and it likes shade and moisture, but must be well drained. Winter daphne is a dwarf shrub and very slow growing. I don't think I have ever seen one much over three feet tall, though it is said to grow to a height of six feet.

Although it is called winter daphne, and blooms all winter at Orton Plantation, and in January at Mrs. Carl Weston's place on the Catawba River, it has never bloomed for me before the first week in February. Last year there was not a flower until the first week in March.

Mine is the variegated form. The slender leaves are tapered at both ends and have wavy cream-colored margins. It is said to be hardier and more floriferous than the type, and certainly couldn't bloom any better. The florets are magenta without and creamy within, and formed in tight little bunches. They pour out what is called the most powerful scent in the plant world, the kind Gertrude Jekyll called "almost intemperate," but no stronger I think than that of the sweet olive or tuberose. It is described as a fruity fragrance. The authors of *The Fragrant Year* say it is a mixture of orange and coconut. In England it is generally given a favorable situation at the foot of a south- or west-facing wall. It was introduced in 1771 from Japan, but is also native to China.

This is the most un-flowering winter we have had for years. It has not really been cold, for it has not been below eighteen degrees, but we haven't had our usual mild spells. *Camellia* 'Dawn' keeps on blooming, but I wish it would not. The misshapen flowers are already brown when they come out, and then they get browner. Hanging on for days they are most unsightly.

Wintersweet, *Chimonanthus praecox*, has been at its best since the first of December. Since we have had so little rain and sleet, none of the flowers have been spoiled and the scent is delicious. *Clematis cirrhosa* is weatherproof too. It came into bloom early in October, and by mid-January, there were still a few flowers and buds while the whole vine was a mass of silky seed heads. Though it is so little known, it has been in cultivation ever since the sixteenth century when it grew in Gerard's garden in London. He called it traveler's joy of Candia, Candia being a town in Crete, as it is a native of the Mediterranean. The flowers are little greenish bells that hang among beautifully cut leaves that persist all winter, dying away in mid-summer when the vine has a short resting period.

Viburnum fragrans [*V. farreri*] opened a few flowers just before Christmas, and the autumn cherry made quite a little show, but both are flowerless now.

The Algerian iris [*Iris unguicularis*] has not produced a single flower all winter long. This means the buds will all open at once in the spring when there are plenty of other things in bloom. I always count on it to produce a violet-scented flower every few days in December and January. Sometimes the slugs find the flowers before I do. They have a horrid way of biting off the top of the bud before it opens. The buds are fawn colored and are hard to see, but if I find them before the slugs get there I pick them and let them unfurl indoors. The flowers are a bright lilac.

There has been only one flower, a puny one, of the white hoop-petticoat daffodil, but lots of pointed buds are waiting for sunny days.

The other day I found the first little crocus, *Crocus laevigatus* 'Fontenayi'. It has been growing among the herbs by the kitchen door for ten years and I think it would spread if it were not disturbed so often by my trowel.

February 2, 1959

THE GREEN WINTER

This has been a green winter. In spite of ice and snow and a lot of cold weather, we have had no very low temperatures. The Japanese climbing fern [*Lygodium japonicum*] was green until Christmas; some of the climbing roses kept their leaves until the end of January; burnet, santolina, and rosemary are still fresh; parsley can still be picked for the kitchen; and every time the fine tufts of fennel are killed back some fresh, feathery aromatic foliage comes to take their place.

As I write, on January 29, Sunday's fine, powdery snow is melting and the winter flowers are, for the most part, as fresh and fragrant as ever. The wintersweet and *Camellia* 'Dawn' have suffered, but they have been in bloom for weeks and were already fading. Still, some fresh buds are coming out. The mahonia and the winter heath are unharmed, the first flowers of January jessamine are still golden, the Chinese witch hazel is pouring out its fragrance, and *Viburnum fragrans* [*V. farreri*] still opens wine-colored buds, as if it were in the garden of the Hesperides. The flowers are as waxy white as those of *Viburnum carlesii*, and even more fragrant. I found the first flower on a bitter day in January. This is the first time it has bloomed, and I hope in time it will begin to bloom in the fall as it does in England.

Harvey's form of the Christmas rose looks as if it likes ice and snow. The very large white flowers are as sparkling as when they first opened, and stand as straight on their sturdy stems. This is a late-flowering hellebore that has never bloomed before January. The Lenten roses are just out. They droop their heads in cold weather, but stiffen up when it gets warmer.

The warm days that came before the storm brought the green and white snowdrop buds from their folded leaves, but they are not yet in bloom. The fragrant flowers of the winter heliotrope will not see January, though their fat spikes are getting ready to bloom. This morning I found two violet flowers of *Crocus imperati* in the melting snow. They are the largest and most brilliant of the winter-flowering species.

February 11, 1962

A HARD WINTER

The early snowstorm saved most of the late summer flowers for a few more days. When I looked out the next morning, the branches of the tea plant were weighted to the ground, all in full bloom, but with buds and open flowers still pearly. Rosy petals on the *Camellia sasanqua* hedge were shining through a white frosting; two late stalks of × *Amarcrinums* were pink and upstanding, and even the bells of the tropical cup-

and-saucer vine [*Cobaea scandens*] looked as if they were not unaccustomed to snowflakes. But after a low of thirty-four degrees the stems of the pink lilies were limp, the purple bells were rather forlorn, though buds continued to open, and only the real winter flowers were left in the garden.

On the day before the storm the slender ivory buds of *Crocus ochroleucus* spring up among the herbs like a fleet of furled sails. I have had them for nearly twenty years, and never before had so much bloom. I think the corms must be too small to tempt chipmunks and I must have scattered them when I was weeding the thyme. Though the flowers look so frail, they were standing as straight as ever when the heavy cover of snow melted and they continue to appear through November and December, and occasionally even into January. They don't in the least mind having thyme, chives, parsley, and marjoram growing on top of them.

After the black frost I found a flowering spray of *Serissa foetida* with tiny white stars and lavender tinted buds, and even tinier bright green leaves. It is a dwarf shrub, not much over three feet tall, but spreading. It blooms freely in May and June with a sprinkling of flowers in summer, and often a few more at the end of the year. *Serissa* is an Indian name and a very pretty one. So far as I know, it has no common name, but it has been listed in the Mississippi Market Bulletin as shrub star jessamine. It is rather common in old gardens throughout the South, especially along the coast, and it is a give-away plant because the branches root wherever they touch the ground.

In Raleigh I rooted enough for a low clipped hedge. It is all the better for clipping and can be kept at any height. Serissa is not entirely evergreen in Charlotte gardens but it would be indoors, and it is a good houseplant because it is not particular as to temperature. It is suitable for bonsai as it takes pruning so well and has such small leaves and flowers. It is fetid only when crushed, and even then the scent is scarcely noticeable.

If there is any truth in the saying that abundant berries foretell a hard winter, we are not in for a very cold one. Even the arbutus is bearing fruit again, for the first time since it was cut back so severely several years ago, just after fruiting freely for the first time. By November, the branches were covered with little bunches of small white flowers and hanging among the flowers little green balls were turning to pale yellow, apricot, and spectrum red. When they were red the birds tasted them, but they did not like the insipid flavor and left them half-eaten.

The cotoneasters have more berries than they have had for years. *Cotoneaster lacteus* has grown to a height of twelve feet or more since I planted it in 1951, and it would be as wide or wider if I had left it room to spread, but I did not know at the time that it was going to be such a monster. Although the berries are not as fiery as those of the pyracanthas, they show up well. The leaves are sparsely spaced on the long flexible branches, and the berries look like clusters of coral beads. The leaves are larger than those of most species, a little over two inches in length and almost round. The berries are rather late in coloring, but they hang on all winter.

In ten years *Cotoneaster wardii* [*C. mairei*] has grown to be a wide-spreading shrub about six feet tall. The long, arching branches are now crowded with berries of a slightly subdued scarlet, and the orange of the older leaves, that color before they fall, adds to the brightness. These two species are evergreen, and *Cotoneaster microphyllus* is said to be, but in my garden it loses its leaves before spring. It hangs over a low rock wall and when the tiny leaves are rimmed with frost, and the red berries have a frosty bloom, I find it charming.

December 1, 1968

BAMBOO

More than a thousand years ago, the Chinese poet Po Chu-I wrote, "What could I do to ease a rustic heart? I planted bamboo, more than a hundred shoots . . . Already I feel that both in garden and house day by day a fresher air moves." Like the poet, I planted bamboo outside a window where I can see the sunlight on the tall green canes, and hear the wind rustle the thin leaves. Birds, especially cardinals and mocking birds, come to it. In winter, they come for the suet I hang there, and in summer they seem to sip something from the leaves.

The leaves are narrow and tapered, like willow leaves, and they have a curious characteristic: they are toothed only on one side. The fine teeth are not visible, at least not to me, but I can feel the roughness of one side and the smoothness of the other. The canes are tall, to twenty-five feet or more, and beautifully straight. The nodes are far apart, except near the base where they are curiously distorted into interesting patterns, no two alike. This is a distinguishing mark of the species I have, *Phyllostachys aurea*, the golden bamboo. The specific name is misleading for it refers to the canes and they are not golden. They are the fresh yellow green of watercress.

Dearly as I love this bamboo, it is more trouble than anything else in the garden. Every summer the wandering rhizomes must be dug and this takes hours of Amorite's time, for I cannot manage it myself. Then the canes (properly called *culm*) must be thinned. For their many garden uses, such as staking, trellises, or fishing poles, they should not be cut until they are three years old or more, when they become strong and durable. The wood of the golden bamboo is particularly strong, but I cannot wait for the canes to mature; I must keep them drastically curtailed or they would make the house too dark.

The shoots come up in spring, May I think, and do their growing all at once, reaching their full height in a few weeks. It is said that those of some species grow half an inch an hour and on a quiet day you can hear them growing, but I never have. "Each breath of South Wind makes a new bamboo," Po Chu-I writes, and so it seems. When the canes are full grown the plant spends the rest of the year sending out rhizomes in all directions. Those of some varieties go underground three to four feet and come up again fifty to sixty feet away. I try to keep mine from growing under the path on one side, and the house on the other. One root went under the terrace at the back of the house and came up on the far side. I suppose some of it is still under there. We work on it all summer.

Some years ago I gave Celia Duncan enough clumps to plant on top of a steep bank, making a hedge nearly a hundred feet long. I have worried about it ever since but she says in the open the rhizomes stay near the surface and she has no trouble controlling them by pulling back the runners.

Bamboo will grow in sun or shade, but should never be planted under or near trees where the roots will be entangled with the rhizomes. Hedges can be kept to any height (not too low) and can be sheared to some extent. Bamboo is supposed to need rich soil and plenty of moisture, but mine is never fed or watered, and I certainly don't want it to grow any better. Leaving a deep mulch of its own leaves and sheaves of its culms is what it needs most.

"The charm of a bamboo grove," David Fairchild writes, "lies in the friendly mystery of its shade with the green sunlight flickering through the thin plumes of leaves onto the soft mat of yellow dead leaves below.

You wander through such a grove feeling that you have never seen anything like it before and the quiet, fairy-like charm of it remains with you long after you have gone away."

November 22, 1964

STORM DAMAGE

The spring has been a lovely one after all. When the dogwood bloomed, burned leaves were still hanging on damaged evergreens, but the dogwood flowers were as snowy as ever, and even more numerous. Most of the azaleas bloomed as usual, in spite of pessimistic predictions, even the tender and beautiful *Azalea vittata* [*Rhododendrum simsii* 'Vittatum'].

The pale pink buds of my *Prunus mume* made a series of attempts to open and were caught each time but the plums, quinces, crabs, and the cherries bloomed in their usual sequence. Even the magnolias had their moment of perfection, though their fragile blossoms seldom escape all of the elements. If they are not torn by March winds, nor blackened by frost nor discolored by rain, they are withered by unseasonable heat.

Although the deciduous trees and shrubs show little damage from the severe winter, it will be a long time before we realize the full extent of damage to the evergreens. Those that look all right now may die later on, and those that are putting out new growth may give up the struggle if we have a hot dry summer or another severe winter. In that late March freeze that we had a number of years ago, my *Osmanthus* × *fortunei* lost a number of branches, but it filled out again, and has never been hurt since. The banana shrub [*Michelia figo*], on the other hand, seemed to recover, but in the next cold weather it was damaged even more severely. When it was killed back the third time, I just had it dug up. I think the pineapple guava [*Acca sellowiana*] will go this time, and I know that my little myrtle, *Myrtus communis*, was killed to the ground, though it may come up from the roots. The bay tree, *Laurus nobilis*, has lost all its leaves, but that has happened before, and I think it will lose little if any wood.

In an article in *The State and Columbia Record*, Mrs. T. D. Simmons reported winter damage in South Carolina. She says *Viburnum tinus* and *Viburnum japonicum* are coming back, though they were badly burned, but the damage to the loquats is greater. I was interested in her comment that variegated shrubs usually fare worse than green ones, but that both the variegated and the green forms of aucuba were untouched. Hollies, yews, and box, plants that like cold weather, are as beautiful as ever, she says and so are the cleyeras.

I noticed that in Charlotte some cleyeras in exposed southern exposures were burned, but on the whole they take cold weather well, though the leaves turn wine-red in the sun. Some color more than others.

In my garden, *Viburnum japonicam* wasn't hurt at all. In shade I think little damage was done to any but very tender shrubs. When Charlotte Trotter and I paid a visit to the camellias on Warren Coleman's pine covered slope, we found the foliage of the camellias untouched and the bushes just coming into bloom. This was in March when daffodils were blooming in sheets of gold in country gardens. Mr. Coleman thinks it best to put off pruning until you can tell the amount of damage the cold has done. He says new growth must never be allowed to come on damaged wood. Branches should always be cut back to sound wood. I know this is true, for I failed to trim my *Magnolia* × *soulangiana* 'Lennei' drastically enough when it was decimated by that late frost several years ago, and now it gets killed back every year. I think I may as well cut it to the ground and let new shoots come up.

I hear people say that we will have to plant hardier shrubs if we continue to have these severe winters. I don't think we will have many more cold ones at present. The cold cycles are always followed by mild ones. I also think the cold kills off a lot of weaklings, and that is not a bad thing. I shall not feel so cheerful though if my handsome arbutus tree that has just begun to flower freely and to fruit proves to be more damaged than I think.

April 21, 1963

THE MERRY MONTH OF MAY

May is Flora's month, the month of flowers. Celebrated in Roman times by the Floralia (April 28 to May 3), when people carried garlands to the grotto of Egeria in honor of the goddess of spring. The Romans must have carried Flora's festival to England, for the celebration was very popular in medieval and Tudor times when the entire world got up at dawn to go a-maying in the woods:

> Upon the first of May,
> With garlands fresh and gay,
> With mirth and music sweet,
> For such a season meet,
> They passed their time away.

The Puritans put a stop to these charming and joyful occasions. The maypole, they said, was a stinking idol and the people leapt and danced about it like heathens but the old customs returned with the Restoration.

In Paris, the first of May is the Feast of the Lily of the Valley, "Something more than an affectation, better than a superstition, almost a religion," Colette writes in *For a Flower Album.* "Its cult excites the entire populace of a capital city to a pitch of effervescence . . . Come to Paris on May Day and watch the flower sellers in the streets . . . The tight bunched lilies brim and foam over the trestle tables. Their long pale-green leaves are always arranged as a coronal round the flowers, a tradition no one dreams of abolishing."

All Paris goes to the woods, returning as the light begins to fade, and all the way to Versailles children blaze the trail, "brandishing by the fistful bunches of lily of the valley, bluebells, wood anemones, Solomon's seal, wood sage, ground ivy, veronica which loses the azure in its blue eyes as soon as picked, wallflowers torn from their ancient habitat, and star of Bethlehem, called eleven o'clock lady, whose eyes closes again whenever a cloud passes across the face of the sun." The crowds carry along with them the scent of fading flowers and "the load of somewhat overtaxed enjoyment and fatigue which, in the month of May, is the reward of a day's sacrifice to the still tender green of the woodland glade and the flowering of the lily of the valley."

The lily of the valley is the Virgin's flower. One of its old names is Our Lady's Tears. Like many other flowers it was once sacred to a pagan goddess, but the Christians gave it to the Virgin along with Flora's month, which became the Month of Mary. Therefore, when lilies of the valley are in bloom they are picked to decorate churches, especially the Lady Chapel. Because they bloom at Whitsuntide, they are associated with that season, which in some places used to take the place of the May Day festival. In fact, I gather that in happier days the merrymaking went on from May Day to the Whit-Monday Fair: "Happy the age . . . When every village did a maypole raise / And Whitsun-ales and May-games did abound."

In England, hawthorn is called May flower, May tree, or May. There and on the continent it is considered a charm against evil because its branches were used to plait the crown of thorns. Blossoms were hung on doorposts to keep the witches away (for the eve of May Day is the time they meet), put in the churches, and woven into wreaths and garlands, as Spenser tells in the *Shepherd's Calendar*:

> Youth's folk now flocken
> To gather May baskets and smelling Breere;
> And home they hasten the posts to dight,
> And all the kirk-pillars ere day-light
> With Hawthorn buds, and sweet Eglantine
> And garlands of Roses, and Sops-in-wine.

Sops-in-wine were little clove pinks used to flavor ale or wine. Other flowers brought to the May Queen were the snowball, sometimes called May rose, the marsh marigold and the cowslip.

In this country we have the May apple, which really does fruit in May, and the Maypop, which doesn't. Anyone who remembers childhood knows why it is called "pop," but I cannot think of any excuse for May, as it blooms and pops in mid-summer. In this country, our May flower is the trailing arbutus, said to be the first flower to greet the pilgrims after the hard winter of their landing. I don't know whether they named it for the month, or their ship, or both, but I like to think of their delight in finding it.

April 30, 1961

TENDER PERENNIALS FOR HOT-WEATHER GARDENS

In April, when I buy petunias and marigolds for the summer garden, I always get some of the tender perennials that thrive in hot weather. One of these is *Pentas lanceolata*. It comes already in bloom and goes on blooming until frost. When I first met pentas I thought that the common mallow pink was its only color. Later, Camilla Truax wrote in the *New York Times* about a collection of color forms that she had made in New Orleans. She sent me, by airmail, cuttings of a white one, a lavender one, and fireman's red. I turned these over to Mrs. Price to root and I hope they did, but I am beginning to find them in the houseplant catalogues, so we can get more if they didn't. I am still hunting a source for the most beautiful one of all, a delicate pink form that I saw in a garden in Monroe, Louisiana, where it was growing in full sun, and blooming much more freely than those in my garden, which I had planted in the shade.

For late summer I depend on lantana to fill in the gaps left by the earlier perennials that have finished blooming. It blooms best when the nights are cool, and comes into its own when its fresh foliage and gay flowers are most needed. Some years it blooms until Thanksgiving. Last year was the first time that I had bloom from the seedlings that come up so freely. I hope they will do it again, but they don't start blooming until September, so I will still need a few greenhouse plants for summer. Some people dislike the gaudy orange and pink that is the characteristic color of the flowers, but by choosing among plants already in bloom, you can get a creamy white, a clear cool yellow, and a very good pink. Lantana grows very fast and needs plenty of room to spread for it takes up at least three or four feet by the end of the season. If it is grown from seed, they should be sown under glass in February.

I never understand why a plant named impatience should be called patience, but that is a common name of *Impatiens sultani* [*I. walleriana*], also called sultana. Sultana is a Victorian houseplant that has come into favor again because it blooms all of the year, indoors in winter and out of doors in summer. Cuttings root easily and plants from seed bloom in about three months. Park Seed offers a pure white form and some named dwarf varieties which are only six inches tall. Sultanas are plants for shady places but Elizabeth Clarkson grows them in large pots in a sunny part of the garden.

The Madagascar periwinkle, *Vinca rosea* [*Catharanthus rosea*], another useful plant for summer, blooms best in the sun although it is supposed to be a plant for moist shady places. In the seed catalogues I find a variety of forms. This year I thought I would try the still more dwarf 'Rose Carpet', sowing the seed where the plants are to grow. Vincas are as easily grown from cuttings as from seed.

In summer I always like some plants with fragrant foliage, lemon verbena, lemon-, apple-, and rose-scented geraniums, peppermint, and some of the salvias with scented leaves. Last year, Mrs. Chalfin sent me *Salvia dorrii*, one I never heard of. It never bloomed, though it is said to have pink flowers, but it grew to be a sprawling plant of three to four feet. The enormous velvet leaves have the most delightful scent of any plant that I know.

In the Mississippi Market Bulletin, a Mrs. Blackwell advertises plants of candle trees, *Cassia alata* [*Senna alata*], that will be ready for shipment after the first of April. I'll be glad to give her address. I put Mr. Saier to a lot of trouble to get me a few seeds last fall and then forgot to send them to Mrs. Price to plant. I did divide them with someone who came begging. I wish I had given her all, for it is too late to plant them now. Nothing is as beautiful as the candle tree.

March 22, 1959

FLOWERS IN THE FALL BORDER

When I paid a visit to Mrs. Zee early in September, though grass was brown and earth parched, a clump of black-eyed Susans was in full bloom, bright, fresh, and crisp in flower and leaf. I always thought of it as native to these parts, but it is really a flower of the plains. "Although now so common in our eastern fields," Mrs. Dana writes in *How to Know the Wild Flowers*, "they were first brought to us with clover-seed from the west and are not altogether acceptable guests as they bid fair to add another anxiety to the already harassed life of the New England farmer." In Mrs. Zee's garden it did not look at all like a weed, but worthy of a place in the summer border. Looking it up in *Britton and Brown*, I found that it is biennial, though sometimes blooming the first year, and that among other things it is called brown Betty and golden Jerusalem.

A hedge of *Malvaviscus arboreus* var. *drummondii* was in full bloom, and this too was untouched by drought. It is called Turk's cap or Mexican apple, and is sometimes advertised in the Mississippi Market Bulletin as ladies' eardrop or red teardrop. The small spectrum-red flowers never open. Their silky petals are furled around a long slender stamen column, and they look like tiny long-handled parasols. I didn't see any fruits, but there should be little red apples nearly an inch in diameter. They can be eaten raw or cooked and are said to be delicious. In Texas, where they are native, Turk's caps grow along shady streams, but they seem to do as well in full sun. In these parts they are killed to the ground in winter and come up again in the spring, and grow to about four feet by the end of the summer.

In my garden late bloom depends upon water, and I have been pretty faithful about watering during the long dry weeks of the summer and early fall. Now, in mid-September, pink Japanese anemones are blooming in deep shade along the far end of the garden path. The last of the small lilac stars of *Hosta lanceolata* [*H. lancifolia*] have just fallen, and the later variety *H. tardiflora* is in bud. The leaves are darker and more polished than those of the type, and the flowers are paler and more crowded in the stem. These are two of the best plantain lilies.

The *Amarcrinums* are usually in bloom by the first of September if not before. One year × *Amarcrinum howardii* [× *Amarcrinum memoria-corsii*] bloomed from the middle of August into the first week of November. The fragrant pink lilies are lovely with the hardy begonia [*Begonia grandis*], *Sedum spectabile*, and false dragonhead [*Physostegia*], and it is nice to have blue masses of the perennial ageratum coming into bloom just as the summer flowers are drying up.

Last spring Mrs. Price gave me a variegated sedum that has been grown in the neighborhood for many years and goes by the name of houseleek. I take it to be the white flowered form of *Sedum spectabile* [*S. alboroseum*]. It has very large heads of off-white flowers, and pale green leaves splashed with cream.

Lantana is the saving grace of the fall borders. The dark leaves keep their color until frost, and the flowers bloom on and on. I noticed that butterflies return to them again and again, after short trips to other flowers. I did not know that it is called butterfly bush until I read about it in *Joe's Bulletin*. Marie Mellinger kept a record of butterflies visiting a bush in her garden in Tiger, Georgia (where it freezes to the ground, but comes up again from the roots), during October and November: "Long-tailed skipper butterflies came every day . . ."

October 6, 1968

FRAGRANCE IN THE GARDEN

It seems to me that this has been the most fragrant summer and fall that I have ever known. Someone suggested that it is because we have had so much more rain than usual. In midsummer I always think honeysuckle is blooming somewhere near, and it turns out to be the white flowers of the glory bower, *Clerodendron trichotomum*. Louise Beebe Wilder agrees with me as to the scent. The author of *The Fragrant Year* describes it as a mixture of lily and nicotine. My little tree, brought from Longview as a sucker fifteen years ago, has been killed back by recent winters. This spring I thought it was dead and wanted to dig it up, but John Rhinehart begged me to give it another chance, and sure enough it put out again and bloomed well. It never fruits well for me, but I have seen it in other gardens in Charlotte when its turquoise berries in their pomegranate-purple saucers really do make it look like a glory bower.

Walking down the garden path on a sultry afternoon in late July, I met a fragrance that took some time to trace. It was the mountain summersweet, *Clethra acuminata*, a delicate, elusive perfume that comes and goes with the breeze. In New England, *Clethra alnifolia* is called sailor's delight because the scent is said to blow out to sea. It is supposed to smell like heliotrope, but to me it is more like vanilla.

The tea olives outdid themselves this year. All through the late summer and fall *Osmanthus fragrans*, the sweet olive (first bloomed on August 21) was better than it had ever been before. The flowers are described as smelling of jasmine and apricot, but to me they are jasmine alone and close kin to the butterfly lily, which blooms at the same time so I could compare them. The holly-leaved tea olive, *Osmanthus ilicifolius* [*O. heterophyllus*], is the last to bloom and at its height in mid-October. E. A. Bowles once likened the scent to an empty chocolate box. The scent of loquat, which blooms at the same time, is pure, full-strength vanilla. I always know when the first flower opens even though I can't see it.

The curious scent of *Elaeagnus pungens*, which is anything but pungent, is described in *The Fragrant Year* as a musty grape-jonquil fragrance and the scent of the variety *E.* 'Fruitlandii' is considered "more refined." The Fruitland form is certainly more fragrant. I came across it in Mrs. Charles Lucas's garden early in October. The shrub is low and spreading with horizontal branches; the leaves are broader than those of the type. Both the leaves and the small silver flowers are spread with copper dots.

November 30, 1969

FALL ADDITIONS TO THE BORDER

Now that fall is at hand, it is time to think of replenishing the flower borders. I am told that no one has flower borders any more, because they are so much trouble to keep, but it seems to me that mine demand comparatively little attention in return for the blooms they provide from early spring until frost. I keep them as full as possible with perennials that take care of themselves: garden forms of phlox, boltonia, loosestrife, pale yellow daylilies in varieties that bloom from May to September, old unimproved shasta daisies, the kind that stays with you, and *Thalictrum flavum* ssp. *glaucum*, Japanese anemones, chrysanthemums, and fennel.

In the shady part of the border, which is increasing in size as the pine tree that shades it grows taller and broader, there are hardy begonias, *Sedum spectabile*, August lilies [*Hosta plantaginea*] and *Heuchera* × *brizoides*. This species of heuchera has prettily mottled leaves and airy flowers of a wonderfully pale, pure pink. They bloomed freely over a long period, beginning early in May and bloomed again in mid-summer. The flowers of the Bressingham hybrids are larger.

With more shade, I shall need more columbines, and as my old garden strain of the vulgaris type has deteriorated, I shall start the fall off with McKenna hybrids. I saw these in bloom with the bearded irises in Mrs. Henderson's garden last May, enormous flowers with spurs to four inches long.

I have Chinese bellflowers, *Platycodon*, on my list because I have not had them for a long time. I need more blue in the borders and they are just as pretty as campanulas and easier to grow. The bells are a soft blue-violet. It is a low plant for the front of the border. A dwarf *Coreopsis* 'Baby Sun', with bright yellow flowers, is a good companion.

Every fall I plant lots of white sweet Williams to bloom with the tulips, but lately they have been waiting for the tulips to fade before they commence. Last spring I had some dwarf sweet Williams in mixed colors. They bloomed earlier and longer than the regular kind, and made nice green mats of foliage. Several plants seem to have every intention of staying another season. There are two dwarf varieties, midget and Indian carpet; the flowers of the first are double, and those of the latter are single and in gay calico colors.

For a long time I have grown a tall allium with a silvery lilac ball of flowers. It comes up in the back of the borders, takes up very little space, makes no trouble and blooms in May. The flower heads look pretty even after they fade, but I cut them for friends who like dried flowers to arrange. I have always called this *Allium giganteum*, but when Billy Hunt was here in May, he said that it could not be that as it has some foliage on the stalks. My allium is about four feet tall but *A. giganteum* is taller. It has bright violet flowers in heads eight inches in diameter, or so the catalogues say, and the perfectly bare scapes rise out of a rosette of wide gray leaves. As it is an expensive bulb, I have been shopping around and have found that De Jager offers the best bargain. They also have *Allium albopilosum* [*A. christophii*] one of the most striking species. It has hairy gray leaves and a flat head of metallic violet flowers on long pedicels. As the flowers mature, the head becomes a sphere, sometimes ten inches across. When the large spheres are dried, they turn the color of sea oats and last almost indefinitely.

Providing color in the borders for so many months of the year is not an easy task. It is accomplished by depending on foliage for a good part of the effect. I find gray plants especially useful, but it is hard to find kinds that do well in our hot, muggy summers. Two of the dusty millers are dependable; 'Diamond', with its coarsely cut leaves, and 'Silver Queen', with its fine, laciniated ones.

October 14, 1962

SOW HARDY ANNUAL SEEDS DURING SEPTEMBER

September is the best time for sowing seed of hardy annuals. Every fall I think I shall order early, and get them sown before the month is out, but spring often finds the little packages on my desk, and then the garden suffers. No amount of pansies make up for the lack of annuals, though of course I want pansies too. If they don't get planted in September, November is the next best time for planting the seed. The success of those that go in the ground in December and January is doubtful. I sow seed only of those annuals that come up readily from seed scattered where they are to grow.

Limnanthes douglasii is a dainty California annual called meadow foam, a name to remind you that it likes moisture. Sown in fall, it blooms in March or early April, myriads of fragrant white and gold cups on low spreading plants with fine pale foliage. Sometimes it self sows, but not freely. I used to buy seeds every year from Carl Purdy. When he died and his business with him, I had no source until I found them again among Mr. Saier's offerings.

California poppies [*Eschscholzia*] seed themselves, but it is better to buy fresh seed each year. I like to sow them early so that the little rosettes of fine gray foliage will come up before Christmas. They look so pretty all winter, and bloom early in the cool weather. As soon as the heat comes they get shabby. The typical orange-flowered form grows best, but this year I am trying a variety called 'White Emperor'.

Nigella damascena, once sown comes back for years. It is not a showy flower, but I like it for the blueness of the petals and for its pretty name, love-in-a mist. It is also called fennel flower, because of its threadlike leaves, and devil-in-a-bush. It is a plant that Miss Jekyll held in high admiration. "Many years ago," she wrote in *Wood and Garden* (1901), "I came upon some of it in a small garden, of a type I thought extremely desirable with a double flower of just the right degree of fullness, and of an unusually fine color. I was fortunate enough to get some seed, and have never grown any other, nor have I ever seen elsewhere any that I think can compare with it." Miss Jekyll has been dead for twenty-five years, but the nigella that she found in an English garden is still available under her name.

One of the best of spring-flowering plants perpetuates itself by seeds, though it is not an annual. This is the common columbine, *Aquilegia vulgaris*, a short-lived perennial that is easily grown from seed scattered on the ground and blooms well in deep shade. A number of forms are available, among them Miss Jekyll's 'Munstead White'. My columbines came from seed saved from those growing in the Busbees' garden in Raleigh. Some are pure white, some in tones of hellebore red and some a very dark mulberry purple.

September 14, 1958

PLANTING ANNUALS IN AUTUMN

The flowers that bloom in the spring must be planted in the fall. If they are annuals, the earlier they are planted the better they will bloom. Some annuals reseed themselves, almost indefinitely, after the first sowing. These I depend on to fill in the bare spaces and to border the walks in the early part of the year.

One that I cannot do without is a low, spreading plant called *Silene pendula*. Every fall I set out pansy plants, English daisies, and *Alyssum saxatile* [*Aurinia saxatilis*] to bloom at tulip time, but it is the clear pink flowers of the silene that makes the garden glow. This year I have at last found a commercial source for the seed, but all of these years in Charlotte, I would have been without silene if I had not met Mrs. Black. The year I started this garden she gave me a strawberry basket full of the gray seedlings, and they have replenished themselves ever since. In fact, one spring when her supply had waned, I was able to give some back to her.

Along with *Silene pendula* I like to plant *Nemophila*, the earliest of spring annuals. From seed sown in September it will begin to flower late in February, and will flower on through March and April. Plants from seeds sown in January will bloom but those from seed sown in early fall are best. Seeds should be sown every year. There may be a few volunteers, but not enough to be effective. The flowers are small cups of cornflower blue.

When I said that nemophila is the earliest annual, I forgot Johnny-jump-ups. They have bloomed for me on the fourth of February. Mine came from Elizabeth Clarkson seven years ago, and have been perpetuating themselves ever since. Those in my Raleigh garden came from Miss Louise Busbee. One spring morning she brought me the little plants along with several right-hand garden gloves, which she always saved for me when the left-hand ones wore out; I always had left-over left-hand ones to go with them. Being so well supplied with plants, I have never bought seed, but I saw little Johnny-jump-ups listed in Park's Flower Book. Sometimes you find them in the catalogues as *Viola tricolor*.

Single-flowered larkspur seeds itself from year to year and blooms in May with irises and peonies. I can't remember ever having planted it in Charlotte. I think it just came over the fence from neighboring gardens. The large double-flowered strains must be planted every fall. For gardens the best of these are the giant imperials, which grow to over five feet tall and produce flower spikes as magnificent as delphiniums. The flowers of 'Blue Spire', a glowing pansy-purple, are the most intense color in the border, those of 'Blue Bell' are palest, 'Dazzler' is almost red, 'Los Angeles' is salmon pink and 'White King' is the finest of all. Seed must be sown in late fall when the temperature is under sixty degrees. Some gardeners put them in the refrigerator for a few days before planting.

I seem to be the only friend of *Calliopsis* [*Coreopsis tinctoria*]. Ann Roe Robbins, in *How to Grow Annuals*, the best book on the subject, writes that the only thing in their favor is that they grow like weeds. But my garden is never as colorful as in June and early July when the small yellow and brown flowers, which seem to float in the green mist of their fine foliage, spread out and spill into the path. They seed so freely, they need never be planted but once, if that. Like the larkspurs, mine volunteered. I think the seed came along in some plants we brought from Raleigh.

A large coarse daisy is *Rudbeckia* 'Gloriosa', a new annual that appeared in Burpee's 1957 catalogue. Mrs. Price gave it to me, saying she planted it in the spring. It began to bloom the first of July and bloomed on all through the heat and drought; a single flower lasted for six weeks. As it is a hardy annual, it will probably bloom earlier from fall sowing. The daisies are five and a half inches across on two-and-a-half-foot stems. Some are brassy yellow with dark metallic centers and some are zoned with dark red.

September 1, 1957

LATE-BLOOMING FLOWERS

It seems to me that this has been the most flowering fall I have ever known. But then, the end of each year is more flowery than the one that went before. Now that gardens are filled with camellias, the end of autumn is like the beginning of spring. After the first black frost early in November, the little autumn cherry dropped its leaves and revealed thin bare branches lightly sprinkled with pale pink flowers.

Beneath it, the autumn snowdrops were coming into bloom. Here and there all over the garden, even in places where I am sure I never planted them, violet-colored crocuses opened in the sun of Indian summer. I don't know what kind of crocus they are, perhaps seedlings, but they bloomed in succession, so that I was never without a flower from the time the first one opened until the first day of December, when the dependable winter-flowering *Crocus laevigatus* 'Fonteneyi' puts up a pale bud under the kitchen window. I thought the chipmunks had eaten all of the corms in the garden, but I have observed that it is a point of honor with them never to touch those in front of the house.

When I went to see Mrs. E. B. Muse early in November, her garden was full of summer flowers as well as masses of chrysanthemums. She dug up a clump of the shasta daisy 'Esther Read' and gave it to me, and it went on blooming, unspotted by frost until after Thanksgiving. It went on blooming even then, but the double white, enameled flowers did look less glistening. I have never seen 'Esther Read' before, but I have read that this endless and bountiful bloom is characteristic. I doubt, however, that in my garden it will do what it does in the rich soil that Mrs. Muse provides it, and I bet her flowers don't know what drought is. They have certainly never met a weed.

Some time before Thanksgiving, a single stalk of the parrot flower, *Alstroemeria psittacina*, sprang up from the shining new leaves that appeared during the last rains. The flowers kept their bright colors well into December while other flowers turned brown. I picked a flower, and held it in my hand in order to stay the narrow, bright red, green-tipped, olive-streaked petals, which looked so unbelievably light and gay on an icy December morning.

Last spring, Mrs. George Tate sent me a late flowering aster from her garden in Belmont. Now, in December, it is in full bloom and the small lilac-tinted flowers, crowded on the long branches, are untouched by a number of hard frosts. I sent a sprig to Dr. Wells, who said he could not place it among the natives. Elizabeth Clarkson's aster which she brought from her mother's garden in Texas is just beginning to bloom. The flowers are deep violet and larger than Mrs. Tate's, but the plant does not bloom as freely.

A queer little flower from the Zephyr Hill Nursery in San Antonio has bloomed with the late flowers for the last two years. It is the green lily, *Schoenocaulon drummondii*, and it is not much to look at, but it takes up no room and causes no trouble, and I like to have it surprise me in late November, when a slender spike of silvery stamens rises on a delicate stem from a clump of grassy leaves.

One thing I have missed this fall is the Chinese violets [*Viola pa-*

trinii]. They sow themselves all through the garden, under the pines and in the borders, and along the edges of the gravel paths and usually in November produce a second crop of pale lavender flowers among narrow unviolet-like leaves. *Viola striata*, on the other hand, usually produces only a stray creamy white flower from time to time in the fall, but this year it bloomed freely and steadily for weeks and weeks.

Counting the late survivors and the newcomers of the season, I made a list of things in bloom—roses, chrysanthemums, camellias, little frost-bitten pinks, and, on Thanksgiving Day, the first fragile and perfect and fragrant Algerian iris—and I thought gardeners are:

> Travelers of the year who faintly say
> How could such beauty walk the common way?

December 15, 1963

THE GARDENING YEAR IS JUST BEGINNING

We usually have a white frost, or rather a black one, before October is over, but this year it was not until November 6 that we said "all out tonight is lost." Not quite all was lost. However, the sasanquas were scarcely touched and, of course, the little bunches of pearls on the arbutus tree were as pearly as ever, and will be until the last one fades in 1968. A few chrysanthemums were left as were the first flowers of the autumnal cherry and the last flowers of the fall snowdrop.

As I cleared away the marigolds and torenias, and cut back the deliciously fragrant dead stalks of the pineapple sage, I felt as I always do when I find new growth beneath dead flowers, that the garden year is not over, it is just beginning. Only the day before, I had found little yellow-throated white flowers of *Crocus ochroleucus* rising above a mat of thyme. They are not spectacular, but they have been faithful to November for nearly twenty years, and while they have not increased, their corms are so small even the chipmunks leave them alone. The crocus always reminds me to look for buds of the paperwhites. I found an unusually good crop, but their chance of not losing the race with the frost is small.

Early in the season the fall colors were disappointing, but it seemed to me that the late fall had never been more glowing. When I was in

Chapel Hill in the middle of November, the white oaks and the red oaks were at their best, especially at sunset.

The leaves of most maples fell without coloring but those of the Southern sugar maple, *Acer floridanum*, were in perfection. It grows in Chapel Hill in ravines and along creek banks, and in Raleigh it is used as a street tree. "The most beautiful thing on the place is *Acer floridanum*," Caroline Dormon once wrote from Louisiana in early November. In *Natives Preferred* she writes that if she could have only one tree this would be it: "The long slightly drooping branches are thickly clothed with prettily cut leaves hanging on long stems. In late autumn the entire tree becomes a clear glowing yellow, which seems to give off light. Here at Briarwood it retains its color until mid-December."

A visit to Chapel Hill always means a walk in the Laurel Hill woods, now the William Lanier Hunt Arboretum. This was the first time I had ever been there when the cyclamen were in bloom. They all came from seed sent to Mr. Hunt from England in 1956. The seedlings began to bloom in three years, and now there is a patch fifteen feet or more across, in flower from early July until Christmas and in leaf from November until late spring.

This species, *Cyclamen neapolitanum* [*C. hederifolium*] has been in my garden for fifteen years and is self-sowing, but it has never produced any variation in color. All flowers are a pale red-violet with a dark red-violet eye. At Laurel Hill they range from pure white through a series of pinks to deep rose.

December 10, 1967

TWO

Perennials and Annuals

PLANTING IN RELAYS

I have decided that it is better to do spring planting in relays rather than to get the plants all at once. Now that they come in peat pots instead of flats, they dry out so fast that they have to be watered at least once a day, and it is not a good idea to get more at one time than you can set out in a few days.

In late March I got petunias, Boston daisies, lemon verbena, pineapple sage (*Salvia rutilans*) [now *Salvia elegans*], and some herbs. In Mrs. Price's garden, pineapple sage lives over the winter, but mine never does so I buy rooted cuttings every spring, for of all the sweet-smelling herbs, this is the most delightful. It smells like a basket of fresh fruit. The little plants come out of the greenhouse in bloom, but the slender carmine flowers don't continue out of doors. Their real blooming period is from September until frost, the very time that a bright note of color is most needed. All summer long I brush my hand over the bush, or pick a scented leaf to put in my pocket. I have ruined lots of blouses by forgetting to take the leaf out. The pineapple sage, Mrs. Chalfin used to say, is a friend of man and bee, and is attractive to hummingbirds.

In spring I always plant *Salvia leucantha*, the Mexican bush sage, for mine always dies, though it does sometimes winter out of doors in protected places. In the fall it is the most admired thing in the garden. The bushes grow to a height of four feet during the summer so they need plenty of room. In September the brilliant hyacinth-violet of the calyx begins to glow, and the tiny white flowers seem to make the purple velvet brighter still. Nearby some single white Japanese anemones bloom at the same time.

The hybrid grandiflora petunias seem to be the thing at the present time. I got lots of 'Apple Blossom' because I admired the delicate pink and white flowers in Mrs. Brenizer's garden last summer, and a few plants of 'Peach Blossom', another pink and white, to see what it is like. I got 'Sky Magic', the blue that goes with ageratum, and 'White Magic'. 'Sunburst', the first grandiflora yellow, is said to be a bright one. The only yellow petunia that I have had is 'Butterscotch' which has proved to be a pale greenish yellow. One year George Ball sent me for trial some plants of pink and white Cascade petunias. The Cascades are particularly good for boxes and planters and hanging baskets. He also sent 'Honey Bunch', a double pink that I did not like very much, but it was effective in the flower border.

Last spring, Burpee sent me a trial package of seed of the pale yellow marigold, 'First Lady', said to be the earliest and most compact of all F1 hybrids. Mrs. Price raised them for me, and as I did not get them to her until late, they did not begin to bloom until the first of July. This year I expect they will be earlier. The flowers are little more than two inches across and did not come up to the three and a half inches promised by the catalogues, and I am sure there were many less than fifty to a plant. However, the plants were stocky and did not need staking and I was glad the flowers weren't so big. Those enormous ones are top-heavy and likely to get their necks broken. It really is the best pale yellow marigold I ever had. The plants were a little more than two feet tall. A new orange flowered marigold, 'Golden Jubilee', is now available.

My sister [Ann Way], who says she likes lots of color all mixed up, set out a mixture of the dwarf snapdragon, 'Floral Carpet'. It also comes in separate colors and so do the 'Rocket Snaps' (horrid name), which are bred for hot weather. She also bought sultana which she is keeping on the screen porch to put out after frost, with ageratum, marigolds, and other tender things.

It is wonderful to have such a variety of large-flowered clematis at hand. We use to have to send off for everything but *Clematis* × *jackmanii* and *C.* 'Henryi'. Now in local nurseries we have 'The President', 'Ernest Markham', 'Duchess of Edinburgh', 'Comtesse de Bouchard', 'Nelly Moser', 'Belle of Woking', 'Lanuginosa', 'Lord Nevill', 'William Kennett', 'Crimson King', 'Mrs. Cholmodeley', *Clematis montana* var. *rubens*, and *C. tangutica*, a late-flowering species with small yellow flowers.

April 14, 1968

BADGE OF GARDENING INCLUDES BLACK KNEES

When the Piedmont Judges' Club met in April with the Charlotte Club of Accredited Flower Show Judges, Mr. W. O. Freeland of Columbia, South Carolina, was their speaker. He talked about gardens and spring and many other things. He says dirty fingernails are not the only badge of the gardener. Little can be accomplished without blackening the knees.

Mr. Freeland doesn't believe in pruning. God knows the proper size for trees and shrubs, he says, and they should be planted where they will have enough room to grow as they were meant to. He suddenly remembered the clipped cherry laurels in my garden and, to avoid hurting my feelings, mentioned them as an exception. Mr. Freeland and I really see eye to eye on the evils of pruning, but I have not found a way to avoid doing it in a small garden. The cherry laurels would take over if they were not clipped.

One year when 'Lady Banks' rose was not cut back severely, the long drooping branches came down and made a thick curtain across the garden path, cutting the garden in two. I once read of a bush in southern France that covered a wall seventy-five feet long and eighteen feet high. It had "50,000 flowers in simultaneous bloom. There is neither height nor width of masonry which it cannot surmount and cover." I think it is at its best on a tall pine on a wide lawn. I have been told that it will kill the tree, but it hasn't done any fatal damage to the pine tree it has been draping itself over in my garden for nearly twenty years.

Mr. Freeland says he likes the old flowers that go from garden to garden and are seldom found in the trade. I have just been reminded of one of these, a low, trailing verbena with lacy white flowers and lacy green leaves. It roots as it goes and used to be the mainstay of my garden but it disappeared and I have not had it for years. Mrs. Brewer, who lives in Monroe, wrote to ask about it. "It spread rapidly," she said, "and in the past has been so plentiful, but now, all at once, it can't be found." If anyone who reads this has any to spare, please let us know. Mrs. Brewer stressed the fact that the flowers are white. There is also a form with bright violet flowers and seed that can be had from Mr. Saier as *Verbena pulchella* [*V. pinnatifida*]. It blooms from seed the first year.

Another garden flower that is not likely to turn up in catalogues is the old white dooryard iris, *Iris albicans*. More than fifty varieties of bearded iris must have gone in and out of my garden in the last twenty years and this is one of the few left. Last spring, like 'Lady Banks' rose, it did not have a single flower, but this year both outdid themselves, and so did a tall yellow iris that came from Sara Kincey's garden, having lost its name on the way. The yellow of the standards is as pale as the rose, but the falls are of a deeper tone, and the flower is lighted from within by the golden beard.

In April the garden is planned around the 'Lady Banks' in the pine tree, with yellow alyssum on the wall, Carolina jessamine on the fence, blue phlox, white phlox, blue and white pansies, white columbine and sweet rocket. This spring I had the white tulips 'Zwanenburg' and the pale yellow 'Nipheto'. Both are Darwins, of the same height and bloom at the same time. I planted twenty-five of each on either side of a path forty feet long and it was too many. They made solid rows. Next fall I shall plant half as many and put them in clumps with wide spaces between.

Mr. Freeland described the Laucklin garden in Aiken, South Carolina, where hedges of white flowering quince border a brick walk, and where there is the largest *Camellia japonica* he has ever seen. He calls the quinces japonicas but camellias are camellias and nothing more. In the Laucklin garden 'Lady Banks' rose grows over a large Southern magnolia. I suppose the rose is evergreen in Aiken. In Charlotte the bare branches would be ugly in winter if they covered glossy green leaves. I think it is better married to a pine.

After the lecture Mr. Freeland produced two lists. "These," he said, handing one to me, "are the plants I brought you, and these are the plants I would like from your garden."

May 5, 1968

GARDENING SURPRISES

For some years I have been getting perennials from a small country nursery in Georgia. They are often things that are difficult to find: the white Stokes aster, rose campion, star jasmine, prickly poppy, and the little old-fashioned, fringed, and delightfully fragrant white grass pink. Some have Latin names and sometimes they are not the right ones, but I never mind that as it is fun to see what turns up.

When *Eranthis hyemalis* bloomed this spring it proved to be a buttercup. And I nearly pulled up the plant described as "erigeron, midsummer daisy, deep blue, aster-like, blooms all summer." It looked to me exactly like a dandelion. I should have guessed what it was, but I didn't know until it bloomed that it was chicory, *Cichorium intybus*. When the first flower opened in the garden, chicory was already in full bloom all over Charlotte along with elder blossoms and Queen Anne's lace. I love seeing roadside flowers in town.

Chicory came to us from Europe. In the Mediterranean countries its value as food and medicine was known from early times, and some scholars consider it one of the bitter herbs of the Passover. Horace took pride in his simple fare of olive, chicory, and the wholesome mallow. The herbalists called chicory a "fine, cleansing, jovial plant."

In the middle of June a regal lily came up and bloomed. I don't remember planting it, and have no idea how it got there, but there it is. A few days later the variety *Lilium* 'Royal Gold' came into bloom. I do know where I got that. Mr. Krippendorf sent me a bulb twelve years ago. It has bloomed faithfully in June ever since but it never increased. It does not look like the color plates in the Wayside Gardens catalogue. The flowers are not red-gold. They are the palest and most delicate yellow with the smoothest and most delicate finish. The Wayside lilies have (they say) eighteen to twenty flowers to a stalk. Mine have only two or three. I am sure they would be more numerous if I took some trouble, but I enjoy them as they are without taking any trouble at all.

Lilium henryi comes next, this year on the seventh of July, which is very early. Gertrude Jekyll describes the flowers as a strong and yet soft orange color. The plant she says impresses one with a feeling of vigor and well-being. Mine, on the contrary, lay themselves out flat on the ground as soon as they are ready to bloom, and I always forget to stake them before that happens. About the time *L. henryi* goes out of bloom, toward the end of July or the first week in August, *L. speciosum* 'Rubrum' begins. Unfortunately the only rubrum lily that I have left is on top of *Hemerocallis* 'Sonata' and is enveloped in a mist of Florence fennel. The raspberry-spattered lilies should have a background of white phlox. They were meant to and they used to, but somehow this last batch was planted in the wrong place.

H. 'Sonata' is the palest yellow daylily I have had except for 'Delta Girl', but that one was always skimpy, and it did not stay with me very long. It blooms from the middle of July through most of August, and once it bloomed again in the fall. The combination of the pale daylilies and the lacy chartreuse umbels of the fennel is something I would never have thought of. The fennel just came up at the right place and bloomed at the right time.

The pink flowers of the *Crinum* 'Cecil Houdyshel' bloomed all through July along with a pale pink mallow and the paler pink plumes of the Japanese meadowsweet. Further on, in a shadier place, there was a peaches-and-cream astilbe that Tempie Franklin gave me years ago. All of these things except the rubrum lily, which must be replaced from time to time, are permanent and self-sustaining.

August 17, 1969

THE LAW OF SUPPLY AND DEMAND

At the January meeting of the Charlotte Garden Club, Fred Galle, president of the American Horticultural Society and director of horticulture at the Callaway Gardens in Pine Mountain, Georgia, showed slides of shrubs growing at the gardens and talked about the difficulty of finding commercial sources for things that we should be growing in the South.

The generation of nurserymen who were also plantsmen is disappearing, and few new ones are coming to take their place. Years ago, when Carl Starker gave up his alpines, Eleanor Chalfin wrote, "It is a pity to see old nurseries curtailed or given up entirely. Soon there will be few field grown plants and almost no sizable stock available for gardens." She died soon afterward, and that was the end of the splendid collection of herbs she and her husband had gathered together during the ten years they were at Plantation Gardens.

Gardeners are unable to find the plants they want, but at the same time nurserymen are unable to sell choice shrubs that they have taken the trouble to propagate. Galle showed a slide of the witch alder, *Fothergilla major*, an early-flowering dwarf shrub found only in the high mountains of North Carolina and Tennessee. He says a New Jersey nurseryman who has grown it for years has discarded it for lack of demand. The witch alder is still listed in the catalogue of the Tingle Nursery Company, but Leamon Tingle, who established the nursery in 1906, retired last fall, and it is doubtful whether his successors will keep up his splendid collection. Already a great many rare plants have been dropped.

Another slide Galle showed was of the bottlebrush buckeye, *Aesculus parviflora*. Although it is native to Georgia, not a single Georgia nurseryman could supply buckeyes when they were needed for research by a government hospital in Maryland. Twenty years ago Henry Hohman sent me the bottlebrush buckeye from the Kingsville nursery. It bloomed the second summer, and ever since has bloomed punctually the second week in June. The flowers are like foxtail lilies, tall spikes of fuzzy anthers. It is not really a shrub for a small garden; it needs room to develop as the plants (imported from Holland!) are allowed to do at Callaway.

Galle is growing two desirable shrubs of the lily family: the Alexandrian laurel, *Danae racemosa* and the butcher's broom, *Ruscus aculeatus*. He is growing the hermaphrodite butcher's broom from seed, and has a plant, either male or female, from an old garden in Athens, Georgia, where it makes a hedge more than 200 feet long. I think this is the form that is generally grown in southern gardens. I have never known it to fruit, though it is described in the catalogue as having "red berries or yellow," but if it is female I hope it will be pollinated by the hermaphrodite form nearby.

Jacques Legendre says he has listed the Alexandrian laurel for years and cannot persuade retail nurserymen to stock it. This is a pity as everyone who sees it in my garden wants to know where to get it.

Galle sent me a form of *Nandina domestica* called 'Harbour Dwarf' that came from a nursery in Winston-Salem. The pretty little plants, some with bright red leaves, are less than a foot tall; and I have another form from the same source called 'True Dwarf' which remains at about two feet. Both make splendid ground covers in sun or shade.

Galle showed slides of interesting hollies, particularly yellow-fruited ones, which he likes because birds allow the berries to hang longer, and because they show up better than the red ones on dark days. Other interesting trees and shrubs at Callaway are: 'Moonglow', a variegated pyracantha that takes on a purplish color in winter; a new fragrant dogwood found in Alabama; a dwarf sweet gum; and the beautiful white redbud.

March 8, 1970

VARIEGATED FOLIAGE

In 1736 John Custis of Williamsburg wrote to Peter Collinson of London to thank him for the plants he had sent from England to Virginia: "It would be difficult if not impossible to say how much I think myself indebted to you for your pretty presents. One striped box has some life in it; I should have been glad of it; being a great admirer of all the tribe of striped gilded and variegated plants; and especially trees. I am told those things are out of fashion but I do not mind that. I always make my fancy my fashion." As an admirer of variegated leaves, John Custis would find himself very much in the fashion now. It seems to me that I find a new variegated leaf every time I go to a nursery or a flower show. Trees, shrubs, vines, and herbaceous plants all have forms with variegated foliage. There is even a variegated nasturtium, or was in the days of Queen Victoria, called 'Tom Thumb'.

Silver or gold trimmings may be inherent in the plant, or they may be caused by a virus. The virus does not add to their beauty. I have a camellia that is disfigured by a scattering of discolored leaves. Even the natural variegation, if you can call it natural, is sometimes very unattractive. "Perhaps more rubbish is foisted on purchasers of trees and shrubs in the shape of variegated sorts than of anything else," [William Jackson] Bean writes. "A variegated plant should have its leaf colouring bright, well-defined and abundant to be of value. Yet by some dealers every spotty or muddy coloured form is thought worthy of a name and flattering description." As thoroughly as I agree with Bean about the prevalence of spotty variegations, especially the aucuba that looks as if yellow paint had been splashed on it, I don't think nurserymen are to be blamed for providing what people want and a great many people want that hideous aucuba.

Among the trees with variegated foliage there are maples with leaves edged in white or yellow, beeches with white or yellow striped leaves, and a form of our native cucumber tree, *Magnolia acuminata,* that has leaves splashed with yellow. The English hollies have more forms with variegated leaves than any *Ilex* I know of. I suppose it is because their silver and gilt trimmings have been prized for so long. One of them, a variegated form of the hedgehog holly, was sent to England from France in the seventeenth century. It is called *I.* 'Silver Porcupine'. The American holly, on the other hand, has (so far as I know) no varieties with white or yellow foliage.

There are variegated forms of the tea olive, *Daphne odora*, euonymus, elaeagnus, *Pieris japonica*, pittosporum, and a number of species of ligustrum. There is also a tricolor variety of the shrub that is in the trade as *Cleyera japonica*, but I have never seen it listed. The leaves are rose tinted with yellow stripes and white margins. For the garden the best variegated ivy is 'Glacier', but it is slow growing and after six years mine is just beginning to spread. The leaves are of medium size and prettily marked with gray and white. They have never been hurt by the cold, but the leaves of the handsome ivy 'Canary Cream' are always ruined by the cold before the winter is over, and in the last severe seasons the plant has been badly hurt.

In the fall flower show, Mrs. Spruce exhibited a yellow-veined form of the common honeysuckle. It is said to be less vigorous than the type and not likely to become a pest, but I think it will bear watching. Ground covers must be considered too. There are variegated forms of both the large and the small periwinkle; these are just as rampant as the typical plants. The variegated pachysandra is said to grow more slowly. I have just gotten some of the pachysandra so I shall see for myself whether this is true.

January 24, 1965

SELECTIONS FOR THE ROCK GARDEN

Lincoln Foster's recent book, *Rock Gardening*, has as a subtitle *A Guide to Growing Alpines and Other Wild Flowers in the American Garden*. It is the other wild flowers that will mainly interest us. Wild flowers from all over the world are saxatile plants, and there are plenty to fill a rock garden in any climate without touching the alpines at all. Sometimes the wild flowers of other countries are easier to grow than our own. I have found *Campanula poscharskyana*, the Dalmatian harebell, the easiest species, and I have never been successful with our own native, *Campanula divaricata*.

The purpose of the book, Foster writes, is "to suggest a number of ways that alpine, saxatile plants and other wild flowers can be grown successfully and in harmony with a variety of sites." One of the advantages of rock plants, he writes, is that a great many can be grown in a small space. A dozen plants would fill thirty-six square feet in the perennial border, but fifty rock plants could be grown in the same space, along with an equal number of little bulbs. The shade of a single dogwood will do for a woodland garden, an outcrop of only three stones will shelter a number of rare and interesting miniatures, and an alpine lawn can be made within the circle of a driveway.

Foster describes the design, construction, planting, and maintenance of all of these, drawing on knowledge gained from his travels in the mountains of this country, Europe, the gardens he and Mrs. Foster have made for others, and from their own garden at Millstream House, Falls Village, Connecticut.

When I opened the book I was already familiar with the Millstream garden, for it is the setting for Mrs. Foster's delightful *Keer-loo—The True Story of a Young Wood Duck*. The little duckling grew up in the garden, following her about while she weeded, napping in her shadow, nibbling lady sorrel, chasing grasshoppers, eating spiders and sow bugs, and paddling in the little brook that comes cascading into the garden at one end and flows through it in a series of little rills and shallow pools. When he was older he learned to swim in a large pond in the woods, where he chased the little trout and pecked at the frogs or sunned himself on the embankment while Mrs. Foster worked in the primrose bog below. While she was weeding he sometimes helped by snipping off the tops of weeds or pulling them up. This was all right, but when he followed Foster to the seed beds, he pulled up gentians and saxifrages that had just been planted and ran off with them like a playful puppy with a ball. For her book she did drawings of Keer-loo and the seedlings, of Keer-loo sitting among the sempervivens on the dry wall, and swimming between the rushes and waterweeds of the woodland pond.

For *Rock Gardening* she did drawings of *Androsace sarmentosa*, *Thalictrum kiusianum*, and *Lewisia tweedyi* and she made diagrams of the construction of outcrops, ledges, and dry walls. More than half of the book is devoted to a descriptive catalogue of plants. Many of these are alpines that I never even heard of, but there are plenty that can be grown in an average rock garden, many that Southerners should become acquainted with, and many more that are already familiar—especially those from our own mountains. Galax and shortia grow as well in Piedmont North Carolina as in Connecticut, and I see that Foster had no better luck with the Japanese shortia than I did.

I was pleased to find the lily-leaf sedge, *Carex fraseri* (now called *C. cymophyllus* by North Carolina taxonomists), a rare endemic of our mountains and a welcome patch of green in the garden in winter. No sources are given for the plants, and I expect the rare ones are to be had only from botanic gardens or collectors or other members of the Rock Garden Society. "From rock gardeners and botanists too numerous to mention," Foster writes, "I have acquired generous gifts of plants and seeds." The seed exchange of the American Rock Garden Society sends a splendid list to members and plants in the trade are advertised in the ARGS Bulletin. Foster is a past president of the society.

March 2, 1969

TROPICAL PLANTS

When Hamilton Mason dropped in last summer on the way to Baltimore, he was surprised to find *Erythrina crista* [*Erythrina crista-galli*] still in bloom. Here it is cut back to the ground every winter, but it rises up again in the spring and grows to eight feet and blooms all summer. In Jacksonville, where Mr. Mason has gardened for ten years, only the new wood is cut back and the plant may grow to the height indicated. Its common name is coral tree. Mr. Mason and I talked about the tropical plants that should be given a trial farther north than they are usually grown in the open.

Some, such as Mrs. Williams's paper plant [*Tetrapanax papyrifer*] and *Jacobinia carnea* [*Justica carnea*] have already proved to be root hardy in Charlotte, and others that have not yet been proven so might be given another trial. Mr. Mason suggested *Calliandra tweedii* which Dr. Mayer has planted without success, but I think I will try it anyway. Mr. Mason wrote after he returned to Florida, "The foliage looks like that of the sensitive plant but it was not damaged in the slightest by eighteen degrees. The bright red puff balls are lovely in spring with minor flowering on new growth during summer and fall."

All calliandras like acid soil and plenty of water. They bloom best in full sun and probably demand it here, though they will take some shade in Florida. In Florida *C. tweedii* gets to be an open shrub to eight or ten feet tall, but Mr. Mason says it is slow growing and could be managed in a container very nicely. Perhaps if we can't get it to grow out of doors someone with a greenhouse will take it on.

Like me, Mr. Mason delights in tropical vines. "My garden is more of a jungle than ever," he wrote on June 27, "perhaps because I have so many vines this year: *Passiflora* × *alato-caerulea*, three species of red passion vines, *Thunbergia grandiflora* (which would be enough just in itself), *Stigmaphyllon*, *Argyreia speciosa* (the woolly morning glory), *Porana paniculata*, and *Solanum seaforthianum*. The last is blooming well now."

The blue passion flower, *Passiflora caerulea*, is said to be as hardy as our Maypop and *P.* × *alato-caerulea* [*P.* × *belotti*] considerably hardier. We should try these and the flowering species.

Thunbergia is root hardy and almost the most beautiful of all flowering vines, but I am going to dig mine up if it doesn't bloom this season. The trouble is that it doesn't get started soon enough in the spring. Perhaps someone with a patio or a very protected place would have better luck than I. The flowers are large, pale blue trumpets that come in the fall.

Dr. Solymosy sent me seeds of the solanum, which I have asked Mrs. Price to start early. If they come up at all there will be some for someone else, as my space is limited. I saw this bloom in Louisiana in mid-October, bunches of charming lilac flowers and brilliant red berries the size of green peas. I'm sure it won't be hardy, but I hope some of the berries will ripen so that I can save seed for another year.

The maurandias can be treated as annuals if the seeds are started indoors and then the plants might as well be left outside to take their chances. "*Maurandya barclayana* [*Asarina barclaiana*] is less rampant," Mr. Mason wrote, "but I think *M. ereubescens* [*Lophospermum erubescens*] is handsomer. It has large, bright pink flowers and is evergreen with me to at least twenty-seven degrees."

All these and many more vines and shrubs, along with palms and ferns, bulbs, perennials, and all sorts of tropical wonders will be found in Mr. Mason's new book, *Your Garden in the South*. I am slowly soaking it up, and shall have more to say on the subject of tropical plants. I am sure it will be most useful to the lucky gardeners with greenhouses and those with patios—I mean those with real patios walled in on four sides—will be able to grow many things that are not hardy here in the outdoor garden.

Mr. Mason has now gone to Des Moines to become garden editor of *Better Homes and Gardens*. He writes that he will miss the tropical plants, but that it will be nice to be able to grow lilacs and peonies again.

January 22, 1961

ANNUALS

Annuals are needed to keep the garden bright and fragrant through the heat of summer. There are annuals that seed themselves year in and year out, and these are indispensable but so are the ones that need to be sown every spring. Larkspur, ageratum and calliopsis [the annual coreopsis] are the never-failing volunteers. Larkspur must be sown in the fall if the seeds come out of packets but seeds of the other two can be scattered in spring if they are not already coming up like weeds. Calliopsis has been with me as long as I can remember, since childhood I think. The tall calliopsis is the one that I like, although the dwarf kinds are said to bloom over a longer period and they would certainly be more practical, as they would not be bent, broken, and bowed down by summer storms. I like the single-flowered ones too. These seem to be hard to find nowadays, but Burpee lists them in mixtures, and the little daisies will be garnet or gold or a combination of the two colors.

Alyssum and ageratum bloom longer than any other annuals. Last spring I planted *Alyssum* 'Pastel Carpet' and 'Tiny Tim' at the end of

February. I forgot to note when they began to bloom, but it was very early, and there were flowers almost until Christmas. *A.* 'Tiny Tim' is really too small. I like *A.* 'Carpet of Snow' better and the violet-flowered *A.* 'Royal Carpet' is the best of all. These two and rosy *A.* 'Rosie O'Day' will be available in peat pots, but seed can be planted at any time, early or late.

I buy plants of ageratum every spring. Last year I had *Ageratum* 'Blue Blazer'. It blooms earlier than other varieties, and I liked it best of the named kinds. I always have lots of volunteers of the old tall floppy kinds, and I am glad to have them coming up and blooming at the end of summer.

Torenias seed themselves indefinitely, but the volunteers do not begin to bloom until mid-summer. Seeds won't germinate until the ground is warm, so I like to get plants that have been grown from seed and grown under glass. Park's catalogue for 1970 lists *T.* 'Alba', a pure white form, and a variety called *T.* 'Gefion' that is said to be more dwarf, eight inches, and more bushy than the typical *Torenia fournieri*. Torenias will bloom in part shade and will keep going in very dry places, but they are at their best when they have lots of moisture and, like the birds, the volunteers cluster around the place where the pool runs over.

V. Sackville-West, in *A Joy of Gardening*, writes she would like to put in a good word for lobelia, so much overplanted in the bedding-out days and then so neglected. She says it should be thought of not as an edging but as a wide blue pool. Gertrude Jekyll had the same notion of planting it in quantity. Dwarf lobelia, she said, should be tucked into every available chink in the rock garden for late summer bloom: "such a filling with one good plant at a time would be found restful and satisfying, and would help correct the slightly disquieting impression so often received in such a place, from too many objects of interest being presented within one's range of vision." *Lobelia* 'Crystal Palace' is an old bedding-out variety that is still in the catalogues. The compact form is six inches tall. A dwarf variety with white flowers is called *L.* 'White Lady'. *L.* 'Sapphire' is a trailing plant for hanging baskets. The flower is deep blue with a white eye.

I see the old magenta spider flower, *Cleome spinosa* [*C. hassleriana*] in bloom in dooryards in our neighborhood, but I haven't had it in my garden for many years. Years ago, when it was not in the trade, Violet Walker gave me seeds of the white flowered cleome. Now I see it in *Park's Flower Book* as *C.* 'Helen Campbell Snow Crown'. It is by far the loveliest, but *C.* 'Pink Queen' was given a Silver Medal All-American Award in 1942. Cleomes are handsome shrublike plants about four feet tall with large palmate leaves. They are delightful when the flowers open late in the afternoon, but look somewhat bedraggled in the heat of the day. They reseed themselves generously and the seedlings are true to color if only one color is planted.

February 22, 1970

SWEET PEAS

Upon looking into the history of the sweet pea, I find that it was described in 1695 by the Italian monk and botanist, Father Cupani, who sent seed to England where they bloomed in 1701. A hundred and fifty years later, Mrs. [Jane] Loudon described six kinds in *The Ladies' Flower Garden of Ornamental Annuals*. There was a pure white form, one of pink and white called *Lathyrus* 'Painted Lady', and the rest were in tones of violet. By the beginning of the twentieth century, the hybridists were at work and there were soon more than 3,000 varieties, most of which have disappeared.

I looked into *My Garden in Summer* to see what kinds Mr. Bowles use to grow and found that he preferred self-colored sweet peas, especially the lilac of 'Grizel Hamilton'; 'Moonstone', a delicate cool lavender gray, endowed with the sweetest scent of any sweet pea, not so strong as to become a burden and lasting until the flower fades; 'Tortoise Shell', an orange-salmon that does not burn in hot weather; and 'Seashell', a delicate shaded pink. None of these are in the modern catalogues, not even in *Thompson and Morgan*.

Elizabeth [von Arnim], she of the German Garden, looks upon the sweet pea as second only to the rose, if not a queen at least a princess royal. "There is something so utterly gentle and tender about sweet peas," she wrote, "something so endearing in their clinging, winding and yielding growth; and then the long straight stalk and the perfect little winged flower at the top, with its soft, pearly texture and wonderful range and combination of colors, all of them pure, all of them satisfying, not an ugly one or even a less beautiful one among them." She must have been reading Cowper, who described the clinging vines as "recompensing well the strength they borrow with the grace they lend." Elizabeth considered sweet peas the easiest annuals to grow. She said they were the only seeds that came up in the first garden that she planted when she was a little girl and for the first season in her German garden. But hers were the old, sturdy, and probably much more fragrant forms, not the modern improved varieties that are considered scarcely worth growing except under ideal conditions and certainly not flowers for the beginner.

The essentials of sweet pea culture are sun, drainage, a rich and preferably heavy soil, and water. The classic method of planting the seed is to trench the soil two feet deep, but this is no longer considered necessary. Digging in manure and a dressing of lime to a depth of six or eight inches is good enough. Some plant the seed in drills five or six inches deep, covering them with two inches of soil until they come up, and filling in gradually as they grow. Some think planting them two inches deep does as well. It is important to put the supports in place when the seeds are planted. Once the vines start to flower the flowers must be faithfully picked.

There have been sweet pea societies since the beginning of the century. They classify the modern varieties as climbing or dwarf, and the flowers as hooded, waved, or open. The waved flowers are the Spencers. They are the prettiest but they stop flowering in hot weather. In the floribunda strain, the less desirable but heat-resistant Cuthbertsons have been improved in color, form, and length of stem, and these are considered the best sweet peas for the South. They begin to flower two weeks ahead of the Spencers and bloom on through the heat.

The dwarf or cupid race, developed in California, is now in the trade as 'Little Sweetheart'. 'Little Sweetheart' comes in a mixture or in a wide range of separate colors. The plants are low mounds, less than a foot tall.

I have wondered if the modern improvements are as fragrant as the old varieties. Evidently they are not, for Park offers a mixture of old-fashioned sweet scented kinds, more fragrant than modern types. In the South, sweet peas should always be planted in the fall.

September 24, 1961

PEONY

When I think of planting peonies, I think of all of the years that people have been planting them, for they are as old as any plant in the garden, maybe older. The first peony was given to Paeon, the physician of the gods, who received it on Mt. Olympus from the hands of Leto, the mother of Apollo. With it he healed Pluto's wound, and so for centuries it was grown as only a medicinal herb. Pliny listed twenty ills that the peony would cure.

It was the Chinese who first appreciated the beauty of the flowers. In the eleventh century, Chinese gardeners began to think of peonies as ornamental, and to fertilize and cultivate the plants to make them produce flowers of a very large size. By the end of the sixteenth century, Chinese growers listed thirty varieties, but English gardeners knew only half a dozen. [John] Parkinson described these and wrote, "We cherish them for the beauty and delight of their goodly flowers as well as for their physical virtues."

Now there is a bewildering variety to choose from, and once chosen, their roots must be planted with care for they are as fragile as old china, and once planted, they must be left alone to grow in grace. The peony-planting season in these parts begins in October. The roots can be set out anytime before Christmas, but all agree that early planting is by far the best, and all agree that planting in spring is not advisable, although potted plants can be put out at any time.

Peonies bloom best in full sun, though some say that shade for part of the day not only does no harm, but is an advantage in that it keeps the flowers fresher. Next to giving them plenty of sun and good drainage, the best thing to do for peonies is to give them plenty of room. They need light and air, and like the bearded irises they do not like to be crowded in the borders with other plants, but want a bed all to themselves. In *The Book of the Peony*, Mrs. Harding says that the minimum distance between plants is two and a half feet and that three and a half or four is far better. But the best plants that I saw last spring were five feet apart. This gives them room to grow and to be admired and be tended to.

In preparing the soil some think well-rotted manure is essential, and some think it is the worst thing that can happen to a peony. Most growers believe in mixing manure with the subsoil and taking care that it never touches the roots. Mrs. Harding believes in manure in small quantities, one part to nine parts of top soil and very thoroughly mixed. She says that manure should never be used as a mulch. Those who are against manure (or who cannot get it) use peat moss or leaf mold for humus (one part to three of top soil) and bone meal (a pound to a plant) or a commercial fertilizer low in nitrogen such as 4-8-8 (half a pound to a plant). All should be thoroughly mixed with the soil. Peonies are tolerant of acidity, but if the soil is very acid lime should be added.

The holes should be three feet in diameter and extremists want them three feet deep, but the celebrated hybridizer, Dr. Saunders, says that eighteen inches is a minimum and two feet is enough. When the roots are planted most peony growers think that the eyes should be exactly two inches below the surface of the soil. Mrs. Harding says the roots should be covered with fine soil and pressed down with the hands. She is horrified at the idea of the rough foot tramping that is often recommended. I picture her as waving the gardener aside and pressing the soil with her own hands.

After they were established, Mrs. Harding fed her peonies every fall with a mixture of bone meal, four ounces to a plant, and wood ashes, six ounces to a plant. She spread these, just before a rain, in a circle just beyond the outside leaves and dug the stuff in lightly. The best peonies that I saw this spring were fertilized twice, early in the season and just before blooming, with 5-10-10.

August 27, 1961

TREE PEONIES AND OTHERS

Like Mrs. [Eleanor Vere] Boyle, I feel that before the parting hours go by, I must quickly set down my delight in the "gone sweet days" and must fix in my memory the thousand glories doomed to die before ever the next month begins.

First the peonies, earliest of all in Mrs. Boyle's garden

> came the crimson-pink single peony with yellow stamens and bluish leaves like a giant Rose of Sharon (the single Scotch Rose); then the pale pink double; then the heavy crimson, that pales so quick in sun or

> rain; then, most beautiful of all, the pure, cold, white peony, with a faint tinge of color on its outer petals. Last of all is the large rose colored one with an evanescent perfume like a dream of the smell of a wild rose, yet in substance so staunch a flower that I have known rose peonies to retain their beauty for two full weeks in a glass of water. All these excepting one or two who here and there outstay the rest, are gone by.

I wonder if those flowers that Mrs. Boyle wrote about in 1884 were not the very ones that are found in old gardens hereabout. Mrs. Forbes has just been telling me of a very old single red variety with white stamens that she saw in Miss Hazel Johnston's garden in Belmont, and of a glorious white one she herself inherited that has moved with her every time she moved. "They say peonies won't bloom if they are moved," Mrs. Forbes said, "but this one always has. It is eighty years old and it has moved a lot."

The earliest peonies to bloom are the tree peonies. These should be grown to lengthen the season, even if they were not more beautiful than all garden flowers. They bloom in April, long before the herbaceous peonies. My earliest date is the eleventh. This was for *Paeonia* 'Yomo-zakura', a most delectable and delicate pink flower with numerous fluted petals and a mass of pale yellow anthers. The rose colored flowers of *P.* 'Kim-Gayo' are delightfully fragrant.

The foliage of tree peonies is as lovely as the flowers, especially when the pale new leaves unfurl in tints of celadon and coral. I don't know why these are called tree peonies for they are low spreading shrubs, usually not much more than three or four feet tall. They are not very well known, perhaps because they are slow growing and expensive, and I should like to hear from anyone who has them.

The herbaceous peonies grow slowly too, but they are as permanent as shrubs. At the present time the single flowers are popular. There are two groups of these; both have five or more petals. The ones called single peonies have pollen-bearing stamens, and those called Japanese peonies have stamens with anthers almost or entirely without pollen. The stamens of the Japanese peonies appear in a number of forms and are called staminodes. *P.* 'Krinkled White' seems to be king of the singles. It is seven inches across by my measurement and stands out in any collection. 'Le Jour' and 'Cygnet' are earlier whites, also large and handsome and of splendid substance. 'Seashell' is like a great pink poppy. The most striking Japanese peony that I know of is *P.* 'Mikado'. It is described as red, but I remember it as I saw it in full bloom early in May as a brilliant red-violet, one of the most telling colors in the garden. 'Roberta' is a late white one, very tall, very fluffy with yellow staminodes. It was in bloom this year on the nineteenth of May, along with 'Shaylor's Sunburst', which has a very high rating with the peony people.

I like these single flowers, but to me the double peony is the peony, and 'Mary E. Nichols' the archetype. It combines the color and perfection of a seashell with the opulence and stately bearing that are characteristic of its race. 'Mme. Jules Dessert' is quite as lovely, an enormous white flower with the tints of the sky at dawn, and it has the same qualities, which only peonies have, of grandeur, purity, and fragility. I think the best pink double that I know is 'Walter Faxon', an early variety with large perfectly formed flowers of a clear tint of rose. Among the semi-doubles, 'Minnie Shaylor' has rows of frilled pink-tinted petals that turn white as they mature and a charming center of golden anthers.

This is the moment to study the catalogues and make a list of peonies for planting next October. Plants grown in the South are best for us.

May 28, 1961

CLEMATIS ALSO FLOWERS IN SHADE

The Arnolds' 1961 clematis list is the most complete that I have ever seen, and their directions for growing the plants are explicit. They even tell you how to pronounce the name, with the accent on the first syllable. It is not a word often mispronounced, but I suppose the Arnolds thought their customers might be misled by Amy Lowell's clematis at her window lattice, or by Tennyson's "Rose, rose and clematis / Trail and twine and clasp and kiss."

Clematis, as everyone hears over and over, likes sun on its head and shade at its feet, and so I am interested to find the Arnolds recommending those of *C. jackmanii*, *C. vitacella* and *C. montana* groups, including *C. lanuginosa* and *C. patens* for open northerly aspects; and *C. alpina*, *C. calycina* [*C. cirrhosa*], *C. chrysocoma* [*C. montana* var. *sericea*], *C. jackmanii*, *C. Montana*, *C.* × *'Nelly Moser'*, *C. spooneri*, and *C. vedrariensis*

'Rosea', for north walls and complete shade. This is something worth knowing and I mean to see if it works for me as it seems to in Oregon, for I have been in search of vines that flower in the shade.

The Arnolds plant clematis in either spring or fall, but I have better luck with those planted in the spring. The ones I have gotten from them came in late March and went right on growing. The Arnolds are very stern about preparing the holes. They want the soil removed from a space two feet square and two feet deep. The bottom of the hole is to have a layer of pebbles, sand or mortar rubble (all kinds of clematis are lime lovers) and then to be filled with a mixture of two parts Blue Whale, three parts soil, and one part coarse sand.

Having read a great deal about Blue Whale, I sat down to telephone and ask a number of seed stores if they carry it. They don't. The Arnolds are prepared for this and they give the address of a place in Canada that ships it "p.p. & d.f." I won't go into the merits of Blue Whale at this time (the part of the liquid which is "the pure essence of the whale") but you can learn all about it from the Arnolds.

Clematis should be planted with two or three inches of earth above the crown, where the stem and roots meet. See that they get plenty of water all through the summer. The species bloom from one year's end to another. In my garden *C. cirrhosa* begins at Thanksgiving and goes on after Christmas. The drooping white flowers are the color of sea foam and the fernlike leaves have warm winter tones of red and bronze. *C. balearica* [*C. cirrhosa* var. *balearica*], which the Arnolds promise for next year, should fill in from January until *C. armandii* blooms, usually in March, and before that is over the pink anemone-like flowers of *C. montana* 'Rubra' come along, *C. texensis* blooms before those come to an end and it goes on readily until frost, if it is never allowed to dry out.

The flowers of *C. texensis* are rose red with a rim of pale yellow. They are followed by clusters of feathered seeds. As soon as the leaves turn brown, the whole vine can be cut away, for it dies at the end of the season and new shoots come up in the spring. As this is a great advantage, I thought I would try some of the texensis hybrids, particularly the 'Duchess of York', which has pale pink flowers, but the only two that I can find in the trade are 'Ville de Lyon' and the 'Duchess of Albany'.

The 'Ville de Lyon' is not typical of the group. The flowers are wide and flat and of a brilliant red with darker tones in the center; the vines do not die back in winter. The 'Duchess of Albany' has the herbaceous habit of its Texas parent. I have planted it beside *Camellia* 'Dawn' where it can be cut to the ground in the fall when the shrub is in bloom and then allowed to cover it in summer with charming rose-pink flowers.

I would never be without the useful, beautiful and fragrant Japanese species *C. paniculata* [*C. terniflora*] and I am now searching out some of the rarer species, each one with its peculiar charm.

March 26, 1961

BEAUTIFUL LILIES

The first speaker of the season for the Charlotte Garden Club was Mr. George Doak, president of the North American Lily Society, who lives in Chapel Hill, North Carolina, where, he says, he once had a lily collection equal to any in the North and would have it still if it weren't for the pine mice. Pine mice are far more destructive than lily diseases and far less easily controlled. They have forced Mr. Doak to plant all his bulbs in baskets and he doesn't like that a bit.

The lily diseases are three: botrytis, which can be entirely controlled by systematic spraying; basal rot, which can be controlled only by discarding infected bulbs and sterilizing the soil; and mosaic, for which there is at present no effective control. Mosaic is a virus that affects lilies in various ways: to some, like tiger and Madonna lilies, it does no harm; others, like the hybrids of *Lilium hansonii*, are immune; and the third group is susceptible and, once infected, the bulbs die immediately. Nothing can be done about it. As none of these diseases are transmitted by seed, planting seed is the best way to grow lilies. Some seed germinates quickly and the bulbs begin to bloom the second season. Some take five or six years. Plant the seeds in the fall, covering with an eighth of an inch of soil and kept moist. Seeds can be had reasonably from the Lily Society and Park Seed Company has a good list.

Lilies, Mr. Doak says, are no harder than pansies to grow from seed. Except for their diseases (and pine mice) their culture is much easier than that of most popular flowers. They have no insect pests; they don't have black spot; they don't have to be disbudded. They are not fussy about the acidity of the soil. With some sun and good drainage, any garden soil will grow just about any lily. They are gross feeders, however, and go downhill if not fertilized.

At the Agricultural Research Center in Beltsville, Maryland, the lilies are given a fair amount of phosphorus after blooming, a fair amount of potash late in the fall and in spring a little nitrogen, but not too much. Mr. Doak simplifies this practice by giving all his lilies a sprinkling of 0-14-14 in September and if he gets to it he gives them a small amount of nitrogen, 8-8-8 or 6-6-6 in spring.

In growing lilies the most important thing is to get bulbs from a specialist who knows how to handle them, for lilies have no dormant period, and bulbs that are allowed to dry out are sure to fail to bloom properly, if at all. Lily books and most of the catalogues are written by the experts for gardeners in the North and on the West Coast. You need to join the North Carolina Lily Society.

In Chapel Hill, the lily seasons last from the third week in April, when *L.* 'Early Bird' comes into bloom, to some time in September when Wilson's form of *Lilium formosanum* is over. Mr. Doak has had flowers the first of October.

October 13, 1963

ASTEROMOEA MONGOLICA—KALIMERIS PINNATIFIDA

Not long ago, I had a letter from Mrs. Joseph Spengler, who said she had been meaning to write to me for more than ten years, and had finally gotten my address from Billy Hunt. She said that when she read about the double Japanese aster in *A Southern Garden*, she was sure that it is the little white flower that had come to her from Clarence Gohdes's old place and has been growing ever since in her garden in Durham. She also found it at Duke University. Professor Sanders of the English department calls it the Oxford Orphanage flower, because that's where he got it. Mrs. Spengler wanted to know what it really is so she "called in the botanists." No one could tell her and at last she wrote to Carroll Wood, assistant curator of the Arnold Arboretum. Mr. Wood replied that the flower is one of the composites, a member of the largest and most difficult family of flowering plants, but it is not an aster. "We have spent a good deal of time in trying to work out its identity," he wrote, "and I think that it is certainly *Boltonia indica*, which has also been known as *Asteromoea indica* [*Asteromoea mongolica* or *Kalimeris pinnatifida*].

"I can find no record of this plant in the current manuals which deal with cultivated plants. However, this and many others which have not struck the popular fancy are certainly around the United States in various gardens, and I hope that they will remain there, cherished, until they are one day rediscovered."

I had the same experience in getting the plant identified. It came to me from Catherine Taylor's garden in Greensboro. Catherine had it from Dreer. Dreer said they got it from Japan and that was all they could tell us. Later on, just before we left Raleigh, Dr. Orland White noticed it in the garden and carried it off to the Blandy Experimental Farm. Some time later he wrote, "At last I have succeeded in getting that aster-like plant identified. Dr. Blake, a specialist on the compositae and one of the taxonomists of the United States Department of Agriculture, says it is *Asteromoea mongolica* (*Franch.*) *Kitam*, a native of China and Japan."

Well, indica or mongolica, I feel we have at last gotten to the root of the matter. And it still blooms in my garden from June until frost. I have given so much away that I haven't much left but I have enough to give Mrs. Price to propagate, if anyone wants it. It is easily propagated by division.

Mrs. Spengler's garden is an acre of woodland where she grows camellias and azaleas under hollies and pine trees along with hundreds of naturalized foxgloves. Foxgloves grown from her seed are thriving at the Villa Serbelloni on Lake Como and in the cloistered garden of the San Domenico Hotel, Taomina, Sicily, overlooking the sea and Mount Etna, a garden once tended by the monks of a fourteenth century monastery. "Right now," Mrs. Spengler wrote in January, "our woods are encased in ice and sleet. I shall have to go out in daylight (it is now 2:00 AM) to see if I can relieve my plants from the weight of ice without breaking them." Camellias grown from cuttings taken from 1947 to 1949, "when no one thought we could grow camellias here," have survived their early smothering with laths and pine bows and some have grown as high as the second story. "Now they're on their own, and no plant likes to be on its own more than a camellia."

In spite of her success with camellias, Mrs. Spengler has no favorites. She calls herself a "general gardener" because she grows everything, and loves everything that grows. "I have had almost every rose that you can grow," she says, "and some died, but at least I have made their acquaintance." She is still expanding. An acre isn't enough for all the things she wants, and so she keeps clearing a little more of the woods. I hope I can get to Durham sometime to poke around in her "primeval forest" with its dogwoods and fringe trees and pines a hundred feet tall. There is no telling what I will find there.

March 3, 1968

HELLEBORES

All these years that I have been looking for *Helleborus viridis*, and not finding it, it has been growing in North Carolina gardens, and now has turned up in Wilson, North Carolina. Linda Lamm says it came into bloom January 25 and bloomed for more than a month. In *Flowering Plants of Great Britain*, a color plate shows a wide-open green flower of *Helleborus viridis* twice the size of the little cup of the other native species, *Helleborus foetidus*.

"No other wild flower, save the daisy and the chickweed, blooms so early in the year," Anne Pratt says, and she quotes from a poem about February: "The crocus, the snowdrop, the starwort appear. The hellebore waited to see me and die."

Gilbert White tells where both are to be found at Selborne: "*Helleborus foetidus*, stinking hellebore, bear's foot, or setterwort, all over the High-Wood and Coney-crofthanger: this continues a great branching plant the winter through, blossoming about January and is very ornamental in shady walks and shrubberies. The good women give the leaves powdered to children troubled with worms; but it is a violent remedy and ought to be administered with caution.

"*Helleborus viridis*, the green hellebore, in the deep stony lane on the left hand just before turning to Norton Farm and at the top of Middle Dorton under the hedge: this plant dies down to the ground early in Autumn and springs again about February, flowering almost as soon as it appears above ground."

The stinking hellebore that Miss Pauline Griffith gave me in the fall of 1968 bloomed last year for the first time, early in February. This year it was almost a month earlier and bloomed on into the spring. I haven't seen the seedlings that are supposed to be so abundant but Miss Pauline's plant has been joined by one from Lawrence Johnson, an Indiana nurseryman, and another from Weezie Smith who says it began to bloom in Alabama before Christmas.

This winter, *Helleborus corsicus* [*H. argutifolius*] came into bloom in Wilson in mid-January and continued into February. Linda thinks it gets too much sun in her garden, and she says it doesn't look like those at Sissinghurst. I have never been able to establish it in my garden, and I think this is due to having always started with mature plants. Last fall, Lawrence Johnson sent me a nice sturdy young plant that has come through the unusually trying winter without a blemish. He says this species has proved hardy in Indiana, though supposed to be tender as it is native to Corsica, and that it grows to shrublike proportions. The flowers are Ridgway's lumiere green. Carl Starker sent me a plant he called *Helleborus lividus* but it must have been closely related to *H. corsicus* [*H. argutifolius*] as the margins of the tri-foliage leaves were sharply toothed, and if true to name they should have been toothless.

In my garden *Helleborus atrorubens* (synonym *atropurpureus*) [probably 'Old Early Purple'], blooms in the latter part of January. The plant is described as deciduous, or might as well be, as the leaves are brown or discolored and should be cut off by the time the buds appear. The clump has increased in the twenty years it has been under a pine tree and I look forward to that early splash of wine when the small purple bells come up.

With me, the earliest Lenten roses bloom before the Christmas roses, at times even in December. E. A. Bowles said that the variety *praecox* is the earliest form of *Helleborus niger*, coming into bloom at Myddelton House by the end of September. I have had this three times from as many sources and never been able to get it established. Again, I think because the plants sent to me were too old. The typical *H. niger* blooms in December. At the present time I have only some hybrids that seldom bloom before the latter part of January.

March 28, 1971

THE CHRISTMAS ROSE AND OTHER HELLEBORES

I read somewhere, or someone told me, that the Christmas rose does not bloom at Christmas. But it does, at least at times, if it is the right variety. The season is variable. Some early forms bloom about Thanksgiving, and some late ones bloom in the New Year. Others bloom at Christmastime; I have known them to do it. The Christmas rose was in cultivation centuries before the English herbalists wrote about it in Tudor times.

"*Helleborus niger* versus the true black hellebore or Christmas flower," Parkinson wrote, "is the same that both Theophrastus and Dioscorides have written of, and which was called Melampodium or Melampus the Goatsheard, that purged and cured the mad or melancholicke daughters of Praetus with the roots thereof." The time of flowering, he wrote, is most rare, "that is in the deepe of winter about Christmas when no other can be seene upon the ground." The flower consists of "five broad white leaves, like unto a great single rose." And it "groweth only in the gardens of those that are curious and delight in all sorts of beautiful flowers in our countrey." Petal seems to be a word that came late to the English language, for the earliest quotation in the Oxford dictionary is 1704. It is defined as "Each of the divisions (modified leaves) of the corolla of a flower."

Gerard describes the Christmas flower as "rose-fashioned, sometimes very white, and oftentimes mixed with a little show of purple. It is good for mad and furious men, dull and heavy persons, and anyone who is molested with melancholy." The Dutch call it Christ's herb because if the weather is mild and warm it "floureth about the birth of our Lord Jesus Christ."

The first time I saw the Christmas rose it was blooming at the front door of a friend of my grandmother's. I wonder if she knew that planting it by the door to keep evil spirits from entering is a very ancient custom. It is not an easy plant to grow. English gardeners say the ground should be trenched three feet deep and well manured. It needs shade, requires moisture, and is said to want lime. Once established it should be let alone and if it flourishes at all it will continue for many years. *Helleborus niger* is called black hellebore because the roots are dark. There seems to be some question as to whether it is really the black hellebore of the ancients. Sir Arthur Hort identifies the hellebore of Theophrastus as *H. cyclophyllus*, a Greek species. Theophrastus has much to say about its poisonous nature and the superstitions connected with it.

Just as all daffodils are commonly called jonquils, there seems to be a general idea that all hellebores are Christmas roses. Lenten roses, hybrids of *Helleborus orientalis* [*H.* × *hybridus*] and other species, are sold locally as the Christmas rose, and Miss Pauline Griffith got *Helleborus foetidus* when she ordered the Christmas rose. *H. foetidus* likes to grow in sun-forsaken places. In spite of its name, the stinking hellebore, it is beloved of bees, and smells bad only at close quarters. The precocious buds appear in November though they seldom open before February or March. They are pale green and velvety and are wrapped at first in pale green, velvety leaves. The root leaves are evergreen and very dark. In *One Man's Garden,* Miles Hadfield says the flower spike withers after blooming and should be cut off. But other spikes continue to appear and mature and there is "nearly always one reaching its third flowering and final year." In my garden the plants have always disappeared after blooming and I have never had any volunteers but Miss Pauline says she always has plenty of seedlings. She really does!

December 21, 1969

GIRIDLIAN . . . A MASTER OF PLANTS

One of the things I most looked forward to in California was seeing Mr. J. N. Giridlian and the Oakhurst Gardens. They are in Arcadia, just across the street from the Los Angeles Arboretum, and they really are a large garden, not at all like a nursery. The plants in the wide circle under the spreading California live oaks were old friends for I have grown many of them, and have seen others pictured in Mr. Giridlian's catalogue of *Botanical Orchids, Bromeliads, and Out of the Ordinary Bulbs.*

Polly Anderson and I were lucky in the day we chose for our visit, as it was the day of the week that the nursery is closed. We telephoned to say we were coming and Mr. Giridlian let down the chain at the entrance and we had him all to ourselves. He is an old friend of mine. We have been exchanging letters for some twenty-five years.

In particular, I was interested in plants that I have grown myself but not long enough to have seen them in a mature state. One of these is *Ophiopogon jaburan.* I had had it just before I left Raleigh, but it had not fruited and I had no idea how handsome the bright blue berries are. The form listed in the catalogue has variegated leaves. Mr. Giridlian also has *O. arabicum* [*O. planiscapus* 'Nigrescens'], the only plant with black foliage that I have ever seen. I had seen it before in Mrs. Dean French's garden in Gastonia. Except for the color of the leaves it is very like mondo grass. The ophiopogons are interesting plants to grow in the shade.

And I was glad to see what can be expected of *Ruscus hypoglossum* in years to come for mine is getting off to a very slow start. At Oakhurst it is a fine thick ground cover, increasing by stolons and growing to a height of well on to two feet. Like *R. aculeatus* it is dioecious and seldom fruits, but there is no better evergreen ground cover for deep shade under trees. It is too expensive to plant in quantity. I was amazed to find that it is a very old plant in gardens, and has been cultivated in England since the sixteenth century.

My interest in the even rarer climbing ruscus, *Semele androgyna*, was somewhat academic as it is very expensive and probably too tender for us, as it comes from the Canary Islands. Still, you never know what a plant will do until it is tried and this is very beautiful with its tall stout canes, and its slender shining leaves that look like the poet's laurel. Mr. Giridlian says it has red berries.

At Oakhurst and elsewhere I saw the evening flower, *Gladiolus tristis*, in bloom. The flowers are very fragrant but only in the dark. Mr. Giridlian has the variety *concolor*, with cream-colored flowers which he considers the best form. The flowers are in long spikes on three-foot stems and all in the spike are open at one time. Although it is fairly hardy, I shall have to report on it later for it comes from South Africa and, as a rule, South African plants do not flourish here as they do in California.

Scilla peruviana, the Cuban lily, was in bloom in Raleigh until the last of the month. The wide umbels of blue violet flowers are a foot or more across when the bulbs are once established, but it has a curious habit of blooming only on alternate years. A handsome rosette of wide flat leaves comes up in the fall and stays green all winter, but it needs some protection from the weather. When Clusius named the species in the sixteenth century he thought it came from South America, but it is really a native of the Mediterranean region.

Mr. Giridlian lists several orchids that can be grown in the garden, and one of them is so easy to please that everyone might have it. It is *Bletilla hyacinthoides* [*B. striata*], a small frilled flower of brilliant red-violet. The pure white form is even lovelier, but does not bloom so freely. Bletilla blooms in April, but not until it is well established and then it is very dependable. It likes shade and some moisture and a soil rich in humus.

I was relieved to find Mr. Giridlian so hale and hearty for he is one of the very few growers offering such a wide variety of rare and beautiful plants. "I am a fortunate man," he says. "I love what I am doing. They ask why I don't sell out and retire, but I am already doing exactly what I would do if I did retire."

September 19, 1965

NIGHT-BLOOMING CEREUS

One night late in August, Hannah Withers and I went out to see Mrs. W. H. Troutman's night-blooming cereus. All my life I have heard about this fantastic flower but this is the first time I have seen it. Hannah was eager to see it too. She said that her mother used to have one in the conservatory of her house in Monroe, but it never bloomed. Mrs. Troutman's plant has just come to her from her mother, who has had it for seven years. Her mother got it from a neighbor who was tired of it. I cannot imagine anyone ever getting tired of a night-blooming cereus.

The flowers begin to open about 8:30, or soon after dark, and watching them slowly unfurl is a fascinating pastime. Unfortunately, I lost my way and by the time we got there, six flowers were wide open and the seventh nearly so. There had been three the night before but there would be no more for a long time, for the only buds left were tiny. The flowers are like enormous and glorious white water lilies of delicate texture and powerful fragrance. The narrow pointed outer petals stand out in a fringe around the wider inner petals, which overlap to form a long delicate cup. The cup seems to glow, almost as if it were mysteriously lighted from within. Mrs. Troutman says she understands what people mean when they say that it reminds them of the manger. The pure white stigma is in the form of a star.

I borrowed a tape and measured a flower and found it to be nearly nine inches across. These heavy flowers on thick, curved, dark red stems spring from the tips of the leaves. The leaves are long, narrow, and so thin that it is unbelievable that they could bear such a weight, but Mrs. Troutman says they are very tough. She says the whole plant is tough, even the flowers, though they look so fragile. Mrs. Troutman's plant is in a five-gallon can. She, her daughter, Hannah, a neighbor, and the neighbor's little boy and I stood around it in awe, as if it were a miracle, and the flowering, so brief and so beautiful, does seem like one. The faded flowers that had bloomed in the darkness of the night before were hanging like three long reddish-brown burrs.

Mrs. Troutman wanted to know if I could tell her something about the plant and its culture. I told her that I could not, but that I would look it up. "You won't find much," she said. And I didn't, not even its name, for it is not a cereus, although it belongs to the cactus family. A number of plants commonly are called night-blooming cereus. The one most common in cultivation is *Hylocereus undatus*, one of the showiest members of the cactus family with flowers almost twelve inches long. It is a tropical American species used for hedges in Florida or to cover walls. It will climb to twenty-five feet with support. The other two that are popular as house plants are *Nyctocereus serpentinus* [*Peniocereus serpentinus*] from Mexico, which sounds more like our plant as the flowers are six inches long, and *Selenicereus macdonaldiae* [*S. grandiflorius*].

The culture of all three is said to be the same as for cactus and for them my houseplant book recommends a potting mixture of coarse builder's sand, one part humus, a little chopped charcoal, and hydrated lime. It needs water in the growing season, rest in winter, and some sun, but not enough to burn the leaves.

Ben Withers says he knows the night-blooming cereus well, as his boyhood chore was to take his mother's out of doors in spring and back up the steep steps in the fall. Once he said his mother was so charmed with a famous opera singer, who gave a concert at the Academy of Music about forty-five years ago, that when she came home from the concert and found a flower in bloom in the dark, she made him cut it and take it to the singer at her hotel. His mother said nothing else was lovely enough to express her gratitude for the pleasure the singer had given her.

September 14, 1960

THE DIVIDENDS OF FALL PLANTING

Any day now we can begin stocking the borders with spring flowers. I always hope to get an early start because it is so miserable to have to set things out in cold wet ground. I think that plants that go in the ground before the first of November get settled, and make better growth before the severe weather comes. My garden is planned to take care of itself and every year I try to see that it makes fewer demands, but fall planting must be done regularly if there is to be any real show in the spring. It is the transitory plants that fill in the gaps and keep color in the garden all through the year.

Arabis and alyssum are short-lived so I add a few every fall when I set out pansies and violas and biennials. The garden would be very forlorn in late spring without foxgloves and sweet William, columbine, and pinks. This year I am going to get some of the little maiden pinks, *Dianthus deltoides*, to plant on the dry wall. I love these small calico flowers that have been in gardens since the days of Queen Elizabeth and even longer.

The painted daisies [*Tanacetum coccineum*] are valuable for cutting. They never have done as well for me as they do in other gardens and I think it is because they like a richer soil than I provide. They are lovely in all their tones of pink and wine.

In the early spring when there is so much yellow—forsythia, alyssum, and daffodils—I just temper it with blue. Very few flowers approach spectrum blue in color, but one that comes very near to it is *Anchusa myosotidiflora* [*Brunnera macrophylla*]. It comes from Siberia and so it is very hardy, but it also survives the heat, and the large round leaves stay green all summer if it is planted in part shade, and not allowed to get too dry. The leaves are very small when the forget-me-not flowers begin to bloom in March, but as the flowers fade the leaves grow wider and some are six inches in diameter. I have never found any seedlings though it is said to seed itself freely, sometimes too freely, when it is in the right place.

The pure blue of the *Anchusa* is not in harmony with the grayed-blue-violets of phlox and violas and the old single blue hyacinths; I try to keep it in a different part of the garden. It is nice with pale yellow primroses and I must remember to get more of those this fall. I am making a list as I write, for if I don't I am sure to forget the things I most want and then when spring comes they aren't there.

I try to look beyond spring to summer and fall, and in looking I was discouraged to see how difficult it is to find sources for some of the common perennials, astilbe for example and Japanese anemones and physostegia. I did find some sources, a perennial nursery in Georgia from which I have gotten well-grown and well-packed plants and several northern nurseries; but if any of these can be had in Charlotte I would be glad to hear about it.

Physostegia is called obedient plant because the florets can be moved about the stem and they will stay in the new position. I wish it would also obey orders to stay where it is put in the flower border, for it is a very good perennial for late summer and early fall. We should use more native plants such as physostegia and Stokes aster [*Stokesia*], for they do well. Stokes aster is available in Charlotte and it has no bad habits.

October 31, 1965

SAVANNAH LANDS OF EAST CAROLINA

When I was a student at State College [now North Carolina State University], I used to go with Dr. B. W. Wells on field trips to the savannah lands of evergreen shrub bogs of East Carolina. Seeing these bog plants in Dr. Hechenbleikner's exhibit at the Flower and Garden Show brought back those happy days and set me to rereading the fifth and sixth chapters of *The Natural Gardens of North Carolina* which Dr. Wells wrote for the Garden Club of North Carolina.

Dr. Wells quotes John Brickell, an early settler in those parts, who wrote of the "Pleasant and delightful Savannahs and Meddows with their green Liveries interwoven with various kinds of beautiful and most glorious Color and fragrant Odours which several Seasons afford." In the distance the savannahs appeared to him like so many pleasure gardens, "being intermixed with a variety of Spontaneous Flowers of various colours such as the Tulip, Trumpet-flower and Princess-feather." I have often wondered what John Brickell took for tulip and princess feather, but there is no mistaking the trumpet flowers, *Sarracenia flava* and *S. rubra*, which Dr. Hechenbleikner grouped so delightfully above a little pool of brown water veiled with a green-gold film of duckweed. Beside the flowering red and yellow trumpets was a clump of pitcher plants, *S. purpurea*, in their bright winter coloring, and creeping through the grass beyond these, the running pine, *Lycopodium alopecuroides*. In the foreground was a patch of Venus flytrap, a semi-bog plant which Darwin called the most wonderful plant in the world. In the entire world it is found nowhere but in North Carolina, in a limited area around Wilmington.

Dr. Hechenbleikner also had in bloom the blue butterwort, *Pinguicula*, which blooms on the Savannah early in April. This is another insect catching plant. The slimy basal leaves trap small victims and roll inward to hold them. The little blue flowers are called bog violets.

Vaccinium crassifolium, the trailing blueberry, is a low evergreen that grows in semi-bogs from North Carolina to Georgia. It has small shining leaves, pink flowers, and red berries that turn black as they mature. In the background were yaupons and dahoon hollies and the pretty white cedar, *Chamaecyparis thyoides*. Gray moss and Carolina jessamine in full bloom hung from the branches of *Smilax laurifolia* from the shrub bogs. The laurel-leaved smilax has thicker, coarser foliage than that of the southern smilax and its black berries take two years to mature.

From the evergreen shrub bog, Dr. Hechenbleikner had brought the red bay, the loblolly bay and a small shoot of the chokecherry, *Aronia arbutifolia*, with pink buds just ready to open. I had forgotten that the chokecherry comes from the swamps, for like so many of the other shrubs from wet places it grows equally well in dry soil. In my garden the loblolly bay has not been a success, though it bloomed for several summers from the end of June into October. I think that in this climate it does not like to be in full sun for I know of several gardens in Charlotte where it is growing well in the shade. The large ivory buds are as lovely as the fragrant flowers, some of them almost four inches wide.

In the introduction to his book, Dr. Wells says that the natural gardens of North Carolina include "the finest examples of the southern Appalachian high mountain plant communities which constitute the southern extension of the Canadian balsam fir forest along with the very extensive developments of typical southern low country plant associations, savannahs, pocosins and swamps."

March 10, 1963

PETASITES

My friend Mr. W. O. Freeland would rather trade than sell. Whenever I order plants from him, they arrive with a list of plants he wants from my garden instead of a bill. Now he wants winter heliotrope. He says the last clump I sent him died, and he never gives up on a plant until he has tried it three times. Mr. Freeland knows that even if he does get the winter heliotrope to grow he will certainly have trouble with it.

He has read *Down the Garden Path* by Beverley Nichols who says some people sneer at *Petasites fragrans* because it spreads alarmingly and does not respect property lines; but "the people next door should be grateful if the roots DO spread into their garden." My petasites came from Mrs. Fred Drane's garden in Edenton, North Carolina, seven years ago and has not yet spread unduly, though I have enough to divide with Mr. Freeland. In that time it has bloomed only twice, both times in January. It is for their delicious midwinter fragrance that the small spikes of pallid flowers are prized and, in a way, their rarity makes them even more desirable. If the season is not just right the blooms are killed by frost. The large round and very decorative leaves are persistent, but they usually crumple up before the New Year, and small new leaves are uncurling when the flowers appear. I expect the plant will grow better in Mr. Freeland's garden in Columbia than with me. It grew better in Mrs. Drane's garden.

I am glad Mr. Freeland wants it, and I hope it will catch on this time, for it is not likely to be found in the trade, and he will see that it gets about. Aside from any merit of their own (and any one who appreciates fragrance in winter will certainly want petasites), I like to see plants in old gardens preserved. A garden with only store-bought flowers is like a house with only store-bought furniture.

Mr. Freeland has collected all sorts of treasures that are not generally available. This winter he sent me a start of the small-leaved fig vine, *Ficus pumila minima*. He says it takes seven leaves to cover a postage stamp. I tried it and he is right. He says the leaves of this variety never turn brown in winter. I suppose it will be very slow growing, and I should think it would please the bonsai fanciers, though I never know what will please them, perhaps it is not woody enough. But perhaps it is.

Along with the dwarf fig vine he sent *Asparagus virgatus*, a hardy species of South Africa, which is said to make a shrubby plant from three to six feet tall. From its looks it will be a long time before it does anything like that. It looks like an ordinary asparagus except that the cladodes (which take the place of leaves) are even more hairlike and the stems even finer. The whole effect is delicate and filmy. Mr. Giridlian, in the Oakhurst Gardens catalogue, says it looks like a smoke tree and "lends itself to spraying with paint for all kinds of arrangements and decorations." I don't think I'd like it sprayed with paint, but I do hope it will prosper in my garden.

Mr. Freeland's latest offerings (I am afraid the balance of trade is sadly in my favor) are *Ophiopogon jaburan*, which I have been wanting for some time and a *Liriope* 'White Giant' from the Bishop's Garden at the National Cathedral. I grew the *Ophiopogon* in Raleigh, but when I left, it had never bloomed. "It is most showy," Mr. Freeland says, "like a little tree of snow, with its flowers on individual stems hanging down gracefully." They are followed by dark blue berries. Mr. Giridlian now lists only the variegated form, which has silver striped leaves. I lost this and must try again. Rereading Mr. Freeland's letter, I see that the liriope is not called 'White Giant'. He describes it as "a giant white *Liriope muscari,* one of the first to bloom, long before 'Monroe No. 1' and about twice as tall." It was given him by Mr. Bloomberg who, before his death, was in charge of the Bishop's Garden.

January 7, 1968

THREE

Bulbs, Corms, and Tubers

PLANTING BULBS, CORMS, AND TUBERS

The time to plant bulbs is as soon as possible after they have been taken up, or as soon as they are available. This is particularly true of daffodils. You will be told about bulbs that grow and bloom after they have been kept out of the ground for a year, but that does not make late planting a good practice. Tulips, hyacinths, and Dutch irises are kept until the last because if they were planted earlier their foliage would come up and get nipped by the frost.

In the South the theory about tulips is that if they are planted eight inches deep (some say twelve) they will not split up into smaller bulbs. If you plant very many, planting them deep is a chore, so I never do. The important thing is to plant all of a kind at the same depth so that they will all be the same height, and will bloom together.

Fall, not spring, is the time to plant lilies. Bulbs come from the Oregon growers in sealed polyethylene bags to keep the live roots from drying out. They are generally available by the end of October. The general rule for planting lilies is to allow twice the diameter of the bulb between its top and the surface of the ground.

The ideal time to plant colchicums and fall-flowering crocus is in July and August, but they are seldom available then. They arrive in the fall with flowers already emerging. The only hope is to get them in the ground as soon as possible. Although the corms of the colchicums are large, they need shallow planting, and the small corms of the crocus are planted comparatively deep. Gladiolus corms are planted deep enough to steady the tall stems and keep them from toppling over.

Gardeners are not agreed on the best depths for planting daffodils. Northerners plant them deeper than we do on account of frost. Three to four inches is all right in the South, but some say that deeper planting keeps the bulbs cool in summer; and the deeper they are planted the less often they will need dividing.

The funny little tubers of *Anemone coronaria* are a puzzle. They are cone shaped, with points that look as if they should go up, but really should go down. After all these years I still hesitate, and usually compromise by planting them on edge. They don't seem to mind.

For the garden or for cutting, dahlias are planted early, but for exhibition they are planted late in May or early in June, so that they will bloom in the cool weather when they are at their best. For garden effect dahlias are planted closer together than when they are grown for exhibition. Plant decorative and cactus dahlias twenty-five inches apart, and 'Mignon' and miniatures about a foot apart.

In the south, montbretias [*Crocosmia*], tuberose, and butterfly lilies (*Hedychium*) are left in the garden all winter. Ismenes [*Hymenocallis narcissiflora*] can be left in the ground too, but I think they bloom better when they are taken up and stored. Plant them deeper if you leave them outside.

On most bulb charts you will find the distances between the bulbs less than those I have given. This is because they are made by bulb growers, and are meant for effect the first year. I like to allow plenty of room for increase. Always remember to plant bulbs deeper in light soil than in heavy soil. Bulbs need little fertilizer if they are in good soil. Bone meal and basic slag are the only ones that are safe.

March 15, 1959

BULBS THROUGH THE SEASONS

Whenever I look something up in an *Enquiry into Plants*, I find myself straying from page to page. Theophrastus seems to be a fellow gardener who might at any moment pay a visit to my garden, and since we grow many plants of the Mediterranean, he would find much that is familiar to him, especially bulbs.

"All bulbous plants are tenacious of life," he wrote more than two thousand years ago, and it is a statement to consider well today, particularly in the South, where bulbs carry the banner of bloom from one year's end to the next. There is scarcely a week when one is not in bloom in my garden, except in winters when we have snow on the ground over a long period.

For the New Year there may be a brilliant violet flower of *Crocus imperati* or the soft mauve of *Crocus sieberi*, and these bloom on at intervals until the height of the crocus season in February. De Jager lists forty-five species and varieties of winter-flowering crocuses.

Before January ends, or even before it begins, the early forms of the broad-leaved snowdrop, *Galanthus elwesii*, are apt to present a few flowers, and the summer snowflake, *Leucojum aestivum*, has bloomed for me at the beginning of the year, though it usually comes much later. I have two later leucojums, both under the name of *L.* 'Gravetye Giant', and these, with the type, provide bloom for several weeks.

The early squills sometimes appear at the end of January, but usually in February. *Scilla siberica* 'Spring Beauty' is gentian blue, and *Scilla tubergiana* [*S. mischtschenkoana*] is silvery with a pale blue stripe. The short spikes begin to bloom almost before they get out of the ground. They are long lasting and almost weatherproof.

About the same time, or a little later, spring star flowers bloom in lawns all over Charlotte, and in gardens where they have been allowed to naturalize. They are lovely where there is plenty of room but must be watched if space is limited. These are in the catalogues as *Triteleia uniflora*, but their proper name is now *Ipheion*.

There are daffodils in February, or even in January on rare occasions when the little early trumpet or 'February Gold' show a flower or two; the various kinds bloom on until the middle of April or later.

Tulips begin in March, with the water lily varieties and some of the early species, but most of them disappear in a few years. *Tulipa clusiana*, the lady tulip, a starry peppermint-striped flower on a slender stem, persists for some years, and I expect it would stay indefinitely in a place that is not disturbed.

The amaryllis family alone pretty much covers the seasons if you count daffodils, for the little white hoop petticoats bloom in winter, and in mild seasons the paperwhites and their kin.

There are atamasco lilies in April, and *Amaryllis johnsonii* [*Hippeastrum × johnsonii*], the red lily with a white star in its center, which is grown in old gardens and blooms in May in North Carolina. Bulbs of atamasco lilies are sold at the curb market in May, and they are listed by

Colonel Wolfe, who grows daylilies and rare bulbs in his garden in Orangeburg. Colonel Wolfe says he will soon have a new catalogue.

Crinums begin to bloom in June and from July through September there are the lycorises, and in September the shining sternbergias that look like buttercup-colored crocus but are really amaryllids.

In the fall there are meadow saffrons, true crocuses, and the Neapolitan cyclamen [*Cyclamen hederifolium*], a delightful miniature in rose or pure white. The most floriferous and effective of the meadow saffrons, and also the first to bloom, is *Colchicum autumnale*. A clump planted nearly twenty years ago still blooms in my garden, but this year I got a dozen new bulbs from Grootendorst. They came at the end of September, and were in bloom in a week. Mr. Grootendorst is a wholesale grower, but he will sell in small amounts and to individuals.

These are only a few of the bulbs that bloom throughout the year, but they are the ones I can depend upon without giving them any care at all.

October 29, 1967

SOME EARLY SPRING BULBS

When southerners speak of snowdrops they really mean snowflakes, for snowdrops are not at all common in these parts, and snowflakes are very common, especially in old gardens where they have bloomed for generations with no care at all.

Our kind is the species that is called the summer snowflake though it is one of the earliest flowers of spring, and I think it must be the *Leucojum* var. *pulchellum* rather than the typical *L. aestivum*. As Mr. E. A. Bowles says, this variety blooms with the daffodils, and so it does only it blooms also with the crocus and also with the tulips. One year it bloomed in my garden from January 28 to April 10.

Its season varies greatly. In the more than twenty years that I have kept records, the date of the first flower has varied from January to the twelfth of March; and I once found a flower on New Year's Day. This year we had real snowflakes when we expected flowers, and on St. Patrick's Day, after the snow had melted, I could find only a few undeveloped buds among the crumpled leaves. I hope the snowflakes have not been hurt by the ice and snow, for I have never known a spring without them since the first year in our Raleigh garden, when every day brought a delightful surprise, since we did not know what had been planted there.

I love those little white bells with the bright green dots on the tips of their petals. They hang in such graceful sprays at the tops of their flat, two-edged scapes. I particularly like them as companions to the old white iris that blooms at the same time in every dooryard and the flowers are of equal purity.

The *L. a.* 'Gravetye' variety is a splendid form that came from William Robinson's garden of the same name. The flowers are larger than those of the common kind, the stems taller, and the season later—from the middle or end of March to the last of April.

The spring snowflake, *Leucojum vernum*, is very rare in this country. The flowers are large, solitary, and on very short stems. They generally come along sometime between the first and last of February.

Although the snowflakes were later than ever before, the flowers of *Iris reticulata* broke through the snow on March 15, a date that had been recorded in 1942, their royal purple petals as brilliant as ever. After the storm, crocus came out again, but not in their former splendor, and when the snow melted there were violet flowers of *Anemone blanda*, wide open and very wan.

Narcissus 'February Gold' went on blooming in the snow, and *N.* 'Peeping Tom' burst into bloom soon afterward. Two tiny, pale flowers of *N.* 'Snipe' were just opening when snow began to fall, and when it was gone there they were as fresh and upstanding and fragile as ever. These three are cyclamineus hybrids, all so very early, so sprightly and so staunch. A few daffodil stems were broken by the weight of ice that covered them, and many flowers are on the ground, but they are gradually rising, and as they come into bloom they seem to have lost nothing in color or grace.

The Lenten roses were at their height when the snow came. Now, on St. Patrick's Day, nearly all of the clumps have emerged. Some of the stems were broken, but like the daffodils, most of the flattened ones are rising up again. Their great leaves are as green as ever, and it seems to me that the color of the flowers—claret, mulberry and grape—are deeper and clearer than before.

My garden is a sad sight, for I have too many tender things. The large, round leaves of *Eucalyptus rostrata* [*E. camaldulensis*] have turned from misty green to dirty brown and are beginning to shrivel. The banana shrub [*Michelia figo*] looks as if a forest fire had passed over it, and all of the branches of the *Osmarea* [*Osmanthus* × *burkwoodii*] are turning yellow at the tips. Quinces are still hung with brown rags, and so is my beautiful *Prunus mume*, which was in full bloom when the cold came.

But this was a good winter until Groundhog Day, and I think that spring will be like a northern spring with everything in bloom at once.

March 27, 1960

DAFFODILS NEED EARLY START

This year daffodils bloomed in my garden from the third of December to the last of April. It was the best daffodil season I have ever known, no hot burning winds, no extremes of temperature—a nice cool spring. For years I have been making a collection of early daffodils, for they are the ones that are most satisfactory in these parts. They bloom in the cool weather that daffodils like. The late ones fade quickly in the heat, and for the most part I have found them hard to keep. Still, I like to stretch the season at both ends, and I shall have more to say of the late ones at another time. One of the very earliest daffodils—not counting the white hoop skirts that bloom before Christmas, or the paperwhite narcissus that blooms all winter in a mild season—is a small pale trumpet called *N.* 'Bambi'. Later on, it would not be noticed, but it blooms so early—this year in January—that it has little competition.

Early in February, I always find the first flowers of *N.* 'February Gold'. This would be an outstanding daffodil at any season. It has the backward-tilted petals, the clean golden color, and the slender, delicately molded trumpet characteristic of the cyclamineus hybrids, but for all its grace there is enough substance in stem and flower to withstand wind and rain and frost. It increases well, but can be left a long time without being divided. And it is in bloom for a long time. Along with *N.* 'February Gold' comes *N.* 'Forerunner', a large golden trumpet. It is an old daffodil (1927) and a good one, but I seem to be its only advocate. I have never seen it in any shows, or in any garden but my own. However, it is still available, though not to be found in the ordinary catalogues.

Very close upon the heels of these comes *N.* 'Ada Finch', which is classed as an all-white trumpet, but the yellow crown never becomes pure white, although it fades to cream after a few days. This very handsome daffodil has one fault. Its nice long stems get very limp when the spring frosts are severe. They usually stiffen again when the sun comes out, but sometimes they don't. It is good for cutting, and lasts a long time in the house.

All of these are too early for the daffodil shows, but one early one that does appear in public, and is a favorite with the judges is a large, well-turned clear yellow trumpet called *N.* 'Golden Harvest'. It is cheap, but it often wins the blue ribbon over more expensive varieties. It is a good bulb for the garden, too, and very long lived.

This year, I indulged in a bulb of the celebrated *N.* 'Kings Court', which is considered the best yellow trumpet for exhibition. I had been watching it since 1948, when it was fifteen dollars, and for the first time it was down to my price, a dollar and a half. But the saddest thing happened. There are no longer choice spots left in my garden for choice flowers, and I had to put *N.* 'Kings Court' in the background. And then, with everything in bloom at once I couldn't find it. When at last I tracked it down, under the Japanese apricot [*Prunus mume*], the flowers were faded. And now I shall have to wait.

Daffodils should be ordered right away, if they have not been ordered earlier, for the growers begin to ship the first of September, and the sooner the bulbs are planted the finer the flowers will be. The bulbs deteriorate if they are left out of the ground very long. They can't be planted too early, and besides, it is a great comfort to have them planted and out of the way when cool weather comes, as there are so many other things to be done. But mark the spot well, and do not, as I have often done, send the spade through the heart of your most expensive (or rare) bulb when something else is being planted.

Most daffodils are easy to grow. Planting is about the only attention that is really necessary. They take care of themselves from then on. Good drainage is about the only thing essential to their well-being, and it is better not to fertilize them too much. One of the best growers in the country recommends cow manure (well rotted, of course) at the time of planting, or preferably ahead of planting time. The only other thing safe to put in the ground with the bulbs is bone meal. For established bulbs a top dressing of manure in winter is recommended, and I usually scatter wood ashes about in early spring. Only I have to be careful not to let them fall near broad-leaved evergreens or other acid-loving plants. Plant the neck about three inches deep. Shallow planting makes them split up, and then they have to be divided sooner. Deep planting allows them to be left undisturbed for a long time. Some of mine are still blooming well after being in the ground for seven or eight years.

August 18, 1957

SPECIALTY BULBS

Early in January, when the bulb catalogues begin to arrive, I make a list of bulbs to plant for summer bloom. Bulbs, filling the garden with fragrance when less enduring flowers are scorched or wilted, are the plants that thrive best through long hot days and short hot nights. The list is added to and subtracted from many times before it is finished, for I always want more than I can afford or have time to plant. This spring I am getting a few expensive bulbs, rather than a lot of cheaper ones. The *Crinum* 'Herald' heads the list. Now that it has come down from ten dollars to seven-fifty, I can wait no longer.

Although I have been gardening for nearly fifty years, and have found that few plants do for me what they do for the people who write catalogues, I still drink in every word written in praise of things that are new to me. Mr. Giridlian says that *C.* 'Herald' is the first crinum to bloom and that, among the many he has grown, it is "by far the finest in every way, robust, five feet tall, very large umbels of wide open outward-facing, purest white flowers."

On another list I found *Montbretia* 'Rheingold' [*Crocosmia* 'Rheingold'], and *Eucomis bicolor*. 'Rheingold' is a montbretia I have sought for many years, as it is the nearest to pure yellow (they say) of any variety, and has beautifully formed flowers, nicely placed on a strong stem. I have never before seen it offered in this country.

Two years ago, I planted the pineapple lily, *Eucomis punctata* [*E. comosa*], and it has bloomed both summers. Mary B. Stewart, whose new book, *The Southern Gardener*, is written for the Lower South, but covers most of the plants we grow, as well as some of the more tender kinds, thinks it is probably the most satisfactory summer bulb she has found. "I plant it in the fall," she writes,

> usually in October, in my north lily bed with the neck showing slightly. Don't be alarmed if it doesn't show immediately in the spring as it is slow to start. The heavy-textured leaves then come up and

> sprawl out like spokes of a wheel and about May first the scape arises from the center and grows to about sixteen inches . . . About May twenty-eighth the buds begin to open from the bottom showing small chartreuse flowers with deep yellow stamens. These bottom flowers remain open as row on row upwards open. At this point I have to stake the flower stem. The bloom remains intact and lovely until about August thirtieth when signs of fading appear.

I neglected to make a note of the date that mine came into bloom. All that I remember is that it was midsummer and that I found the staking necessary. I planted it in March in semi-shade, where it did very well though it is said to tolerate full sun. Any soil will do, and the crown of the bulbs should be an inch deep. The spotted leaves and the slender scapes with their pineapple topknot of short crisp foliage are prized for flower arrangements.

If gladiolus corms are planted every ten days from early April to early July, there will be a succession of bloom until frost. I like to plant all of one kind, and my favorite is an old one called *G.* 'White Gold'.

Among the new varieties listed are three All-American selections for 1961: *G.* 'China Blue', a soft tone, deeper at the tips, lighter at the throat; *G.* 'Gypsy Dancer', orange with yellow on lower petals; and *G.* 'Rusty', a silver picotee with a bright red mark on the lip. The rosy-purple, white-throated *G.* 'Emperor' is one of the best. Plant gladiolus corms deep enough to give the stems good anchorage so they won't need staking. Six inches is not too deep.

February 26, 1961

CROWN IMPERIALS

The crown imperial is the crown of an emperor, as distinguished from that of a mere king, so it is not strange that *Fritillaria imperialis*, the flower that bears that name, was once very proud: "No flower aspires in pomp and state so high."

No wonder it held itself stiffly erect when our Lord walked through the Garden of Gethsemane, though all the other flowers bowed their heads. But when it was rebuked, the white flowers drooped and blushed with shame, and tears gathered on the petals, but did not fall. The flowers have never again been white, the color of innocence, and the drooping cups still hold the pearly tears that no human hand can wipe away.

"In the bottome of each of the bells," Gerard wrote in his *Herbal*, "there is placed six drops of most cleere shining sweet water, in taste like sugar, resembling in shew faire Orient pearles, the which drops if you take away, there do immediately appeare the like; notwithstanding, if they may be suffered to stand still in the floure according to his owne nature, they wil never fall away, no, not if you strike the plant until it be broken."

As long as I have known about it I have wanted to grow the crown imperial, and I have tried it many times without success, but now, on Passion Sunday, it is in bloom in my garden, and if it blooms for a month, as it is said to do, it will be there in Holy Week.

In England, it is supposed to bloom on the eighteenth of March in memory of St. Edward, who was murdered on that day in 978. Thus, it honors one king and is said to have sprung from the blood of another, Augustus Adolphus of Sweden, who died so mysteriously in the mist that hung over the battlefield on the sixth of November 1632.

Various reasons are given for its name; one is that it "hath the true shape of the Imperial Crown," and another that it was so named by Alphonsus Pancus, because it grew in the Imperial Gardens of Vienna, having been brought there by Clusius in 1576. Its provenance is Persia, and there it is associated with royalty; the flower they say is the spirit of a queen falsely accused of infidelity. The ever-flowing drops are her tears.

My crown imperial is the variety *F. i.* 'Orange Brilliant'. The flowers are a sort of burnt orange, covered with very fine red veins, and the general effect is English red—or as an early eighteenth-century gardener described it, "of a colour like to that of a boiled lobster."

When I knelt in the April sunshine to look up into the cups, I noticed that they had a very strong smell, which the herbalist describe as a stink, and which Mr. E. A. Bowles says is a mixture of "mangy fox, dirty dog-Kennel, the small cat's house at the Zoo, and Exeter Railway Station." But this does not keep Miss Rohde from including them in *The Scented Garden*, for, she says, "their foxy smell is sweetness of most spring's scents, and has an attraction of its own."

There is a scentless form, the variety 'Inordora', but Mr. Bowles says it is a dwarf plant that never did well in his garden. He was most successful with the variety *F. i.* 'Maxima Rubra', though the yellow-flowered form, which he could never keep, was of course his favorite.

Perhaps it was because I got the red one, not the yellow, that at last I had this flower in bloom. But I got it because it was cheaper. I find if you get the cheaper plant it usually does better than the more expensive kinds. I think that another reason that I was at last successful is that I got the bulb from the West Coast. Heretofore I had planted imported bulbs.

They should be set in deep, rich loam, some recommend old manure, in sun or part shade, but the important point is to see that the bulbs are out of the ground as short a time as possible, and once planted, that they are left undisturbed.

After the flowers have faded and the seed pods have formed, they rise up until at last, as Canon Ellacombe says, "they range themselves in perfect order on the top of the flower stem, forming what it requires little fancy to liken to a well-formed crown with sharp jeweled points."

April 15, 1962

LYCORIS RADIATA

Some years ago Sam Caldwell sent me the fertile form of *Lycoris radiata*, that blooms in mid-August, if it blooms at all. It lingered for several seasons, bloomed twice and disappeared—I can't think why, for W. O. Freeland says it flourishes at the The Garden Spot in Columbia. He says this and the common infertile form, which blooms in September, were brought back to South Carolina by Dr. Morrow, a naval surgeon who was with Commodore Perry on an expedition to Japan.

This must have been the first expedition, as Dr. Morrow says in his journal that they found red lilies in bloom when they sailed along the east coast of China on their way to Hong Kong. Since the American fleet left Japan toward the end of July, they must have reached there about the time the lycoris were in bloom.

Freeland says the early form is now considered a separate species, *Lycoris morrowi* [*L. radiata* var. *pumila*]. "The flowers are a bit redder and a little smaller than the later flowering one. It has proven itself to be a true species for it sets seed, and the seedlings are true to the mother plant. Increasing by seed and division of the bulbs it would seem that it should be more plentiful than the other one, which increases by division only, but such is not the case. It is not in the trade, and the only way to get a start is to watch for its brilliant blooms in August and to beg, borrow, or steal a handful." I shall start by begging.

Many years ago I had some correspondence with Mrs. Wentworth Simmons and her sister Miss Mary Roberts about *Lycoris radiata*.

"I have always been told," Miss Mary wrote, "that our uncle, Captain W. W. Roberts, who was with Commodore Perry on his second cruise, brought them from Japan, and planted them in his mother's garden. Later, about 1868, he gave a bulb to my mother. They are peculiar. Sometimes they bloom soon after being transplanted, and sometimes they stay in the ground many years. I have read that they grow wild in Japan, and are called by many names in many places. The Japanese love to plant them in their cemeteries, and the children make chains as we make clover chains. I don't like to call them spider lily." Mrs. Simmons said they were called the Sacred Lily of Japan. "Our garden at this time is aflame with them," she wrote. "We have given hundreds of bulbs away, and it is wonderful to think they all came from one bulb. I am glad you wrote to ask about them."

Earlier in the fall Caroline wrote, "Like all flowers this fall, the lycoris are acting crazy. My favorite, the cream from Russell Wolfe, is as faithful as *L. radiata*." And just now, on the first day of October, Caroline Dorman wrote from Louisiana, "The garden is ablaze with *Lycoris radiata*. What would we do without them at this time?" But it has been a poor season in North Carolina. Rose Wharton wrote that she found three scapes where there are usually dozens, and in my garden there was only one. At least that one was perfect.

Only three clumps bloomed for me, but these bloomed freely. The first flower opened September 22, the earliest date I have recorded. I have them from various sources, and they usually fill the September garden with creamy apricot-tinted flowers. I have never had them from Colonel Wolfe, however, and I have now ordered from him what he lists as *Lycoris radiata* 'Alba'.

In late summer Sam Caldwell sent me half a dozen bulbs of his *L.* × *jacksoniana* (*Lycoris radiata* × *L. sprengeri*), his first cross and (he says) his best. I was not surprised that these did not bloom their first season. They are peculiar. Sometimes it takes bulbs several years to become adjusted.

October 15, 1970

AMARYLLIS FAMILY

This has been a wonderful season for the amaryllis family. Those that always bloom well have bloomed even better, and those that are temperamental have done better than usual.

The beautiful white crinum that smells like a water lily has not bloomed so freely for years. So far, no one has been able to put a Latin name to it, but it goes from garden to garden with the name of the donor. I have several clumps, all with different names: Catherine came from Haphazard Plantation in Louisiana; Miss Elsie came from a beautiful garden in Atlanta; Mrs. Parsley came from a Charlotte garden, and was one of the first plants that I begged after I came here. Mrs. Parsley said I was very welcome to a start, and added, "You dig it." If you have ever divided a *Crinum*, you will understand that this is only fair.

Another crinum that has been at its best this summer is *C.* 'Frank Leach', a superior form of *C. moorei*. It is superior in flower and in foliage, but some years it does not bloom at all. I keep a clump anyway because the foliage is so good and the pale pink, fragrant bells so lovely when they do appear. It is a good plant for shade.

As a rule, the *Ismene* [*Hymenocallis*] bloom much better if they are taken up in the fall, stored over winter, and planted again in April, but this summer all of mine bloomed beautifully though they have not been divided for several years. Ismenes belong to the South American section of *Hymenocallis*. They have larger cups than the North American species. *Hymenocallis occidentalis* [*H. caroliniana*], one of our natives, blooms late in July or early in August. Several flowers, all lovely, have come to me under this name. The one that bloomed in my garden this summer is from a California grower.

Now that so many kinds of lycoris are available, I have them in bloom from the middle of July until October. Hall's amaryllis, *Lycoris squamigera*, comes first, and before the pink flowers are gone the paler, smaller umbels of *L. incarnata* are out. *Lycoris incarnata* is one of the temperamental species, but it bloomed its best this year, and the last scapes were still fresh when *L. caldwellii* came along, followed by the strange bluish flowers of *L. sprengeri*.

Four years ago Wyndham Hayward (feeling guilty for former neglect) sent me a bulb of *L. caldwellii*, named for Sam Caldwell. Just before the Communists took over, Mr. Hayward had imported it from China, as *L. aurea*. Fortunately for us, it was not *L. aurea*, which is unsatisfactory here, but a lovely, pale buttercup-yellow flower that is hardy and a dependable bloomer. Mine is increasing, and it blooms better every year.

Lycoris albiflora blooms next. The cream-colored flowers are tinged with peach when they first come out. Caroline Dormon, who has had this for years, says that it is as prolific and indispensable as the old red spider lily *L. radiata* that everyone has, and that blooms last of all. My experience is that *L. albiflora* takes a long time to become established. Once settled it blooms freely, and as long as it blooms well, the clumps had better be left alone

The only lycoris that has not done well (with the exception of the hurricane lily, *L. aurea*, which is too tender for this climate) is *L. sanguinea*, which has small, scarlet flowers. Last year I thought I would give it another trial, and I planted a dozen bulbs in various parts of the garden, but I have had no bloom. They may pop up some time when I have forgotten all about them.

I often wonder why people say that you cannot expect bloom in southern gardens in the summer time.

October 4, 1959

THE SURPRISE LILY

In midsummer, when heat and drought have drained all color from leaf and blossom—in spite of all of the city water that is poured on them—the surprise lily rises mysteriously from the ground. One day there is nothing, and the next there is a tall, pale stem that grows to about three feet and then produces, at the top, a circle of flowers of the most luminous and delicate pink. The surprise lily is not really a lily. It is a lycoris, as lovely as the nymph it was named for, and it belongs to the amaryllis family. It is sometimes called Hall's amaryllis for the New England doctor who brought it back from a Japanese garden nearly one hundred years ago. Dr. Hall also brought the "queen of the lilies," *Lilium auratum*, to this country, and the star magnolia, which was once called *Magnolia halleana* [*M. stellata*]. Japan is a good place for things to come from if you garden in this part of the country.

Although it has been in gardens so long, and is one of the easiest bulbs to grow, the surprise lily has never become common. One reason is that it has always been expensive. People who wouldn't hesitate to pay ten dollars for a camellia won't consider paying a dollar for a single bulb. This year the bulbs are cheaper. I see in a catalogue that three can be had for a dollar, and I shall remind you when the time comes to order them. The bulbs do their growing in late winter when the wide, gray-green leaves come up. The time to plant new ones, or to dig and divide old clumps, is when the leaves die. The bulbs need not be dug unless you want to increase the supply. They will go on blooming indefinitely in the same spot. The flowers bloom whether they are watered or not, even in the driest season, and no spraying is required.

Perhaps the last is a little too careless. The other night when I went out at dusk to move the hose, I found one of those repulsive red and black grasshoppers—the ones that look like prehistoric monsters—gnawing the base of the stem of a lycoris whose buds were just breaking through the sheath. I shut my eyes, and stepped on the grasshopper, and then I picked the ruined stalk and put it in the pool. Several days later I found that it has come out almost as well as the ones that were still unpicked. This is worth knowing, for sometimes the crisp scapes are broken by storms or pets before the flowers open.

I think the other reason that surprise lilies are so little known is that their specific name, *squamigera*, is so long and so ugly. It means scaly, which sounds equally unattractive, and means that with a hand lens small scales can be seen in the throat of the flower—a fact of no interest to the gardener. Nevertheless the Latin name will be needed when the bulbs are bought, for they will be listed by the bulb growers as *Lycoris squamigera*.

August 18, 1957

LILIES GROW WHERE NONE WERE

"Remember, we agreed that we couldn't have lilies in the South?" Miss Caroline Dormon wrote this spring. "Have you tried the new hybrids? Last year my Olympic and Sunburst hybrids were exquisite, and some have come back in spite of gophers—whose favorite food are members of the lily family. *Lilium formosanum* comes up all over the place, and I would have thousands but the gophers have to live."

Miss Dormon has a plantation of 120 acres near Shreveport, Louisiana, where she says she plants only such things as can take drought and rains as they come. You are going to hear from her from time to time, for she is always sending me bits of horticultural gossip.

As she says, the hybridizers have now made it possible to grow lilies where they would not grow before. Through years I have had more than thirty species and varieties, but it was not until the Olympic hybrids came along that I found a lily dependable enough to be considered a permanent part of the flower border. They have now bloomed in my garden for seven summers, glistening white trumpets—bigger even than the regal lilies [*L. regale*]—towering on five-foot stalks. Since these stalks must not be cut when the lilies are gone, I have learned to plant the bulbs in the back of the border, where the dying foliage is soon hidden in the white mist of Bolton's aster [*Boltonia asteroides*]. If the Olympic hybrids bloom for me, they will bloom even better for anyone else.

The sunburst hybrids have been too expensive for me, but after some catalogue shopping I have decided to invest this fall in three bulbs at $1.15 each. A single bulb would not give you an idea of their color, which varies in this group from cream to pale yellow and orange. These hybrids belong to one of the groups that resulted from crossing trumpet lilies with *L. henryi*, a handsome orange-flowered species from China. The flowers of the hybrids are larger than those of their parents. Their colors are softer, and their stalks stronger. Some of the experts consider them the most important of the new strains. Dr. [Augustine] Henry's lily has bloomed for me many a July. It is at its best in light shade, as the flowers fade in strong sunlight, and this is true of the hybrids.

Lilies are heir to two diseases: botrytis, to which the Madonna lily [*L. candidum*] is particularly susceptible, and which can be controlled by spraying with Bordeaux mixture every ten days and mosaic, for which no control is known; plants infected by the virus must be destroyed at once. To prevent mosaic, be sure that you are getting clean bulbs raised from disease-free seed; keep the garden free of aphids, which spread the virus; and refuse to have tiger lilies [*L. tigrinum*] near you—without showing any sign of disease themselves, they may have it and pass it on to other bulbs. I never had the heart to root them out of my Raleigh garden, where they grew for years and bloomed magnificently through the entire month of July, but I have not allowed them in my new garden. *L. speciosum* and *L. auratum* are among the species especially susceptible to mosaic.

I have read that *L. formosanum* is also a victim of mosaic, but if Miss Dormon raises them for gophers they must be disease-resistant strains. I have a healthy clump—I don't remember having planted it, but I suppose I must have done so—that has grown under a pine tree for several years, and blooms July or early August.

This fall I am going to try the late-flowering variety *L. wilsonii* which I have found after a prolonged search. I want it because it is said to be the last lily to bloom—even blooming in November, though I doubt that it will do that here. Dates given in catalogues and magazines seldom apply to our part of the country.

I am writing about lilies now, because this is the time to plant them, although *L. formosanum*, *L. longiflorum* and the regals can also be planted in the spring. Madonna lilies should have been planted in August or early September, but even these have bloomed when the bulbs were planted very late. All lily bulbs should be planted the minute they come. Reliable growers pack them so they will not dry out on the way, but this is all in vain if the gardener lets them lie around in a heated house. The ones that I have mentioned (except the Madonnas) are all stem rooting and should be planted with five inches of soil on top of the bulb.

October 13, 1957

GARDEN CASUALTIES

There have been even fewer crocus than usual this fall (and the rodents, I suppose, better fed) but a flower in the hand is worth ten thousand at a glance, and all through October I picked them as they came out, one by one, and kept them beside me. They come up in odd places, one in the midst of a maidenhair fern, the fern protecting it from the gourmands. It was a large flower of a pale tint of pure violet with fine veining of a deeper tone. I think it must be a seedling of *Crocus speciosus*, for it has the characteristic fragrance, but it has a yellow throat so must be a hybrid. *Crocus speciosus* 'Albus' has been for fifteen years as faithful as the catalogue promised, though not so floriferous. In mid-October, I found a single large white flower with pointed petals "fair as a star when only one is shining in the sky." I don't know why the chipmunks have overlooked it.

There were a number of garden casualties from last winter's low temperatures, especially among the amarcrinums. × *Amarcrinum* 'Deikin's Find' was killed outright, not a great loss as it seldom bloomed, and only two or three bulbs of my twelve-year-old clump of *A.* 'Dorothy Hannibal' survived. The survivors did not bloom. It will be years before they will recover, and another winter like the last would kill them entirely—which would be a real tragedy as it is no longer in the trade.

Even my original clump of × *A. howardii* [*A. memoria-corsii* 'Howardii'], which has never suffered in winter in the thirty years I have had it, lost a few outer bulbs and only two scapes bloomed this fall; another hybrid, a nameless one that Polly Anderson sent me several years ago, did bloom though it often doesn't, and did not seem to suffer at all.

I don't think any crinums were killed but the blooms of some were poor. Only *Crinum moorei* var. *Schmidtii* bloomed as well as usual.

There was no bloom from *Habranthus brachyandrus*, and I think it is gone. The hybrid *H.* 'Grace Primo', more reliable as to bloom than its parent, seemed unharmed. Whenever the flowers appear, like large amaranth-pink rain lilies, I think of its originator, Mrs. Primo, who died so many years ago. At the time that I corresponded with her, she was building a collection of amaryllids, especially crinums, in her garden in Mobile, but she had moved to the Gulf Coast from Missouri and so had knowledge of our zone as well as the warmer one.

This fall the butterfly lily, *Hedychium coronarium*, bloomed better than ever, though it often loses a good proportion of its rhizomes in winters that leave crinums and amarcrinum unscathed. This was due to the heavy mulch of pine needles it had last winter. If these severe winters are to continue we shall have to mulch a lot of half-hardy bulbs that never needed it before.

John Rinehart says his Mexican sage, *Salvia leucantha*, is a large bush seven feet tall. He planted it at the same time (early May I think) that I set out two in the borders. Mine are spindly things and scarcely more than three feet tall. John says he gave his a thorough watering every week, and that he could afford to as he has his own well. I thought I had kept mine well watered too, but evidently I was not as systematic. Seven feet of those velvet, violet spikes and small white flowers must be a fine sight.

November 1, 1970

FOUR

Trees and Shrubs

PLANTING FOR ICE STORMS

When the sun came out on the morning after Christmas, and I looked out on a glittering garden, I thought the Japanese cherries the most beautiful of the storm's creations. Their delicacy in ice is sufficient reason for planting *Prunus subhirtella* and *P. incisa*. Their twigs are so fine that they don't show at all, and the whole tree seems to be made of glass. Their beauty made me think that some thought might be given to planting for ice storms. Consideration must be given to vulnerability as well as to effect.

The cherries came through without losing a twig (I can't remember their ever having been broken by snow or ice), and *P. serrulata*, which is the winter-flowering form, went on with its meager blooming. Pines are beautiful but brittle. Willow oaks are beautiful and strong. Weeping willows are fountains of ice, but I expect they will grow less green in the spring.

There was much less damage to blooming plants than I had feared. This was because the ice melted so quickly when the storm was over. When Robert Talley and Jacques Legendre came by a few days later, a wintersweet was still in full, fresh, and fragrant bloom in my garden as well as at the W. B. Mayers' and the Edwin Clarksons'.

Mr. Legendre was interested in the variations in the flowers, and he said their scents differed too. Perhaps this is why there is so much difference of opinion as to what wintersweet smells like. It is described as smelling of honeysuckle, of a mixture of jonquil and violet, and of poet's jasmine. Mr. Legendre says he and Mr. Talley have the yellow-flowering wintersweet at their Gulf Stream Nursery in Wachapreague, Virginia. It came from England, and it is the one Graham Thomas describes in *Colour in the Winter Garden*.

"One dull afternoon in January," he writes, "I went to Kew: the most lovely sight greeted me on the wall of the Duke of Cambridge's garden, where a plant of the superlative *Chimonanthus praecox* var. *luteus* had been trained to cover many square feet. The flowers open wider than those of the other varieties and all the petals are broader, of a clear light yellow, heralding the glory of the forsythia in March. The scent is not as strong as that of the species, but it is sweet and lovely, even so." I told Mr. Legendre about the yellow-flowered wintersweet that Mrs. Dan Beckham brought me from her great-aunt's garden on Elizabeth Avenue where it had been growing for seventy years. Her aunt grew it from a seed she brought from Columbia, South Carolina. The flowers match Ridgway's color chart wax-yellow, and as the inner petals are marked with wine, the plant cannot be the variety *luteus* whose petals are all pure yellow. The fragrance is very different from the honey-scented flowers of mine; it is spicy, and reminds me of clove pinks.

Wintersweet seldom fruits here, but it fruited in the Mayers' garden this year, and I saw the apple-green velvet pods for the first time. Cuttings will not strike, and it is propagated by layering, but even that is difficult. Some say it should be done in the spring, and some say in the fall—but it should be done, for wintersweet is scarce in the trade, and its flowers delight from Thanksgiving until well into the New Year. E. A. Bowles says it should be in every garden that is large enough to hold two plants. He doesn't say what the second plant should be—perhaps another wintersweet.

Our native witch hazel, *Hamamelis virginiana*, has a long and fragrant winter season too. When the North Carolina Wild Flower Preservation Society visited White Oak Mountain (near Tryon, North Carolina) on October 18, it was just coming into bloom on the edge of the lookout, the earliest date in my records. It was a small wind-swept shrub with the palest flowers I have ever seen.

The usual color is mustard yellow, but Caroline Dormon says the colors at Briarwood range from off-white to deep gold. The flowers light the woods and fill the air with a refreshing perfume. "I have never seen them so exquisite," she wrote at the end of the old year. "Hard freezes spoil the blossoms, but we have not had a hard freeze in over a month. Today is dark and cold and drizzling, and I love it. I have no patience with folk who call such weather gloomy."

January 18, 1970

PLANTS FOR PARKING STRIPS

As I could never have room for all the trees and shrubs I want to grow, and in my small garden there is room for so few, I have planted as many as possible on the parking strip at 348 Ridgewood Avenue. It is not an ideal spot, being hot and dry in summer and swept by cold winds in winter, but at least the flowering trees get all the sun they need to make them bloom.

Next to the driveway I have planted *Pyrus calleryana*. I chose it because I love pear trees, and Caroline Dormon praises this one. "Why don't people ever plant pears for ornament?" she once wrote early in December. "I wish you could see my big old Keiffer pears right now, glowing with the tones that shade from yellow to apricot and the little *Pyrus calleryana*—which the nurserymen graft on, but never offer for sale. I enclose some leaves of the latter, for you could not believe the color, and their lovely shining quality."

If I had not seen them, I certainly could not have believed the deep wine color of those shining leaves, or that they looked like that in December. So far, my little Callery pear has not held its leaves long enough for fall color, perhaps because it is so dry or because of its youth. Last spring, on the twentieth of March, its first white flowers opened. Of all the pears, this one is supposed to be most resistant to fire blight. The sidewalk may seem a strange place for a pear tree, but the fruits of this species are the size of very small berries. And nurserymen do sell it. I can give a source.

Next to the pear is *Prunus sargentii*, planted because E. H. Wilson considered it the most beautiful of the Asiatic cherries. In Japan it is a huge tree, wide spreading and reaching a height of seventy-five feet. I doubt whether mine will be half so tall. At present, after ten years in the parking strip, it is still vase-shaped, and has a height of little more than fifteen feet. It looks as if it will be just the right size and shape for a narrow street like ours. It bloomed a little the fourth year after it was planted, and now, around the first of April, it is a bower of frail pink single flowers that seem even more frail against the dark branches. The red-brown bark is well polished, and is very beautiful in winter when the leaves have fallen. The leaves are a shining bronze as the buds unfurl, but they become green at once.

The third tree is *Malus* × *micromalus*, the midget crabapple. It is not a midget at all, being almost as tall as the cherry, and still growing, but it is very slender in spite of having several trunks. Around the middle of March the long branches are like wands wreathed in rose-red buds that break into a froth of dainty white flowers. The small round yellow fruits are borne very freely and are rather a nuisance. I think I may replace this when I find something I like better.

Between the pear and the cherry is a dwarf Chinese holly, *Ilex cornuta* 'Rotunda', that makes a neat, compact, and prickly mound, four feet or more in width, and wider than tall. Although this clone has been in the trade for twenty years, I have never heard of its fruiting.

Between the cherry and the crab is a small specimen of *Pyracantha* 'Santa Cruz', a low and spreading form of *Pyracantha koidzumi* (which we call 'Formosana'). 'Santa Cruz' comes from California, but I got mine from James Patterson who found it in a Georgia nursery. I must say it doesn't look like much at present, but I am willing to be patient, and I hope for bright red berries.

The last shrub is Mr. Patterson's graceful little cotoneaster, which is a hybrid between *Cotoneaster bullatus* and *C. salicifolius*, with the fine dark foliage of its willow-leaved parent. It is too soon to tell what its fruit will be, if any, and how tall it will grow. At present it gives promise of being the sort of low and spreading evergreen that is needed—a shrub that never outgrows its allotted space and is at its best in all seasons.

March 31, 1963

FLOWERING TREES FOR THE CITY

Dr. Herbert Hechenbleikner sent me a copy of a letter he wrote to Mrs. James Hadden, president of the Charlotte Council of Garden Clubs, proposing the crape myrtle for citywide planting. He says we should feature it because it is characteristic of the South, varies in color, has a long period of bloom in summer, beautiful color in fall, and beauty in winter in the pale bark of the slender trunks. Its small size, seldom more than twenty feet, makes it suitable for curb strips, and it is not particular as to soil or situation as long as it is in the sun. Dr. Hechenbleikner does not consider occasional attacks of mildew a serious drawback. Mildew disfigures the foliage only in damp and shady places, and only late in the year, and it does not harm the plant.

I agree that crape myrtle is one of the loveliest of flowering trees. I admit that small plants in containers are available at low prices for community projects, but it will take these a long time to grow. I have two objections to their wholesale planting on city streets. One is that the colors most likely to appeal to the general public are the hot rose reds and watermelon pinks. We already have too many of these. The other reason is that few householders are likely to allow crape myrtles to grow into graceful little trees. Most of them are going to grow them as shrubs, butchering them every year so that all winter long they are a bunch of hideous sticks, and in summer a menace to traffic as they block the view of oncoming cars.

If crape myrtles are planted I would like to see some of Mr. K. Sawada's pale pink ones, which are now in the trade as 'Near East'. Mr. Sawada gave me a small plant years ago, before it was introduced, but it got lost in the confusion of making a new garden.

I side with Mrs. Huffman [another writer for the *Charlotte Observer*] in a preference for cherries. They are not characteristic of the South and their bloom, though glorious, is brief. But they are the most beautiful flowering trees in Charlotte. Dr. Hechenbleikner's argument is that what we need is uniformity, and that too many kinds of cherries would be planted if they were chosen as the city tree. It seems to me that it would be a good thing to plant a number of kinds. 'Yoshino', 'Kwanzan', and 'Mt. Fuji' are available locally. Tingle lists 'Hally Jolivette', a hybrid with pink buds and very double white flowers.

I planted *Prunus sargentii* on the curb in front of my house in 1953. It grew to the height of fifteen feet in ten years, and looks to be about twenty now. I have had to do very little pruning, as the upright growth of the branches leaves the sidewalk clear, and the view of the street open. The large pink single flowers open between the middle of March and the first of April, before the leaves come out. A columnar form of Sargent's cherry is listed in the catalogues.

It seems to me a good thing to plant not only a variety of cherries, but also more kinds of flowering trees. Pears, I think have a bad name because they are subject to fire blight, but the Chinese species, *Pyrus calleryana*, a small, upright, fast-growing tree, is not susceptible.

One fall, Caroline Dormon sent me some wine-colored leaves in a letter. "It is lovely in flower," she wrote, "and sprays of the tiny russet fruits are charming in a copper bowl. The leaves keep their color until after Thanksgiving. Birds like the fruits so they are never a nuisance." With me the flowers come in the second half of March. 'Bradford' pear, a new variety introduced by the Department of Agriculture, is said to be superior to the type in bloom and in fall color.

For the sake of variety, the golden rain tree, *Koelreuteria paniculata*, might be considered. Though it is not long lived, it is fast growing. It has large compound leaves, and the large panicles of yellow flowers that bloom in June are followed by decorative fruits.

May 19, 1968

STREET TREES

Requirements for street trees limit the choice. We would like for them to be long lived, quick growing, free of pests, of easy culture, and tolerant of traffic fumes. They should be of suitable size for the allotted space, not easily damaged by storms, needing no pruning, having no messy fruits nor ill-smelling flowers nor litter of leaves, and beautiful at all seasons. Few fill these requirements and so street plantings become monotonous. I should like to see more variety, even if some sacrifice has to be made for the sake of beauty.

"In Washington, U.S.A. (where some of the most interesting street planting in the world has been done)," Bean writes in his *Trees and Shrubs Hardy in the British Isles*, "there is an avenue of maidenhair tree [*Ginkgo biloba*]—one of the most striking objects of that city." This is high praise from an Englishman and a curator of the Royal Botanic Garden at Kew. "Its habit is perfect, it thrives in towns, and in autumn its foliage invariably turns a lovely pale gold." The ginkgo is a good tree for this climate because it does better where the summers are hot.

In *Trees and Shrubs for the Coastal Plain*, Brooks Wigginton suggests giving a trial to a Japanese tree, *Zelkova serrata*, as a substitute for the American elm, and it is being grown in a local nursery. Another exotic that might be tried in a small way is the evergreen oak, *Quercus ilex*; this also is available in Charlotte.

Certainly the native trees come first, and where there is room for them to spread, nothing is better than the willow oak, *Quercus phellos*; but I do wonder, as I drive about under its dense shade, why the ground can't be covered with lilyturf [*Liriope*] instead of being left bare under the pretense that grass will grow there. If grass is wanted, it is better to plant a tree like the 'Moraine' locust [*Gleditsia triacanthos* 'Morain'], which gives light shade. In addition to *Quercus phellos*, three good oaks are *Q. palustris*, *Q. rubra*, and *Q. coccinea*.

There are other good native trees that could be planted between the sidewalk and the curb. One is the cucumber tree [*Magnolia acuminata*], a quick-growing magnolia; and another the silver bell, *Halesia monticola*. The maple that has the least number of drawbacks is *Acer saccharum*, but it is slow to get started, and when it does grow you will have to choose between the tree and the grass.

It seems to me that much might be sacrificed for the sake of flowers, and I would like to see more flowering trees in public places. Perhaps oaks live longer than cherries, but E. H. Wilson tells of a Japanese village with a three-mile avenue of cherry trees planted in 1735.

When I see magnificent oaks coming down all over town, I think that a quick-growing cherry like 'Yoshino' [*Prunus × yedoensis*] might give more pleasure. Two other quick-growing cherries are *Prunus lannesiana*, with single white flowers, and *P.* 'Shirotae' with double white flowers. Since Wilson considered *P. sargentii* the most beautiful of the Asiatic species and one of the best street trees, I planted two on Ridgewood Avenue. So far they have proved to be slow growing, but they are grafted. Seedlings are said to grow more freely and be more satisfactory. I should like to see 'Yoshino' planted all along the center of the Plaza. The objection that it costs too much to mow the grass around trees could be overcome by allowing the branches to grow to the ground and planting a ground cover such as liriope next to the curb. Then the grass could be done away with and wouldn't cost anything at all.

The cherries are beautiful at all seasons because of the picturesque branching habit and showy bark, but if an evergreen is wanted, *Magnolia grandiflora* could be used the same way.

In Rochester, New York, the lovely Yulan, *Magnolia denudata*, has been successful in a planting between two lanes of traffic. It is a slow-growing tree, but blooms when small, producing large, creamy flowers in mid-March, before the leaves come out.

The rows of winged elms on Colville Road show the advantage of uniform planting over a hodge-podge of trees and shrubs. On new and treeless streets, where the planting is left to the householders, how simple it would be for them all to get together and plant the same tree.

August 24, 1958

TREES WITH COLORED BARK

I seem to remember having said rather often that I would never plant any but flowering trees in a small garden, but now I have become interested in trees with colored bark. As English gardeners have always paid more attention to horticultural detail than we do, I looked into Graham Thomas's *Colour in the Winter Garden* to see what he has to say on the subject. He begins, of course, with the silver birch, but that is not a tree for us, and even our native paper birch, which occurs in North Carolina only at altitudes of 5,000 and 6,000 feet, barely tolerates hot summers.

However he appreciates the considerable beauty of the river birch, *Betula nigra*, which has been used so skillfully and effectively in the Flower and Garden Show. It looks like such a weedy tree along the creek banks in winter, but the warm rosewood color and the delicacy of the branches has an unexpected charm among the spring flowers. "Fine young trees by the lake at Wisley," Mr. Thomas writes, "show how this graceful tree does not shed its light brown bark, but retains it in a furry mass round the branches." The river birch is not apt to be long lived in cultivation, but it is good for a quick effect.

Mr. Thomas does not mention our sweet birch, *Betula lenta*, which has dark, aromatic cherry-like bark, or the yellow birch, *B. lutea* [*B. alleghaniensis*]. The yellow birch has finely cut leaves, and its bark peels away in thin strips leaving a yellowish layer beneath. "In certain lights," Alice Lounsberry writes, "it looks ruddy gold, always with a silvery sheen." Both species are listed by the Gardens of the Blue Ridge.

Mr. Thomas singles out the snakebark maples for the winter effect of the young trees. The trunks and branches of most species are at their best, he writes, from four to ten years. After that only the upper branches are colored, but the trees have a peculiar beauty of leaf and a graceful habit suited to small gardens. The original snakebark maple is our moosewood, *Acer pensylvanicum*; in North Carolina it is a tree of the high mountains. It was introduced into England in the mid-eighteenth century, and has been enlivening English winters ever since. "The most wonderful bark coloration I have ever seen," Mr. Thomas writes, "is to be found in some of the maples, one of which has thereby earned the name of the snakebark. It is *A. pensylvanicum*, and the variety 'Erythrocladum', whose young shoots are of the most brilliant crimson imaginable, and look as though they had just received a new coat of varnish on top of their paint."

Some southern nurseries list *A. pensylvanicum*, but the brilliant variety does not seem to be in the American trade at the present time. The Tingle Nursery lists two Chinese snakebarks, *Acer davidii* and *A. grosseri* var. *hersii*. Edward Scanlon considers *A. davidii* a good street tree; its large leaves turn red in the fall, and it is extremely tolerant of drought.

Most cherries have beautiful bark. In particular, I admire the silvery trunks of *Prunus serrulata* and its varieties, and the trunk of *P. sargentii* is like old pewter. I have never seen any mention of the autumnal cherry in this respect, but the trunk has curious and attractive golden marks, and my little tree, now on to ten years old, is beginning to peel. I skinned off a piece of old bark just now, and found the surface beneath it pale and shining. The most striking cherry as to bark is *Prunus serrula*, but its flowers and foliage are not outstanding.

Every one who sees the Wayside catalogue knows the colored photograph of *Cornus alba* 'Atrosanguinea' in the snow. This is a shrub that should be cut to the ground annually to encourage strong bright shoots.

The lacebark pine, *Pinus bungeana*, has been cultivated in this country for more than a hundred years, and the horticulturists are always luring gardeners to plant it, but very few nurserymen grow it. Mr. Hobman describes it as bushy and slow growing, but in time it will probably reach a height of thirty feet. The dark bark begins to peel when the tree is young, in a lacy pattern like that of the sycamore, showing the white surface beneath. When the tree gets to be some fifty years old, the trunk is all white.

November 27, 1966

WITCH HAZELS

Celia Duncan says I should write more about flowering shrubs, and I think she is right. She means the ones that drop their leaves. These are being forgotten now that we have so many broad-leaved evergreens, but the garden needs some bare branches in winter, and at all seasons it needs more color than evergreens alone can give.

In my own small garden I try to have some shrub in bloom every day of the year, and with so little space, I must choose each one with care. I look for a long season of bloom, ornamental fruits, handsome foliage, autumn color, any interesting form, attractive bark, easy culture, and freedom from disease. It is not likely that all of these will be found in a single shrub, but one that has only flowers to offer must be really outstanding when it is in bloom.

And now I have to confess that my choice for the first month of the year, the Chinese witch hazel, *Hamamelis mollis*, has none of the things I look for—except that it gives no trouble and stays in bloom for weeks. Its flowers, though utterly charming, are not spectacular; its habit is not graceful, its bark is dull, and its leaves are coarse. The books say that the fall color is fine, and mine does turn a warm apricot in a favorable season, but usually the large felt leaves (to six inches long and over four inches across) dry up before they color.

In spite of these failings, I consider this one of the ten or twelve best flowering shrubs and one that I could not be without. I like it because the flowers, thin shreds of gold bunched in wine-red cups, are able to defy the furious winter's rages and bloom on and on through frost, cold, ice, and snow.

The Chinese witch hazel has been in cultivation since 1879 when Charles Maries brought it to England from the mountains of central China. Through all these years it has been much praised, but little grown (in this country at least), and I have never seen it outside of my own garden. This is partly because there are many people who take no joy in a garden until the year is well advanced, and partly because most people must see things in bloom before they want them for themselves. In China, the witch hazel grows to a height of thirty feet, but in cultivation it is more likely to be a shrub of six to eight feet or less. The one in my garden has been there for twelve years, but I still look down on it. It branches near the base at a curiously low angle that seems to be characteristic. It began to bloom when very small, and blooms well in shade, though I should have planted it in the sun. When it turns to gold in the "dreadful dawn of the year" (Reginald Farrer's phrase) the garden is filled with fragrance.

Getting rid of poor plants is as important as seeking out the best. Nearly every garden in the South has a large ungainly Christmas honeysuckle, *Lonicera fragrantissima*, that is dull at its best, shabby at its worst, and never the least bit beautiful, even when in full bloom. There is no place for it in a small garden, and yet its nostalgic perfume on a warm day in January makes me think regretfully of the one left behind in Raleigh. Nothing would have induced my mother to part with it if we had not parted with the garden too. I doubt whether there is a southern nursery without a dull row of Christmas honeysuckles, and if there is a single one this side of Maryland that grows the Chinese witch hazel, I would like to know about it. This I hasten to say is not the fault of the nurserymen. It is the fault of gardeners, who should learn to know good plants and to demand them.

January 28, 1962

FLOWERING CHERRIES

The flowering cherries are the loveliest of trees, and their being relatively short-lived is not a drawback in these restless days. Their quick growth and their habits of blooming when young are greatly in their favor.

The Manchu cherry, *Prunus tomentosa*, is the first to bloom. In my Raleigh garden I often found a few flowers at the end of February. It is a shrub to about ten feet tall, and not pretty enough to plant for flowers, but the bright red cherries are edible and are attractive to birds. It takes two to produce fruit.

The Higan cherry, *P. subhirtella*, blooms in March. In an early season one in our neighborhood blooms the first week in March, but the weeping form is usually at its height between the middle and last of the month. The weeping cherry is a large tree, but the type—though it varies greatly and no two are alike—is usually rather small and often bushy. In my garden the autumn-flowering form shows a scattering of pale blossoms when the leaves fall, and unless the weather is very severe, we have a few until Christmas. In shape it is something like a crape myrtle, usually with more than one trunk. It blooms again in March, along with the Fuji cherry and the Hitoye cherry.

I bought Fuji cherry, *P. incisa*, for a small tree, and it is only fifteen or twenty feet tall, but it is wider than it is high and its spreading branches take up more room than a small garden can afford. In bloom it is the prettiest tree that I have, the myriad of little shell-tinted bells topped with dark red calycles, hanging from branches that would sweep the ground if I did not cut them back every spring. It is beautiful in summer when the small, fine-toothed leaves are green, and in fall when they turn to gold, and again in winter when the warm brown tones of the multiple trunks show up, and the fine twigs glitter in the sun. They say the birds are fond of the tiny cherries, but mine has never borne fruit—none of my cherries have ever fruited—except for the wild ones, and a little pink-flowered shrub, *P. humilis*.

The flowers of the Hitoye cherry, *P. lannesiana*, are single, sweet smelling, and two inches across. They are typically pink, but pure white in the wild form, which is the one I have. Mr. Sawada [of Overlook Nursery in Mobile, Alabama] gave it to me years ago, because he thinks it one of the best for the South. It is large, shapely, and wide spreading.

Prunus × *yedoensis*, the Yoshino cherry, is the one planted around the Tidal Basin in Washington, and the one that is so beautiful and so plentiful in Myers Park. It grows very fast and blooms when young. The flowers are pale pink and single.

Sargent's cherry, *P. sargentii*, grows slowly and does not bloom until it is well established. Mine (planted in the parking strip in front of the house) began to produce a few flowers after four years, but it did not bloom freely until ten years ago. The flowers are rose colored and single.

The double-flowered cherries come when the single-flowered ones are past. *P. serrulata* 'Shirotae', sometimes listed as 'Mount Fuji', is one of the best white ones. The flowers are large, to two inches, and semi-double when the tree is young. As it grows older they become more double. 'Kwanzan' and 'Naden' are the two double pink cherries seen all over town in early April, and 'Amanogawa' is the one with pale pink flowers, and the slender form of a Lombardy poplar. I love the pretty Japanese names. 'Amanogawa' means milky way; 'Shirotae' is snow white; 'Shogetsu', moon hanging low by a pine tree.

Once, when the emperor of Japan was returning to the palace after viewing his cherry blossoms, there was a discussion as to whether the pale pink flowers of his favorite were single or double. He ordered the coachman to turn back, and so the cherry was called 'Mikuruma-gaeshi', the royal carriage returns. The flowers proved to be single.

February 21, 1964

SERVICEBERRIES AND SLOES

I have always been told that the shadblows get their name from the fact that they bloom in the early spring when the shad are running, and that they are called June berries because they fruit in June, but I wondered about their other name, serviceberry (sarviceberry in the mountains). I read somewhere that they bloom in the mountains in spring when the itinerant preachers make their rounds and hold burial services for those who died during the winter when no one could get through to them, but it seems to me more likely that they are called serviceberry because they are of service, that is, they are edible. Birds eat the small sweet fruits, and so do bears, and so do people.

"Those that find it eat it as eagerly as they would cherries," Alice Lounsberry writes, in *Southern Wildflowers and Trees*. "It is even made into pies. The mountaineers' vigorous method of procuring it, however, is usually to chop the tree down, so in many places they are becoming rather scarce." Before the white men came the fruits were eaten by the Indians and were also made into a paste that could be kept for winter. I doubt whether very many mountain people chopped down shadblows in order to pick their fruit.

The native species are much confused because they hybridize freely, and there are many intermediate forms. In gardens the common shadblows, *Amelanchier canadensis* and *A. laevis*, are usually shrubs or small trees, but in the woods they may grow to a height of forty-five feet. The apple serviceberry [*Amelanchier* × *grandiflora*], a hybrid between these two, is considered an improvement over both parents.

Mr. Tingle lists it and also a selection called 'Robin Hill', which is new this season. He says it is much pinker than pink varieties, with a red bud that turns bright pink and gradually fades to white. He also lists *A.* × *grandiflora* 'Rosea' which I take to be the *rubescens* of other catalogues.

All of these shadblows bloom briefly, but they are usually beautiful again in the fall in autumn colors of red or clear lemon yellow. In *Natives Preferred*, Caroline Dormon's drawing "Shadblow in Winter" shows the charm of their graceful form and mottled bark when leaves are down.

Mr. Tingle considers the western shadblow *Amelanchier cusickii* [*A. alnifolia* var. *semi-integrifolia*] superior to the eastern species. It is a shrub to ten feet with heavy masses of white flowers followed by ornamental fruits. It comes from the far West, Washington and Oregon, and I have only recently found it in the trade.

Amelanchier stolonifera is native to the eastern states as far south as Virginia. I have found it in the trade only in Ohio nurseries. It is a good undercover tree for woodsy places, grows to a height of three or four feet, blooms a little later than *A. laevis*, and produces sweet juicy fruits in summer.

Most of the shadblows are American shrubs, but there are species in Europe and in Asia. The genus takes its name from *Amelanchier vulgaris*, now called *A. ovalis*, which is called amelancier in Savoy. It does not seem to be in the American trade, but it is popular in England. They call it the snowy mespillus. It flowers late, and the fruit is not palatable.

Amelanchier asiatica, a Chinese species but introduced from Japan, is said to be the first to flower and the last to shed its bright leaves. Mr. Tingle lists it, and in the Wayside catalogue, the almond-scented flowers are described as repeating in the fall. It seems to vary in size from a large shrub (to ten feet) to a medium sized tree.

Nearly always in March—early or late—but occasionally the first of April, Caroline Dormon writes that the sloes and shadblows are in bloom at Briarwood. The sloe is the hog plum, *Prunus umbellata*, which ranges along the coastal plain as far north as North Carolina. [William C.] Coker and [Henry Roland] Totten say that it grows near Myrtle Beach (where "an excellent, tart jelly" was made by Mrs. D. R. Coker from the sour fruits), and that it was in bloom in Chapel Hill on the twenty-fourth of February, 1933.

Caroline asks, and so do I, "Why does no one grow the lovely sloes?"

March 20, 1966

DOGWOODS

Never pluck the flower that blooms before the leaf.
It will bring you grief;
It has curious power in its blossoming hour,
Mystical and brief.
Down through the years there comes a tale of tears
About the flower that blows white as the last late snows
Before the leaf appears.

Ever since I came upon Louise Driscoll's poem, I have wondered what the threat of dogwood is, but I have never found out, although I have searched all the books of flower lore that I have at hand. The only clue I have came from a child who said, "But didn't you know? The Cross was made of dogwood—that's why the petals are notched and tipped with red for the four wounds." Many trees are said to be the ones that the cross was made from, but dogwood is not native to the Holy Land. Still, the symbol stands, and supports the warning:

Oh, be careful how you break the dogwood now.
No one ever should!
You break more than wood with the dogwood bough.

It seems to me that this is a good thing for conservationists to stress, for dogwoods grow very slowly, and there is reason for keeping your hand "aloof from leafless blossoming." The common name comes from a European species, *Cornus sanguinea*; its bark was used to wash mangy dogs.

The bark of flowering dogwood, *Cornus florida*, can be used as a substitute for quinine and Alfred Rehder says that merely chewing the twigs will sometimes ward off fevers. He says the bark can be used for tooth powder, for ink, and the root yields a red dye.

Coker and Totten say that the largest dogwood they have measured is forty feet high with a spread of fifty-three feet. It is usually a small tree not over twenty-five or thirty feet tall. There is considerable variation in the size and quality of the blossoms. A tree at Chapel Hill has flower heads that measure five and a half inches across, and another has bracts that persist a week or ten days longer than those of the type.

The thousands of dogwoods set out as a war memorial at Valley Forge have stimulated public planting all through the country. This is a good thing for parks, lawns, roadsides, woodsy places, and wide parkways. I hope no more will be planted in narrow parking strips where low, spreading branches are hazards to cars coming out of driveways, and where there is not room for the trees to develop naturally.

Glenn Park and the Rotary Club have asked for a citywide effort to plant dogwoods in Charlotte. The unusual beauty of the trees will make everyone eager to support the project, but there are several things to take into consideration. One is that dogwoods are not easy to transplant, even when balled and burlapped, and planted in the spring, which is considered the proper time. Trees from three to four feet tall are the best size to set out for they grow slowly.

One that Elizabeth Clarkson gave me more than ten years ago has not quite reached a height of fifteen feet. However, the trees begin to bloom when they are small, and they are long lived, which is very important in public planting.

Dogwoods have their troubles. Some springs the blossoms are marred by late frosts, and in some seasons the leaves are disfigured by brown splotches. The beauty of dogwoods in April makes these drawbacks seem unimportant. Other good points are the rich autumn color of the foliage, the bright fruits that hang on after the leaves fall, the lovely form of the bare trees, and the winter pattern of the bud-tipped branches.

May 14, 1961

BUCKEYES

When Osmond L. Barringer comes to garden club meetings, he fills his pockets with buckeyes to hand out to fellow members, who keep them for good luck charms or plant them in the garden. Mr. Barringer has a tree nearly fifteen feet tall, grown from a seed planted twelve years ago. His seed came from a tree (fifty to sixty feet tall) that Mrs. Barringer's grandfather, Mr. Cowles, planted in front of the Charlotte Mint about 1866. When the mint was moved the tree was cut down but you can still see it in the mural in the American Commercial Bank.

Mr. Barringer calls this tree the red buckeye. From its size I take it to be *Aesculus* × *carnea*, a cross between our native *A. pavia* and the European horse chestnut, *A. hippocastanum*. There must be a good deal of variation in the hybrids, for the flowers of Mr. Barringer's tree are Etruscan red and in open panicles, but Mr. Sam Caldwell—when he was here lecturing to the garden club—told me that the trees he knew as *A.* × *carnea* look as if they are covered with pink hyacinths when they are in bloom. In either form it is a shapely tree, decorative in flower and leaf. Though slow growing, it begins to bloom very early in life, even at eighteen inches.

If Mr. Barringer offers you any buckeyes, you had better take them and plant them, for trees of this species are seldom found in nurseries. Mr. Barringer, who knows every tree in Charlotte, told me about the European horse chestnut in front of the City Hall, at the northwest corner of East Trade Street. He says it is about twelve inches in diameter and fifty feet tall, the only large one in Charlotte, and that no one knows how old it is, though he has watched it bloom for twenty-five years or more. On the twenty-eighth of April he offered to go by to see if any flowers had come out and found it in full bloom.

In Raleigh I used to watch every spring for the white cones of a young tree in Capitol Square, and another on the campus of Shaw University. When in bloom, the horse chestnut is one of the loveliest of flowering trees.

Aesculus pavia is a shrub or small tree (to twenty feet) that grows in moist woods, mostly along the coast, and likes a shady place. It blooms in my garden in subdued gaiety late in April or early in May.

Mine was bought as the variety *humilis*, which is described as prostrate. But it is an upright shrub, already six feet tall, and still growing. For some time before it blooms, the developing flower panicles, the persistent scales of the winter buds, and the uncurling leaves are in warm tones of rose and bronze; and then it blooms in a soft rosy glow. Dr. Totten says that it is a difficult shrub to transplant, and should be grown from seed, but I had no trouble with it.

Aesculus parviflorum, the bottlebrush buckeye, is another native shrub with handsome palmate leaves. This also is a valuable shrub for blooming in the shade. It suckers freely, and keeps growing in girth until it makes a mass, sixteen feet or more in diameter, but is seldom more than four or five feet tall. It needs room to spread, and if it isn't given room, it takes over anyway. The tall candles of bloom, sometimes sixteen inches long, with creamy flowers and apricot-tipped stamens, stand high above the leaves. Buckeyes are poisonous and narcotic, but I shouldn't think anyone would be tempted to eat them.

I have always wondered how buckeyes got their name. Mrs. Loudon says they are so called because the large pale scar of the seed makes it look like the eye of a stag.

The genus, Gerard says in his herbal, is called horse chestnut "for that the people of the East countries do with the fruit thereof cure their horses of cough . . . and such like diseases." It belongs to the soapberry family, whose members often have saponin in bark or fruit or root. In the buckeye saponin is in the root, which is used to wash and whiten cloth. The bark cures toothache and ulcers, and crushed branches thrown in the water stupefy fish so that they are easily caught. Altogether, it is a very useful as well as an ornamental genus.

May 4, 1958

EUCALYPTUS

I am always being asked about the Australian gum tree, *Eucalyptus pulverulenta*, that grows by our front door, and I have fallen into the habit of saying that I really don't know much about it, except that it is not dependably hardy. Saying you don't know is easier than taking the trouble to sum up what you do know, which is often more than you think—as I found when I sat down to make up for my negligence.

The Australian gums are among the tallest trees in the world. Early travelers told of having seen some over 500 feet, but the tallest—when accurately measured—proved to be only a little over 300. *E. pulverulenta* is described in the Royal Horticultural Society's *Dictionary of Gardening* as a small tree up to thirty feet, and the one by our door must be well on to that, but I have read of a tree in Ireland at Mount Usher (near Dublin) that is ninety feet tall. The Fruitland catalogue allows it fifty feet.

I bought my first eucalyptus from Fruitland in a small pot. Mr. Baillie wouldn't let me pay for it. He said it wouldn't be hardy in Charlotte, but I put it out in November, and it survived the winter and in a year it had grown to ten feet. The second winter was one of early and disastrous cold that came before new growth was hardened. My eucalyptus was killed, and so were three young ones on Belvedere, as were many in Augusta, including the stock at Fruitland.

I had to send to California for the next one, which came in a gallon can. It was put out in April, the best time for plants of doubtful hardiness, and has now survived six winters. I think it was the second winter that we had a heavy, wet snow that came before daylight. By the time I got out with a broom to brush off the eucalyptus, the branches had been too heavily laden, and the trunk was broken off six feet from the ground, but by the next summer it had come out again and was more beautiful than ever.

I have since learned that the branches should be cut back half way after the first year, and March is the time to do it. I think it should be cut back severely every spring if it is grown for foliage, which is what most people want, for this is one whose branches are sold by the florists.

Only the new growth has the round, silver-blue leaves that give it the name silver dollar gum. Some of the leaves really are as large as silver dollars, but most of them are only like dimes and quarters. They come in pairs, at intervals of two or three inches, along white stems to a yard or more long. The mature leaves are narrow and tapered, and of a dull yellow-green.

The Mayers cut their gum trees to the ground every spring, and this is probably the most satisfactory way of growing them in this climate, for the foliage is very unsightly after a spell of severe cold, and it does not come out again until very late in the spring.

Gum trees are grown from imported seed. Several people have tried them from cuttings without any success. Seeds of *E. pulverulenta* are very hard to find. The plants that Mrs. Price has had were from seeds that came under another name in a batch that she raised for Dr. Mayer. They gave me several, which I put on the west side of house for cutting. Last fall I gave most of the foliage away, and this spring I trimmed off the rest. It was soon out again, and as fast as I cut it, more comes. I am amazed that it will grow so well in a place that gets only a few hours of afternoon sun.

Last fall the tree by the door bloomed. I looked up one day in October, and saw little, pointed green buds which soon opened into tiny white flowers. I think I was the only person who admired them. I don't think any seed ripened, and last year there were no flowers—at least I couldn't see any.

When a eucalyptus is planted, a stake should be driven into the hole first, and the trunk should be securely tied to it, as it is hard to keep the tree well anchored. In a book called *The Australian Gardener* the author says that manure in any form is fatal, and applications of fertilizer likely to cause failure, but the *R. H. S. Dictionary* recommends decayed manure. The trees are drought resistant, and will grow in very dry soil, though not as fast. I think it is better not to give them too much water or too rich a diet. They are not particular as to soil.

January 26, 1958

HONEY LOCUST

Eight years ago, when we came here to live, Charlotte was full of mimosas [*Albizia julibrissin*]. A great many fine, wide-spreading trees grew in our neighborhood, and between us and a neighbor there were seven beauties all in a row. Early in June they were a wall of tender green, embroidered with pink and yellow silk. I felt as if I were living in a Japanese print. But two or three years later they began to droop, and one by one they died slow, lingering deaths.

Now there are few trees left in this part of town. The mimosa wilt had come to Charlotte along with us. No practical control has been found for this disease, and until a wilt-resistant strain is developed a gardener will think twice before planting a mimosa.

In the meantime the best substitute is the native honey locust, *Gleditsia triacanthos*. Like the mimosa it has fine lacy foliage, leafs out late in the spring and sheds its leaves early in the fall, allowing grass and other plants to grow underneath it. It grows rapidly, is long lived, deep rooted, reasonably pest free, easily transplanted, and not particular as to soil. Unfortunately, the flowers are meager greenish tassels instead of balls of silky fluff.

The strain called the 'Moraine' locust is now appearing in southern nurseries. It originated in Ohio, but is just as tolerant of hot, dry summers as of long, cold winters. It has two advantages over the type—no dirty seed pods and no horrid thorns. There may be some who will not consider the first a virtue. I see in *Trees of the Southeastern States* (Coker and Totten) that the fruits "are often mixed with persimmons to form what is known in the South as locust or persimmon beer." But the vicious three-pronged thorns—which give the tree its specific name, *triacanthos*—are well rid of, for when they fall to the ground they can be a menace to small bare feet.

It must be remembered that the honey locust sometimes grows to be a very large tree. The American Forestry Association has recorded one with a spread of 112 feet, and a height of ninety. A tree in our neighborhood (which has probably not finished growing yet, as the trees hereabout were mostly planted around thirty years ago) looks to me as if its branches spread thirty to forty feet, and it is as tall as it is wide.

The 'Moraine' locust is said to grow to forty-five or fifty feet, and the one pictured in the catalogues fills a small front yard, and spreads over the sidewalk and parking strip. I expect it is still growing for the strain is of fairly recent development. It makes a shapely tree where it is allowed room to grow naturally.

A new form of the honey locust appeared recently in the gaudiest of the illustrated catalogues. It is called 'Sunburst', because the branches end in great plumes of bright yellow foliage. This too came from an Ohio nursery, and it grows to a considerable size although it is described as a "graceful small tree." In the early part of the summer I was startled to see a pair of these trees in front of a house on Queen's Road West, on either side of the door, and I was interested to find that they came from a local nursery. Seeing a plant that you have known only in catalogues is like recognizing a celebrity in a crowd. The 'Sunburst' locust is said to keep its bright plumage throughout the summer, but at the end of July it seems to me that its glow is somewhat dimmed.

September 15, 1957

OSMANTHUS

Long-sought plants have a way of turning up in the backyard—or at least in the neighborhood. All the while that I have been searching for *Osmanthus aurantiacus* [*Osmanthus fragrans* f. *aurantiacus*] it was growing in Laura Braswell's garden—in fact, I put it there.

In spite of the fact that its leaves are longer (to seven inches), narrower and more tapered, it never occurred to me that it was not the sweet olive for which it was bought until last September, when Laura said, "The sweet olive you got for me has orange flowers. Do you think its being in the shade makes it a deeper color?" To find an extremely rare shrub substituted for a common one is wonder enough, but it is even more wonderful that it has survived some bitter winters when even shrubs that are supposedly hardy have been injured, for it is not considered reliable above zone nine. The orange *Osmanthus* is said to be native to China. It is known only in cultivation and grows in the old Imperial Gardens of Tokyo, which are now a public park. I think it was introduced into this country by Walter Clarke—at any rate it was first mentioned, so far as I know, in his *Garden Aristocrats for 1940* and his successors (W. B. Clarke and Co.) are the only source I know of, although an Alabama nursery lists a "Yellow Osmanthus" which may be this.

Bean says that the flowers vary in value; those of the only other specimen that I have seen (in Inez Conger's garden in Louisiana) were very pale. However, they were the last of the season, in mid-October, and may have been faded. Laura's are of the soft clear tint called Mikado orange, not far from the pure spectrum color. The flowers are slightly larger than those of the sweet olive, of firmer substance and equally fragrant. They are in round, compact clusters in the axils of the leaves.

Laura cut a branch to show a friend at the Curb Market, who took it home and found it rooted readily in the damp soil under a spigot. There may be some difficulty in getting young plants through their first winters, but I hope the nurserymen will try, for California is a long way off.

Osmanthus 'San Jose' is Mr. Clarke's hybrid between *Osmanthus aurantiacus* [*Osmanthus fragrans* f. *aurantiacus*] and *O. ilicifolius* [*O. heterophyllus*]. He considered it faster growing than either of its parents, and I expect it is, for a tiny plant that came to me in a pot has grown to a height of six feet in ten years. It is still very slender and not at all compact, but I can't tell whether this will be its characteristic form. It is said to produce comparatively large creamy yellow flowers in fall and winter; so far mine has not had any. I think the leaves are the most decorative of any of the tea olives. They are small, spiny ovals of a deep shining green—some of the large ones to more than three inches long.

Osmanthus fragrans blooms in August and September, again in the spring, and at intervals through the year. *Osmanthus ilicifolius* [*O. heterophyllus*], the holly-leaved tea olive, blooms late in September or early in October. All are wonderfully fragrant.

These are tall evergreens to fifteen or twenty feet, but *Osmanthus delavayi* is low and spreading. It is said to grow to six feet or more, but it can be kept to any height by pruning. Mine has never been pruned. After twelve years it is still only three feet tall and not very much wider. It is somewhat tender, and late freezes cut it back severely. It is a graceful, spreading shrub, well furnished with small, finely toothed oval leaves that are seldom over an inch long. In mild seasons it blooms for weeks, beginning in late February or soon afterward, and the small, white, tubular flowers are outstanding for numbers and fragrance.

October 15, 1961

HOLLIES

There must be greater variety among the hollies than in any other genus of broad-leaved evergreens, which is not strange as there are up to five hundred species scattered throughout the temperate and tropical parts of the world.

The species vary in fruit, foliage, and form. The berries vary in size from a large pinhead to a large pea, and in color from black, red, orange, and yellow and from opaqueness to translucence. They are borne singly or in bunches, and on long or short stalks or none at all. The leaves are shiny or dull; entire or toothed or spiny; light green, dark green, gray, or variegated; and range in size from the minute ones of the dwarf Japanese hollies to the wide ones of *Ilex latifolia*, which in some forms are as large as an average leaf of *Magnolia grandiflora*. In form the hollies vary from the low and spreading, to the tall and spreading, the globe, the column, and the pyramid. They have everything to offer except conspicuous flowers, and here they are not entirely lacking for some species, such as *I. pernyi*, put on a good show when in bloom.

Visitors to the Flower and Garden Show had a chance to see a cross section of native and exotic hollies, in the exhibit of the Department of Horticultural Science of the North Carolina State College. The native species include one deciduous holly, *I. decidua*, the typical and dwarf forms of yaupon, several varieties of *I. opaca*, and the beautiful little yellow-berried *I. cassine*. (I'll never be happy until I have that.)

Ilex decidua, the possumhaw holly, is a Southern species native from Virginia to Florida. It is the best of the kinds that drop their leaves, because the berries, as is evident from the fact that the specimen at the exhibit was in perfect fruit in the middle of February, hang on in good condition all winter. In spite of its beauty in fruit, it must be remembered that it does not bear freely until it gets to be a big shrub, and that both male and female plants must be present if it is to fruit at all. It is not a shrub for a small garden, but it is one to watch for in the winter woods.

Among the American hollies in the exhibit were 'Savannah' and 'Tinga'. 'Savannah' is valuable as a slender, almost columnar female form that has light green leaves and well displayed berries. This winter its foliage has suffered in exposed places, but I hope winters like this will be rare. 'Tinga', which comes from a Wilmington nursery, has dark green leaves with a few spines, and an abundance of large red berries.

Among the varieties of the Chinese holly, *I. cornuta*, were two dwarf forms, one loose and spreading, the other round and compact; a spreading form with large golden berries; and the favorite Burford holly [*Ilex cornuta* 'Burfordii']. The Burford holly is a female form that fruits without pollination. The leaves are entire and of a deep and shining green.

The Japanese hollies were the typical *I. crenata* showing the black fruit, and three dwarf varieties: 'Repandens', 'Helleri' and 'Stokes', all three having tiny leaves. Those of 'Stokes' originally came from the Stokes Nursery in Pittsburgh, are dark green and very hardy. Those of 'Repandens' are light green. It is to be remembered that all three of these hollies, though very dwarf, keep spreading, and though they spread slowly they must be pruned if they are to be kept to a narrow space.

Two of the Foster hybrids were shown. These hybrids are seedlings of a Dahoon holly [*I. cassine*] pollinated by an American holly. They have narrow, glossy leaves, and quantities of small red berries, and very gray stems. The Foster hybrids grow very fast, and although they came from an Alabama nursery those in Charlotte have not been hurt by this cold winter. All these hollies are to be had in nurseries hereabouts.

March 24, 1963

CONIFERS

Conifers have been neglected since the broad-leaved evergreens have become so popular, but Warren Redd is one man who has never wavered in his enthusiasm for the cone bearers. I went about with him in a showery day last spring, and after studying the varying shades and shapes, I could understand his partiality. He is also a great admirer of rocks and rocks and conifers go together. Junipers in particular look well with rocks as companions.

The Chinese juniper, like most Asiatic plants, adapts itself to our part of the world, and grows better in cultivation than our native *Juniperus virginiana*. It is the most variable of the species, with nursery forms from Fruitland in Georgia, to San Jose in California. *Juniperus chinensis* 'Fruitlandii' is a sport of the Pfitzer juniper [*Juniperus chinensis* 'Pfitzeriana'] but more compact, bluer, and more feathery.

Mr. Clarke describes the 'San Jose' variety as sage green, showing no variegation, but having a mixture of adult and juvenile foliage. It is a creeping form. Another and better-known creeper is Sargent's juniper, one of the best and greenest of the prostrate kinds. It keeps to a height of less than three feet, but gradually spreads itself over an area of eight or ten feet. As it is wonderfully drought resistant, it makes a good cover for steep slopes. I particularly like the way it keeps its color in winter.

The Pfitzer juniper, the most commonly planted of the Chinese forms, is a large ungainly shrub, six feet tall, and very wide spreading. The variety 'Hetzii' is a more compact shrub, with blue foliage; the variety 'Nana' is perfectly dwarf, dense, and extremely slow growing, a good subject for the rock garden.

Last fall I ordered three very low and slow-growing conifers that fit into the pockets of the rock garden or grow on a dry wall. They came in little plastic pots, looking perfectly charming, though only two or three inches in diameter, and now they look very gay with the season's growth.

One of these is *Juniperus squamata* 'Prostrata', a stiff, compact little blue–gray shrub that keeps to a height of about six inches, and will be many years in reaching a spread of three feet. It comes from the Himalayas, but does not seem to mind our summers. Another is *J. procumbens* 'Nana', a dense, irregular, silvery cushion with sharp bluish needles. The type makes a very wide-spreading shrub in time, to four or five yards across. Unlike most junipers it requires shade. My third little pot held *J. horizontalis* 'Bar Harbor', which is considered the best of the prostrate forms for covering the ground. They describe it as "a quick growing mass of attractive steel blue." It is now a small fern-like fan on the edge of the terrace.

At the Flower and Garden Show in Raleigh, the Andorra juniper, *J. horizontalis* 'Plumossa', was used lavishly in planters, and I must say it looked attractive, though I have never liked the purplish color it usually assumes after frost. Perhaps it should be used with brick and stone only, and not with green grass and evergreen shrubs.

One of my favorite dwarf species is the shore juniper, *J. conferta*, which is planted at the entrances of the Nalle Clinic. It is such a cheerful green, and the shiny needles have somewhat the effect of yew. Although it comes from the seashore and thrives in sand, it grows equally well in Mecklenburg clay.

The Savin juniper, *J. sabina* 'Tamariscifolia', is an aromatic, upright, and spreading evergreen with dark feathery foliage. Mr. Redd has an interesting form that I have never seen before, the cultivar 'Von Erhon', which has very fine needles. The better-known *J. sabina* var. *tamariscifolia* grows fast and keeps its regular contour.

Mr. Redd thinks that one reason the junipers have been out of favor is that they are not properly and regularly pruned; pruning should be done in the spring, with a knife, just before new growth starts.

September 9, 1962

FIRS AND CEDARS

I am concerned about the fir tree at the corner of Mecklenburg and Belvedere. I am ashamed to say that I never noticed this tree until it was pointed out to me, but I think it is the most beautiful conifer that I have ever seen. As I stood before it, looking up at its perfect symmetry, I felt that tree worship is understandable. It is the Caucasian fir, *Abies nordmanniana*, one of the best conifers for this part of the country. Planted about fifty years ago by Fred Laxton, it is now more than thirty feet tall, with horizontal branches all the way to the ground, and the narrow, almost columnar habit that is characteristic of the species. The dark, glossy green needles—an inch or more in length—are notched at the end, making it easy to identify.

The Caucasian fir is a rare tree in American nurseries. It has taken me some time to track down a few sources in Maryland, New England, and California. I suppose few people in this restless age are willing to wait for it to mature. Now that Mr. Laxton's fir tree has come into the hands of the Charlotte Country Club, I hope it will be treasured as it has been in the past, and left to increase in beauty against the long view across the golf course. The nearby pecan should be cut down before it crowds the fir.

The Caucasian fir needs sun, but the Chinese fir, *Cunninghamia lanceolata*, will also grow in shade, though it is best with some of both. The *Cunninghamia* is not uncommon in Charlotte, but when Dr. Nehrling wrote about it in the first quarter of the century, he said that the two trees in his Florida garden were the only ones he had ever seen. Mr. Berckmans had sent them to him, and Fruitland Nurseries list them still.

The genus is one of the oldest types of vegetation. Its glossy needles have something of the strong but delicate pattern of a fossil. They are two inches or more long, slender, and tapered to a very sharp point. The branches are decorative in winter bouquets but most unpleasant to handle.

The Chinese fir grows almost as fast as a deodar cedar [*Cedrus deodara*] and its strict habit makes it more suitable for a small place. Its one fault is that the dead needles hang on, making it look shabby. I asked Helen Mayer why hers never has brown branches, and she said that is because she keeps them pruned.

There is a blue form of the Chinese fir, the variety *glauca*, which I have seen at the Blandy Experimental Farm in northern Virginia. I see that it is listed by a Richmond nurseryman.

I see that a local nursery offers the incense cedar, *Libocedrus decurrens* [*Calocedrus decurrens*]. A lofty one in Mrs. Odell's garden in Concord was planted in 1880. She says that it is the tallest tree in town, which it may well be. There is one in Hillsborough that I have been told is seventy feet tall and on the West Coast, where it is native, it grows to a hundred feet. The incense cedar has the distinct and formal habit of a cypress; the lacy foliage and frondlike branches of an arborvitae, and tiny, curious cones in the shape of a fleur-de-lis. The fragrant wood that gives it its name has been used for cedar pencils.

It seems a pity that the popularity of broad-leaved evergreens has made these good conifers go out of fashion. I wish they could come back in favor.

May 3, 1959

FLOWERING SHRUBS

When it comes to choosing flowering shrubs, it is more a matter of taking what you can get than of getting what you like—which, as the March Hare pointed out, is a very different thing. Emphasis on evergreens has made people lose interest in deciduous things. When these are not in demand the nurserymen cannot afford to grow them, and then they become more and more rare and often go out of existence.

When I think of flowering shrubs I think first of the quince, and the loveliest of all is 'Apple Blossom'. It is not really a shrub for a garden as small as mine, for it has long since outgrown its allotted space, and has to be cut back savagely every spring to keep it from covering the flower border. It is more than ten feet tall and has a spread of more than fifteen feet and it is still growing. Fortunately it came from Mr. Hohman, who grows quinces on their own roots, so the suckers come true, and I give them away as soon as they come up. They begin to flower at once, and grow very fast.

If this quince is in any southern nursery, I should like to hear about it. Kingsville and two Massachusetts nurseries are the only sources I know of. I am surprised at finding it in New England for I thought it would not be hardy there. The pink buds usually begin to open soon after the middle of January or early February and continue through March. Some of the flowers are caught by the cold, but there are always more to come.

The flowering almond, *Prunus triloba*, is a larger, more woody, and grander shrub than *Prunus glandulosa*, the flowering almond of southern gardens, which is really a cherry. Unfortunately most nurseries graft *P. triloba* on some horrible sort of plum that suckers in the most devastating manner. As the suckers increase, the shrub dwindles. Miles Hadfield, in *One Man's Garden*, writes he overcame this difficulty by layering the branches. In any case it is a shrub that wears itself out blooming and needs to be replaced after a number of years. One reason for this is that heavily flowered shoots cannot be counted on to bloom freely again, and should be cut back to the base immediately after blooming. This drastic pruning makes, in time, an ungainly bush. The flowering almond blooms at the end of March.

Sargent's crab, *Malus sargentii*, is a charming and little-known shrub from Japan. The faintly pink buds open in late March into pure white flowers. These are followed by small bright red fruits that are said to persist until the following spring. I remember Caroline Dormon's having arranged a jar of the branches with fruit still hanging on them when I was at Briarwood in October. I am sure that the apples disappeared very quickly in our Raleigh garden and I suppose the birds ate them. Though the books say the leaves are brilliant in autumn, mine never were. I grew the shrub under the high branches of white oaks, where it probably got too little sun, though it bloomed and fruited, and was a pretty woodsy sort of thing among the native shrubs and wild flowers. I remember it as three or four feet tall, with a wider spread.

Spiraea × *arguta* is the only species I care enough about to grow in a small garden. It can be held to a reasonable size without any trouble, but it will grow to six or eight feet tall if left alone, and will continue to spread as the branches touch the ground and take root. After a sprinkling of flowers all through the winter, it comes into snowy bloom about the end of February in company with the flowering quince. Wayside is offering a compact form called 'Foam of May', which with us would be 'Foam of February'.

March 12, 1967

MARCH-FLOWERING SHRUBS

One of the beautiful flowering shrubs of March is the pearl bush, *Exochorda racemosa*. "I can most conscientiously say, 'Get it'," Mrs. Earle wrote in 1896, half a century after its introduction. "The flowers, full-blown and in bud, are of an exquisitely pure white, and the foliage is light green, delicate and refined."

In *Shrubs and Vines for American Gardens*, Donald Wyman relegates this species to the secondary list as inferior in flower, fruit and habit. He recommends, reluctantly, *E. giraldi* var. *wilsonii*, and writes, "Many shrubs, more serviceable in flower, and during other seasons as well, might be used to better advantage."

I am on the side of Mrs. Earle and of Reginald Farrer, who considers *E. racemosa* "one of the most glorious of all flowering shrubs." I used to visit one in Raleigh that was just that. It was as beautiful as white quince, perhaps more so, for the buds of the pearl bush break out all at once, and the quince comes into bloom slowly, blossom by blossom. It was a large bush, six feet or more in height, and spreads its whiteness over at least sixteen feet of a grimy embankment.

The pearl bush is a member of the rose family, closely related to the spiraeas, but Mr. Farrer says, "To call it by its old name of *Spiraea grandiflora* is to give an entirely misleading impression. For what one associates with the spiraeas, every one of them is a distinctive grace of multitudinous fluffiness; whereas the blossoms of *Exochorda* are individuals, and very remarkable individuals, too—large pearly white stars of remarkable beauty, gathered together in very loose spikes, so that you can see each flower outline completely."

The pearl bush blooms the last half of March, *Abeliophyllum distichum*, the white forsythia, at the beginning. In my garden *Abeliophyllum* is a low, shapeless, slow-growing shrub that has not reached a height of more than three feet in the twelve years that I have had it. Against a wall, and with support, it will grow to eight or ten feet. It is not much of a plant, but the flowers are so delicate and so delightfully fragrant that having once had them in Raleigh, I felt I must have them again. At that time the Princeton Nursery was the only source that I knew. Later another nursery offered *Abeliophyllum* as something new, at ten dollars a plant. Now blooming-size plants are available at three or four dollars, and Tingle offers small ones for thirty-five cents.

Abeliophyllum is a very hardy shrub, but it wants warmth and protection as the buds are tender, and full sun is essential for good bloom. It would be a good shrub to plant on a bank as the tips of the branches take root where they touch the ground. I cannot imagine why it is called abelia-leaf, for the leaves are twice as large as those of the abelia, and not at all shiny; or why it is called white forsythia, for the flowers are like those of its showy golden cousin only in that they are four-parted and in spikes. They are distinguished from other early shrubs by their delicacy, their delightful fragrance, and the way they are arranged along the thin, dark red stems.

Although it is considered winter blooming, the *Abeliophyllum* blooms for me around the first of March. The tiny wine-colored buds come out so suddenly that I can never catch them at it, no matter how closely I watch, but always find them in full bloom just after I have thought them nowhere near ready.

The early spring shrubs have been at their best this year. In spite of all of the snow they have bloomed steadily, and have been damaged very little. The early daffodils have been splendid. With these and the Lenten roses and the snowflakes, the garden has been full of bloom since the last week in February.

March 25, 1962

VIBURNUMS AND OTHER FLOWERING SHRUBS

In April, the most spectacular plant in my garden is the sterile form of *Viburnum macrocephalum*, the Chinese snowball. The buds begin to color early in the month, or sometimes late in March, and they slowly increase in size and beauty as they turn from apple-green corymbs to glass-green balls, and finally to enormous spheres of dazzling white. Some years I have counted a hundred or more flower heads, some of them seven inches in diameter. The shrub is semi-evergreen, which means that the leaves persist through mild winters; but they always drop off before the new ones come and the flower buds appear on bare branches. Then, as the flowers develop, there is just a trimming of bright green where the new foliage follows.

Robert Fortune found this snowball in a Chinese garden and sent it back to England in 1844. In all these years it has never become common there or in this country, probably because it is somewhat tender and apt to be killed to the ground in northern winters. Fortune found shrubs twenty feet tall in China. I think the one in my garden is well on to that. My Chinese snowball is planted in an out-of-the-way place under pines. It is a gaunt and angular shrub, not handsome when out of bloom. It blooms there in deep shade and puts up very well with the situation, though it likes rich moist loam.

Wayside Gardens offers *Viburnum* × *carlcephalum*, a hybrid between *V. macrocephalum* and *V. carlesii*. It is a smaller and more compact shrub with the added charm of fragrance, but to me it has neither the grace of the one parent nor the magnificence of the other. *Viburnum plicatum* var. *tomentosum* blooms about the same time or a little later. Mr. Bean puts this in "the very first rank of deciduous shrubs," probably in the first twelve. I am partial to the lacy white flowers of the type, and especially the cultivar 'Mariesii' which begins to bloom when very small, quickly growing into a large bush, and is covered with flowers all the way to the ground. This will bloom in shade too, but it is at its best when in full sun with plenty of room to spread. V. 'Mariesii' has a second season of beauty when the berries turn red, another reason for preferring it to the sterile form. I am not sure just when this is, for it never fruited with me.

Prunus triloba plena [*P. triloba* var. *multiplex*], another shrub that Fortune introduced from China, usually blooms in my garden the first of April or a little earlier. I never saw or heard of this until we came to Charlotte, and I began a systematic search for the best flowering shrubs. In 1916 Mrs. Wilder wrote of it in *My Garden* as lovely indeed and "wreathing itself from top to bottom with gay pink rosettes resembling but larger than those affected by the Flowering Almond. We have two great bushes in front of the garden-house porch with a fine clump of gray-white Florentine Iris and some cherry-colored tulips 'Pride of Haarlem' as its neighbors." I wouldn't choose cherry-colored tulips to go with this bright pink shrub.

Prunus triloba (which seems not to have a common name) is a much larger and more impressive shrub than our old flowering almond, and grows to a height of twelve or fifteen feet if given room. It should be cut back immediately after flowering, and if, as mine has, it has been grafted on plum stock, the suckers should be removed the minute they appear.

A dear shrub that flowers in old gardens along with the flowering almond is the Persian lilac, *Syringa × persica*, the only species that is really satisfactory and long lived in these parts. Celia Duncan has the pretty cut-leafed form, which she says is known in gardens as Spanish spiraea.

April 22, 1962

JUNE-FLOWERING SHRUBS

If the garden could have only one deciduous shrub to flower in June, it would be hard to choose between the oakleaf hydrangea and the dwarf horse chestnut. Both are native to the southeast; both like shade and a deep loamy soil, and need plenty of room to display their full beauty. They are slow growing, but in time they become very large shrubs.

When he visited Mount Vernon in 1824, Lafayette is said to have set out an oakleaf hydrangea, *Hydrangea quercifolia*, on either side of the palm house and the gate. It is a shrub that is found in old gardens more than in modern ones, but there must be a demand for it in Charlotte, for it is being grown in at least one nursery.

The most beautiful specimen I have ever seen is in the Mayers' garden, where it begins to bloom in late May with the 'Chugai' azaleas, presenting great gleaming white bouquets that stay fresh for more than a month, and then take on tones of green and purple. The dried flowers are cut for arrangements and winter decoration, and the garden club ladies once fashioned some very charming hats from them. The shrub has another season in the fall when the large leaves turn dark red. The leaves are so handsome that the shrub is grown for foliage in parts of the country where it is too cold for it to flower well.

Now, in mid-June, various forms of *Hydrangea macrophylla* are in bloom all over town, delicate pink ones, and some that look as if they had been left in the bluing too long. The best white one that I know came to me from the old Kohankie nursery as *H.* × *anthoneura* 'Thomas Hogg', but I think it must be the one that Alfred Rehder describes (in *Bailey's Cyclopedia*) as one of the macrophylla varieties, and one of the hardiest. The shrub is little more than three feet tall, but the heavy flower heads make the branches lean, and wherever they touch the ground they take root.

It was a sad day for me, and for all gardeners, when Mr. Kohankie sold his nursery. His successor has dropped this hydrangea (and many other rare plants) from his list, and I no longer know a source for it. I have urged rooted branches on my friends, and I wish some enterprising nurseryman would propagate it.

The dwarf bottlebrush buckeye, *Aesculus parviflora*, is not really small flowered. The specific name applies only to the individual flowers. The inflorescence is an impressive slender spike, like a foxtail lily, from twelve to sixteen inches long, with apricot-tipped stamens standing out beyond the white flowers. They bloom punctually the first part of June, almost always beginning on the eighth. The tapered plumes cover the bush from top to bottom, standing well above the yellow-green five-fingered leaves. The only thing they lack is fragrance. In spite of the fact that the flowers are so plentiful, there are very few buckeyes, and those few disappear before I can gather them. Last summer I found out where they go. I caught a chipmunk lugging one to his tunnel. Lacking seed, propagation is by division. Nuts of the other species are poisonous, though the Indians roasted buckeyes and ate them. Mrs. Loundon writes in *Botany for Ladies* that those of this species are edible, and that when boiled in milk they taste like chestnuts. She says the shiny red-brown nut is like the eye of a stag, the scar being the pupil. So that's where the name comes from.

The dwarf buckeye is a rather slow-growing shrub, but it blooms freely when small. Mine bloomed, when less than two feet tall, the second season after I planted it. By the fourth season it was impressive, and now, after twelve years it is six feet tall, with a spread of ten feet or more and graceful branches sweeping the ground.

These June-flowering shrubs make no demands beyond shade and water.

June 24, 1962

VIBURNUMS

One day this past summer (I suddenly realized that it has passed) I went to the Nalle Clinic to see how *Viburnum* × *pragense* is getting along. It is flourishing. In the four years since it came as a small plant in a container, a present to me from Mr. Hohman, it has grown to be a striking shrub about five feet tall.

I wrote to Dr. Donald Egolf, at the National Arboretum, to ask why it is called *pragense*. It is because it was developed at the Prague Municipal Gardens. "The plant has thrived at the National Arboretum," he writes, "and has developed into a fine specimen. Although it has good foliage and growth habit, the flowering and fruiting attributes are inferior to other cultivars." I missed the flowering of our plant this spring, so I shall have to wait until next April to see for myself what the flowers are like.

Viburnum × *pragense* is described in *Gardeners Chronicle / Gardening Illustrated*, April 30, 1960, by the Czechoslovakian horticulturists Jaromir Hajcek and J. P. Krouman. It is a hybrid between two Chinese species, *V. utile* (the pollen parent) and *V. rhytidophyllum*, a cross made by Josef Vik. "The new *Viburnum* has a light and elegant shape and is only slightly larger than *V. utile*, from which it has inherited the overhanging side branches and the glossy upper side of its leaves which are, however, bigger (two to four inches) . . . From *V. rhytidophyllum* it has inherited the felt-like lower side of its leaves, and marked vitality, and ability to resist frost."

It grows readily from cuttings taken in the late fall. After a three-year test in the arboretum of evergreen plants at Malonya, and in other gardens, the new hybrid was given in 1959 the name *Viburnum* × *pragense*. As both parents are shrubs to ten feet or more in height, I expect it will be at least that tall and more spreading than *V. rhytidophyllum*, but more strict than *V. utile*.

I did not think to see how the foliage of the plant at the clinic stood last winter's bitter weather, but I will try to remember to check it this year. So far it has not fruited.

I have never been able to find out why *V. utile* is called the service viburnum, for I have never heard of its ever being of any use other than as an ornament. In the eighteen years since it came to me from Hohman it has never fruited, though it flowers very freely. The large clusters of off-white flowers are rather like Queen Anne's lace. Ernest Wilson, who introduced the species in 1901, described them as fragrant, but I have never noticed any scent.

Hohman says *V. rhytidophyllum*, the leatherleaf viburnum, will not fruit unless two or more plants are close together. I have only seen it in fruit once, in mid-August, at the Carolina Nurseries. The fruit is red but its brilliance doesn't last long as it soon turns black. As soon as they turn black the birds get them. Since the leaves suffer from cutting winds and severe cold, this is apt to be a gaunt and ragged shrub unless it is grown in good soil and in protected places.

Dr. Egolf says it is common that the seedlings vary greatly. Leaves may vary in length from three to fifteen or more inches. He says the best fruiting form is one grown in Scotland at Crathes Castle.

Dr. Egolf says the true *Viburnum japonicum* (syn. *V. macrophyllum*) is a first-rate evergreen, but almost unknown in this country, and that the one sold under those names is a variation of *odoratissimum* with leathery leaves. I sent leaves of mine to him, and he identified them as belonging to this form of the fragrant viburnum.

It is one of the most beautiful of all broad-leaved evergreens and tall shrubs, well on to twenty feet. In the twenty years I have had it, it has never fruited, and in all that time has only once borne a few flowers in early June.

November 8, 1970

PYRACANTHAS

Hannah Withers won't have firethorn in her garden. She says it brings bad luck. This notion probably came from the connection between firethorn and hawthorn. Hawthorns have always worn an aura of superstition—only the ill luck is supposed to fall on those who cut them down, not on those who plant them. I am thankful that I have no such fear. The only thing I am afraid to plant is parsley seed. Mammy always said, "Sow parsley, sow trouble."

Firethorns are most useful. For a quick-growing screen I don't know of any evergreen that equals *Pyracantha formosana* [*P. koidzumii*]. The first one I had came from Fruitland Nursery in January and by fall it was nine feet tall. They don't always grow so fast. One planted five or six years ago is scarcely nine feet now. Where it is planted in the open, firethorn makes a very large shrub. One in the Mayers' garden has grown in twelve years or so to a height of over sixteen feet and is twenty-one feet in diameter. It is not a shrub to plant in front of a window or on a small lawn.

The Formosan firethorn is one of the handsomest in fruit. Its large berries begin to color in August and by early September they are already a brilliant scarlet, but the branches are so heavily fruited that the weight of berries bends them down, and sometimes breaks them, and so the small-berried *P. yunnanensis* [*P. crenato-serria*] has something in its favor.

The Yunnan firethorn colors later and is prettiest in September when the berries take on warm tones of apricot and coral. They stay in good condition until spring. In my garden this is a tall, upright shrub that has grown to a height of sixteen or eighteen feet in six years. It differs from the other kinds in the shape of leaves, which are rounded and very broad at the end, and taper sharply toward the base.

Seven years ago Dr. K. Sawada sent Dr. Mayer a dwarf form of the Formosan firethorn that originated in his nursery, and has recently been patented under the name *P.* 'Low-Dense'—not Lodense, as I misinformed the Monroe Garden Club the other day, having read it that way in *The Flower Grower*. It is said to grow no more than eight feet tall. Dr Mayer's is now six feet, and is full of huge red berries. It has some thorns, although this variety is supposed to be practically thornless.

Small plants in the nursery are two feet wide by one foot tall, and so dense that the berries are lost in the foliage. I have read that they can be kept under two feet for several years by pruning, but I am more interested in seeing some of the prostrate firethorns grown on the West Coast than in trying to keep this one so low.

Another patented firethorn is *P.* 'Rosedale', an upright grower with deep green leaves and bright red berries. This was introduced by a California nurseryman. The variety *P.* 'Clemsoni', introduced by Clemson College, is also upright, with dark red berries and excellent foliage. There is even a firethorn with a rather large variegated leaf, grown more for the foliage than the fruit. It is slow growing, and takes some years to reach a height of six feet. I was delighted to find all of these firethorns in a local nursery. I hope that they will soon be in gardens, and that we will see more of them, and less of the hideous orange-berried *Pyracantha coccinea* 'Lalandei'.

On the whole, firethorns are very healthy shrubs, but they are sometimes troubled by the hawthorn lacebug. Dr. Westcott says that this can be controlled by spraying with Malathion, or nicotine sulphate in the nymph stage. Not knowing when the nymph stage is, I asked Mr. Patterson when to spray. He said April, and again in July. He says nicotine sulphate doesn't do any good, and that Malathion, in the strength sold in seed stores, is probably not harmful if you hold your breath and spray fast. Unless things get much worse, I think I shall just learn to live with the lacebugs.

December 15, 1957

NANDINAS

Heavenly bamboo is an ironic name for the forlorn and naked plant most often seen in crowded foundation plantings, but nandina is a sacred shrub to the Chinese and praised by the discriminating English gardener Gertrude Jekyll. "The Chinese plant it for good luck near their houses," she says in *Wood and Garden*. "If it is as lucky as it is pretty, it ought to do one good! I first made acquaintance with this beautiful plant in Canon Ellacombe's most interesting garden at Bitton, where it struck me as one of the most beautiful growing things I had ever seen; the beauty being mostly in the form and coloring of the leaves. It is not perhaps a plant for everybody, and barely hardy; it seems to get a slow hold, and its full beauty only shows when it is well established, and throws up its wonderfully-coloured leaves on tall bamboo-like stalks."

When they are planted in moist and fertile soil and comfortably mulched, nandinas deserve Miss Jekyll's praise but the fact that they will survive almost any amount of ill treatment makes them anybody's plant, and this has been their undoing.

They grow equally well in sun or shade, but will not prosper in hot, dry places and in poor soil. They will grow to a height of six to eight feet, but if they are not kept down to about five feet they get leggy. Cutting out the tall canes in early spring before growth starts will keep the plants bushy and furnished all of the way to the ground. Cutting them back part way only makes matters worse.

Some nandinas have few if any berries. I have read that their fruiting depends upon cross-pollination and that two distinct plants are needed for berries. Two suckers from the same plant won't help. I have also read that an application of muriate of potash makes them berry. A thorough watering in spring may save the season's crop, for drought at the time the fruits are being set may make them drop off. I find that plants in the shade never berry heavily and their leaves never take on warm red tones in winter.

As the berries are left untouched by birds and frost, they are decorative all winter. The common bright red ones are most colorful in the garden, but the form with ivory berries is useful for bouquets. I have never seen this, but I found it listed by a Maryland nurseryman, and if he still has it I think I shall give it a trial.

Nandinas, as every one who has self-sown seedlings knows, vary in height and in texture. Forms with small leaflets are usually more dwarf and more compact. Last spring, Mrs. Oscar gave me a little plant that is less than a foot tall, which spreads laterally, but grows no taller. I had seen it advertised in *Flower Grower* as 'True Dwarf' by a Winston-Salem nurseryman. Though it has few berries, it seems to be a delightful addition to the rapidly growing list of small evergreens.

It seems to me that gardeners would do well to reconsider the beauty and usefulness of an evergreen that has dainty flowers and spectacular fruits, that grows so readily, and needs no spraying. Its only fault is that it grows slowly, and that is common to most good evergreens.

January 4, 1959

1. Elizabeth Lawrence with her nephew Warren Way.

2. Gate of the Charlotte garden.

3. Plan of the Charlotte garden.

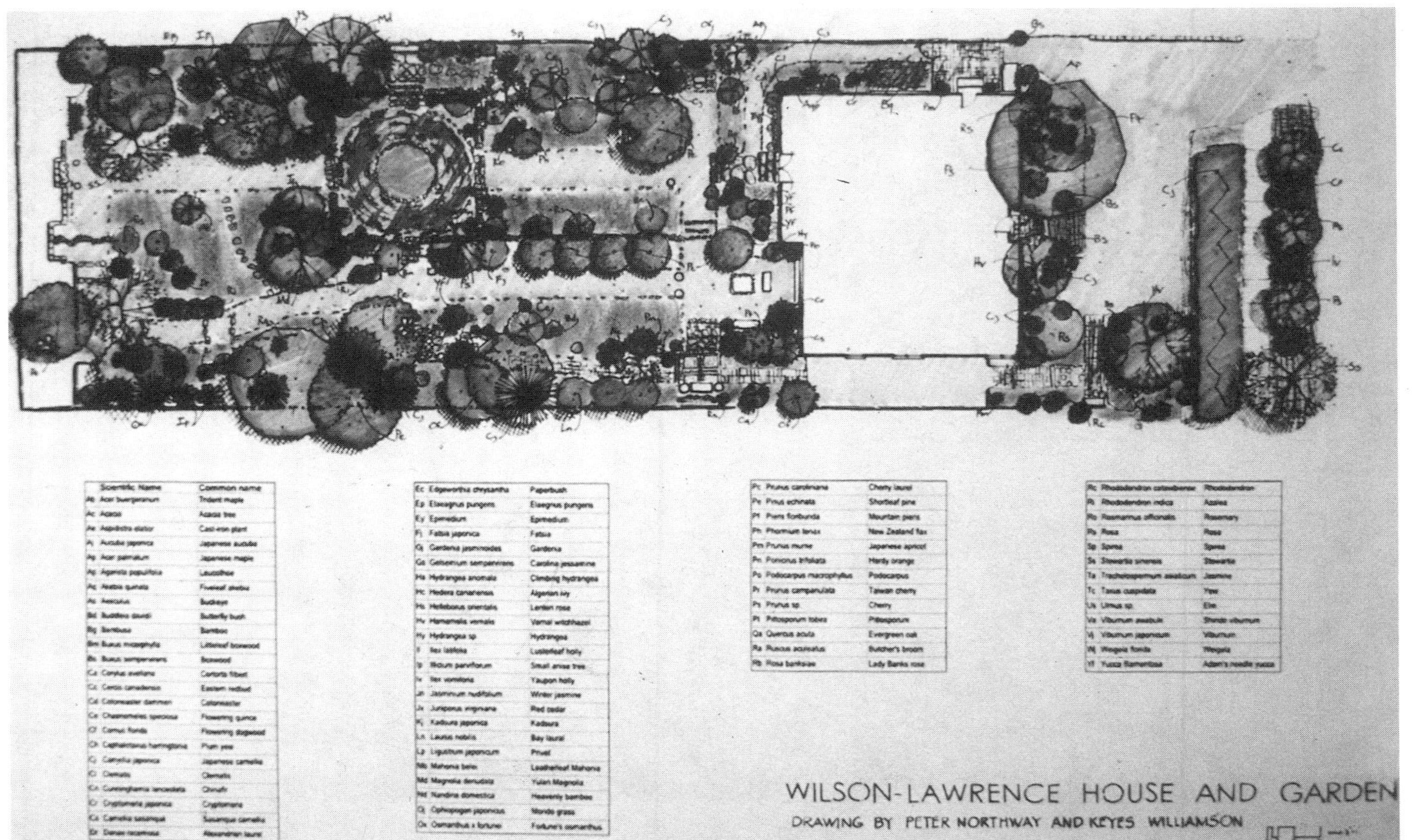
WILSON-LAWRENCE HOUSE AND GARDEN
DRAWING BY PETER NORTHWAY AND KEYES WILLIAMSON
Scientific Name / Common name
Ab Acer buergeranum / Trident maple
Ac Acacia / Acacia tree
Ae Aspidistra elatior / Cast-iron plant
Aj Aucuba japonica / Japanese aucuba
Ap Acer palmatum / Japanese maple
Ap Agarista populifolia / Leucothoe
Aq Akebia quinata / Fiveleaf akebia
Ae Aesculus / Buckeye
Bd Buddleia davidii / Butterfly bush
Bg Bambusa / Bamboo
Bm Buxus microphylla / Littleleaf boxwood
Bs Buxus sempervirens / Boxwood
Ca Corylus avellana / Contorta filbert
Cc Cercis canadensis / Eastern redbud
Cd Cotoneaster dammeri / Cotoneaster
Cs Chaenomeles speciosa / Flowering quince
Cf Cornus florida / Flowering dogwood
Ch Cephalotaxus harringtonia / Plum yew
Cj Camellia japonica / Japanese camellia
Cl Clematis / Clematis
Cn Cunninghamia lanceolata / China fir
Cr Cryptomeria japonica / Cryptomeria
Cs Camellia sasanqua / Sasanqua camellia
Dr Danae racemosa / Alexandrian laurel
Ec Edgeworthia chrysantha / Paperbush
Ep Elaeagnus pungens / Elaegnus pungens
Ey Epimedium / Epimedium
Fj Fatsia japonica / Fatsia
Gj Gardenia jasminoides / Gardenia
Gs Gelsemium sempervirens / Carolina jessamine
Ha Hydrangea anomala / Climbing hydrangea
Hc Hedera canariensis / Algerian ivy
Ho Helleborus orientalis / Lenten rose
Hv Hamamelis vernalis / Vernal witchhazel
Hy Hydrangea sp. / Hydrangea
Il Ilex latifolia / Lusterleaf holly
Ip Illicium parviflorum / Small anise tree
Iv Ilex vomitoria / Yaupon holly
Jn Jasminum nudiflorum / Winter jasmine
Jv Juniperus virginiana / Red cedar
Kj Kadsura japonica / Kadsura
Ln Laurus nobilis / Bay laurel
Lj Ligustrum japonicum / Privet
Mb Mahonia bealei / Leatherleaf Mahonia
Md Magnolia denudata / Yulan Magnolia
Nd Nandina domestica / Heavenly bamboo
Oj Ophiopogon japonicus / Mondo grass
Ox Osmanthus x fortunei / Fortune's osmanthus
Pc Prunus caroliniana / Cherry laurel
Pe Pinus echinata / Shortleaf pine
Pf Pieris floribunda / Mountain pieris
Pt Phormium tenax / New Zealand flax
Pm Prunus mume / Japanese apricot
Pt Poncirus trifoliata / Hardy orange
Pm Podocarpus macrophyllus / Podocarpus
Pc Prunus campanulata / Taiwan cherry
Ps Prunus sp. / Cherry
Pt Pittosporum tobira / Pittosporum
Qa Quercus acuta / Evergreen oak
Ra Ruscus aculeatus / Butcher's broom
Rb Rosa banksiae / Lady Banks rose
Rc Rhododendron catawbiense / Rhododendron
Ri Rhododendron indica / Azalea
Ro Rosmarinus officinalis / Rosemary
Rs Rosa / Rosa
Sp Spirea / Spirea
Ss Stewartia sinensis / Stewartia
Ta Trachelospermum asiaticum / Jasmine
Tc Taxus cuspidata / Yew
Us Ulmus sp. / Elm
Va Viburnum awabuki / Shinde viburnum
Vj Viburnum japonicum / Viburnum
Wj Weigela florida / Weigela
Yf Yucca filamentosa / Adam's needle yucca

4. Pink petals of the Oriental magnolias
on the paths of the garden in early spring.

5. Rear wall of the Charlotte garden
with a plaque of the Madonna and Child.

6. Elizabeth Lawrence's study with window looking out into the garden.

INVOICE

KINGSVILLE NURSERIES
KINGSVILLE, MARYLAND

Our Order No. 9388

Date Shipped October 25, 1949.

ORDERED BY

Miss Elizabeth Lawrence
348 Ridgewood Ave
Charlotte, N.C.

ARTICLE	PRICE	AMOUNT
Ceanothus Arnoldi 4ft B&B		$ 5.00
" GL.de.Vers. 2ft " died		2.00
Cot. salicifolia		1.50
" Franchetti		1.50
Cledrastris Lutea		1.50
Chaenomeles Apple Blossom-only plant on hand 3-3½ft		2.50
Euonymus nana 18" B&B		2.50
Ham. Mollis		2.00
Mag.Conspicua 2yr graft		2.00
Osmaria Burkwoodi 18"	2.00	4.00
Pieris Taiwanensis		1.00
Phyllera decora		2.00
Siphonosmanthus delaveyi		2.00
Stewartia pseudo-cam.		1.50
Vib.cinnomonifolium		2.50
Wisteria sinensis alba		4.00
Syringa swegen.suberba		1.50
Boxing at cost		2.50
		$ 42.50

7. An invoice for plants dated 1949. Some of the plants on this invoice remain in the Charlotte garden.

8. *Rosa* 'Old Blush' at the front
of the Lawrence house in Charlotte in April.

9. View of the garden from the study window.

10. Elizabeth Lawrence with Elizabeth Clarkson and Carl Starker
at the front door of her Charlotte house in 1957.

HYDRANGEAS

The relatively cool damp weather of June and early July brought the hydrangeas in my garden to perfection, particularly two lace-flowered Chinese species that Dr. Mayer got from England ten years ago. These are not for gardeners who want a sure thing. Like camellias they are dependent on the season; in a poor one they come to nothing, but in a good one they are magnificent.

In mid-July, when *Hydrangea aspera macropylla* [*H. a.* ssp. *strigosa*] was at its best, the bees and I hovered over it all day, and at night I took a candle and went out to look again. It is a graceful, spreading shrub (six feet tall) with large, rough, light-green leaves, and well-presented corymbs of lacy, violet flowers; the fuzzy, blue-violet fertile florets are encircled by pale sterile florets that are almost pink.

The flowers of *H. villosa* [*H. aspera villosa* group] are larger (to nine inches across), more open, and even more beautiful, for the violet tones of the florets are deeper and more glowing. But the shrub itself is not so graceful or so free flowering as the above hydrangea, perhaps because it is cut back more severely in cold winters, sometimes to the ground.

Both varieties need protection, light shade, and an abundance of moisture, and a thorough soaking every few days when they are ready to bloom. With water and shade they are easy to grow and seem to have no troubles. Neither one is in the American trade, which is very sad, especially as *H. villosa* [*H. aspera*] was introduced from China by Ernest Wilson when he was collecting for the Arnold Arboretum; it now grows in English gardens but not in ours. It has been neglected in this country because it is not hardy in the North, and southern nurserymen have never carried it, although it is easily propagated from half-ripe side shoots and now is the time to take them.

Another good summer flowering shrub that is not in the trade is *H.* × *anthoneura* 'Thomas Hogg' [*Hydrangea macrophylla* 'Thomas Hogg']. Perhaps the dazzling white heads of sterile flowers are no more beautiful than those of the common hydrangea, but they seem whiter to me and the glossy deep green foliage certainly is far handsomer. It is about the same height as *H. macrophylla* to three or four feet, but it is wide spreading, and the branches root where they touch the ground, so I have been able to give rooted pieces to friends. It begins to bloom late in May and goes on until the end of July. This year it has bloomed better than ever, and I think this is because the winter did my pruning and did it well.

The PeeGee hydrangea, *H. paniculata* 'Grandiflora', as common as 'Thomas Hogg' is rare, is the last to bloom. The panicles of sterile flowers are large and handsome, but not so graceful as those of the type or the variety 'Praecox' which have both fertile and sterile florets. The variety 'Praecox' begins to flower several weeks earlier and blooms for a month or more. The type grows to a height of twenty-five feet in Japan, but in gardens it is about ten. The shrub that nurserymen call 'Hills of Snow', a variety of our native *H. paniculata*, produces large heads of sterile white flowers early in June. They may be ineffective in the garden for the stems are not always stiff enough to hold up the heavy panicles, but I find them very useful for cutting.

The oakleaf hydrangea [*H. quercifolia*], earliest of all, comes as early as the first week in May. With so many good shrubs it is possible to have blooms all summer and no one need complain of having nothing in bloom in the shade.

July 31, 1960

SASANQUAS

This is the year of the *Camellia sasanqua*. Frost usually catches the flowers before they reach their peak, but this fall, beginning with a pink seedling the first day of September, they bloomed on and on, and by the middle of November all of the varieties in the garden were in full and glorious bloom. *Sasanquas* have been in American gardens for a long time. As early as 1832 William Prince, a Long Island nurseryman, introduced the variety *C. s.* var. *rosea*, and in 1897 Dr. Henry Nehrling imported five named varieties from Japan, and planted them in his Palm Cottage Gardens in Florida.

"Hundreds of plants are still in full bloom," he wrote on a morning early in November. "The single red *Camellia sasanqua*, however, is the glory of the day. It is in full bloom and is the brightest, most brilliant and most conspicuous of all the flowering plants near the house. The blossoms exhale a pleasant delicate fragrance when we pass the shrubs, but on taking one in your hand you will find the scent a little musty."

Early in this century, K. Sawada introduced a number of *C. sasanquas* from Japan. When he came here in 1950 to talk to the garden club, he said he was disappointed in the variety of *sasanquas* in Charlotte gardens. I, on the other hand, was much impressed by the number new to me, for I had just come from Raleigh where I grew only *C. s.* var. *rosea* and *C. s.* 'Mine-no-yuki'. I think even Sawada would be pleased with the varieties growing here now.

Early varieties of *Camellia sasanqua*, 'Apple Blossom', 'Blush Pink', 'Papaver', 'Floribunda', and 'White Glory' come into bloom in September, and usually all varieties are in bloom before the end of October or by early November. 'Velvety', one of Sawada's favorites, blooms in late September. The rose-red flowers are like very large wild roses, and so are the pink and white flowers of *Camellia oleifera*. These, and Sawada's pure white 'Gulf Glory' and the pale pink 'Gulf Breeze' are the best of the single *sasanquas*. 'Gulf Glory' is a late one. It comes into bloom some time in October, and if the weather isn't too cold, continues into December.

For weeks, I have been enjoying a hedge of 'Mine-no-yuki' and a hedge of a single pink variety 'Blush Pink' or something similar. The double varieties are later than the single ones. In my garden 'Pink Snow' comes into bloom at the end of October or early in November, with flowers like small pink roses that withstand a lot of frost. 'Jean May' and 'Cotton Candy' are larger and a clearer pink. 'Sparkling Burgundy', double and wine red, was introduced in 1959. It blooms when very small. I first saw the flowers in Linda Lamm's garden in Wilson in October 1960. In the ten years since its introduction it has made good growth in Charlotte gardens and is characteristically upright, strict, and tall.

'Mine-no-yuki', usually in the catalogues as 'Snow on the Mountain' or sometimes as 'White Doves', is the only double white *Camellia sasanqua* that I know. There are others, but I doubt that any of them are better. In my Raleigh garden I grew this in a protected place where it sometimes produced perfect flowers very late, once even on Christmas Eve. In this garden it gets morning sun, and several degrees of frost puts an end to bloom. It is a wide-spreading shrub and needs plenty of room—fifteen feet or more.

December 27, 1970

CAMELLIA SALUENENSIS

In the six years that *Camellia saluenensis* has been in my garden it has bloomed earlier and earlier: at first soon after the New Year, then before Christmas, and this year in late October. This year the flowers were much larger than ever before—I suppose this was due to the warm weather, for they have mostly bloomed in frosty times. They are single, and delicately modeled with a slender column of pale yellow stamens. The petals are ivory with a flush of wine. They usually withstand frost very well, but the severe freeze before Thanksgiving ruined not only the open flowers but all of the buds as well.

The species is called *saluenensis* because it is native to mountains along the Salwin River in the province of Yunnan in southern China. It was introduced into England in 1924 by George Forrest, who sent seeds to Mr. J. C. Williams. Three plants from these seeds, grown at Caerhays Castle in Cornwall, were more than fifteen feet tall in 1948. Flowers of the species vary in color from white to rose, but these are pink.

A number of crosses made at Caerhays between *Camellia saluenensis* and *C. japonica* are called *C.* × 'Williamsii'. They are said to bloom in Cornwall in February and March, with a few flowers lasting until April, but some must bloom earlier as one is called 'November Pink'. I made a note of one of these, 'J. C. Williams', in full bloom in Dr. W. B. Mayer's garden in mid-March. The flowers are single, a clear tint of lilac, and three and a half inches across.

In my garden 'Williams Lavender' usually blooms in mid-March. The flowers are a bright rose color, not all lavender. They are single, and irregular in shape. This variety was raised by Fruitland Nurseries from seed from Caerhays.

After the freeze all of the camellias in my garden looked, as Miles Hadfield says, as if they had been boiled in strong tea, but early in December I found a bunch of delicate pink flowers in the Mayers' living room. Dr. Mayer said they were from a graft he had made of 'Berenice Boddy', but they looked more like a *saluenensis* hybrid.

'Berenice Boddy', Mrs. Joseph Spengler wrote in her Christmas letter, "is the hardiest known camellia, and 'Magnoliaeflora' ['Hagoromo'] is also very hardy, and as a low border, 'Shishi-Gashira'." She says the low in Durham in October was eleven degrees, which was worse than the zero temperatures last January because it came so early. 'Bernice Boddy' hasn't even thought of blooming in my garden yet, and I hope the buds are all sound. I am afraid that every bud of 'Magnoliaeflora' is ruined.

'Shishi-Gashira' ('Beni-Kan Tsubaki') is one of the winter-flowering forms of *Camellia* × *hiemalis*. I have found it in bloom as early as the first week in October. I have notes of bloom in various gardens in November, December, and January. Sara Kincey's was in bloom before Thanksgiving, and just before Christmas she said it was trying to bloom again. It is probably fifteen years old and is only four feet tall. The semi-double flowers (three inches across by measurement) are rose red. The leaves are comparatively large, very thick, bright green, and glossy.

'Showa-No-Sakae', which we used to call a sasanqua, is another dwarf and slow-growing form of *C.* × *hiemalis*, but it doesn't bloom over as long a season. The rose-colored flowers have from fifteen to seventeen petals, and they are as large as a medium-sized *Camellia japonica*.

I like the Japanese names. 'Moon at the Window' is prettier I think than 'Bonsai Baby' or 'Mutt's Watermelon Pink'.

January 3, 1971

E. A. BOWLES'S LUNATICS

One of the interesting plants in W. H. Parker's garden is Harry Lauder's walking stick, *Corylus avellana* 'Contorta', a twisted form of the common hazel. The original plant was found by Lord Ducie in a Gloucestershire hedgerow. He gave a plant to Canon Ellacombe, who passed it on to E. A. Bowles, and now, one hundred years later, it is in the trade and anyone can have it—but few do.

I must say that at first sight I was not favorably impressed by this celebrated shrub. I thought that it had some sort of blight, although I was too polite to say so, for every leaf as well as every stem is curled and twisted. Mr. Parker explained, with a note of apology, that it comes into its own in winter when the leaves are down. The curious interlacing of the twisted branches has the grace of those little stunted trees that the Japanese like to grow in pots.

I remembered some notes on the twisted hazel in an old issue of the *Royal Horticultural Society Journal*, and looking back I found a photograph of Mr. Bowles's shrub, taken in early spring when the bare branches were hung with silken tassels. It really is beautiful. When Mr. Bowles described his shrub in *My Garden in Spring*, he said that it had never bloomed. He wondered whether the catkins would be curly lambs' tails and the nuts curled like rams' horns. In the picture the catkins are perfectly straight, but the branches twist and turn as wildly as ever, so that the whole bush is "a collection of various curves and spirals, a tangle of crooks and corkscrews from root to tip." The reason for these contortions is that the outer bark of one of the parent plants was slow growing, and the inner bark of the other grew fast. The wood of the offspring never has a chance to straighten out, but is always being pulled in the opposite direction.

Perhaps the popular name needs some explanation to the present generation, which may not know about Harry Lauder's crooked cane. The twisted hazel was the first and the most interesting inmate of the part of Mr. Bowles's garden that he called the "Lunatic Asylum," a home for demented plants. Freaks of nature interested and amused him. He collected all that he could find or hear of, and gave them the greatest care. He had a green-flowered strawberry that Parkinson had written about, an elder that thought it was a mulberry, and a laburnum that pretended to be an oak. One of his favorite lunatics was a pigmy elder that grew as a witch's broom on a tree of normal size. Cuttings made from it remained dwarf, and curiously enough they were almost evergreen.

In the asylum there was a dwarf form of *Viburnum opulus*, a round, compact shrub with small, bright, maple leaves. Where an evergreen is not wanted this makes a perfect little hedge that keeps a neat form without clipping, and never grows to a height of more than two feet—if that. I see nothing abnormal about this useful and attractive little viburnum, which grows in places too wet and shady for other plants, but Mr. Bowles insisted that it is a "seriously minded lunatic, suffering from melancholy madness, for it never flowers."

I see even less reason for "certifying" (as Mr. Bowles writes) the insanity of either the white-flowered ajuga, or the one with crinkled wine-colored leaves. I consider these perfectly sane. I will grant, however, that a black-leaved ash is something of a freak. It is quite a dwarf, Mr. Bowles writes, and has crimped leaves that are nearly black, and beautifully polished.

How he would have loved *Ophiopogon arabicum* [*O. planiscapus* 'Nigrescens'], which the Oakhurst Gardens describe as having black foliage: "Yes, we said BLACK leaves, you read it correctly." They are right too, for I saw the plant in Mrs. French's garden in Gastonia. But it is still expensive, and not really worth the price to any but real plant lovers like Mr. Bowles and Mrs. French.

I ask, with the keeper of the lunatics, does the notion of a home for demented plants appeal to you? Or does it appall you?

July 30, 1961

FIVE

Vegetables and Herbs, Climbers and Creepers

FALL VEGETABLES

When I was eight, I planted a ten-cent package of radish seeds with a view of selling the crop to my mother. Only three came up. They were small, tough, and hotter than red pepper. Except for a feeble attempt at a "victory garden," I have never planted a vegetable since. But every time I go to see my friends the Richardsons, and come home laden with good things in jars and baskets, I wish I were more like them and less like myself.

Vegetables are far more difficult to grow than flowers. They must have full sun, and the rows should run north and south to give them the full benefit of it. They need a rich, deeply dug soil. Five-ten-five and quantities of rotted leaves make good fertilizers.

I have a friend who raised a large family on vegetables grown on a narrow strip between her driveway and her neighbor's. But the gardener with a small space must stick to such things as peas, beans, lettuce, beets, carrots, and radishes. A good gardener can get a lot of tomatoes from a few plants.

August and September are the months for planting vegetables for late fall and winter. I was amazed at the length of the list of those that can be planted now. For winter greens you can sow seed of kale, rape, chard, mustard, spinach, and turnip greens. 'Purple Top' and 'White Flat Dutch' turnips are good varieties for both tops and roots. 'Seven Top' is one for greens only. Turnips can be left in the ground all winter, but the greens are ruined when the temperature gets below twenty degrees. This is too much for collards and mustard, too. Collard plants can be put out now, and most winters there will be plenty of time to enjoy them.

Kale is used as a salad, with French dressing, or cooked like spinach and served with sour cream and capers. The kind of Swiss chard that is grown for greens only keeps growing from the center as the leaves are cut. Another green for winter is the kind of cress that the country people call creasy. This, too, can be eaten hot or as a salad.

Carrots as well as turnips can be planted now and left in the ground. Parsnips and salsify can be left in the ground, too, but their seeds must be sown in early spring. I don't suppose that many people grow salsify nowadays, but when there were no fresh vegetables to be bought, we used to have salsify all winter.

Radishes can be planted now, but the varieties are different from those that are planted in the spring. A local seedsman offers two winter radishes, the 'China Rose' ("skin a deep rose color, flesh pure white, crisp, of pungent flavor. Good keeper") and the 'Black Spanish' ("crisp white flesh and black skin").

I was amazed to find that bush beans can still be sown, although it would have been better to get them in in August. Mr. Richardson says that cauliflower and broccoli are cold-weather plants and that it isn't too late to sow them. Seed must be sown in a seed bed, and the seedlings transplanted. Broccoli is much easier to grow than cauliflower. Cabbage plants can be set out still, but it is too late to sow seed.

Sow English peas in September for an early spring crop. They make much better roots when they are sown in the fall instead of the spring.

September 8, 1957

TWO VEGETABLE GARDENS

On an afternoon in July, which in ordinary summers would have been considered cool, but in this cool season was called sweltering, I went with Morgan Johnston to a hilltop garden in the Rocky River section. The sun was hot on the hilltop, but a light breeze was blowing across fields of daisies and Queen Anne's lace. A partridge was calling "bob-white" across the field, and being answered from the other side, called again. The hilltop belongs to D. V. Walker; his and the Johnston garden are side by side, their rows of flowers and vegetables divided by a central path shaded by some peach trees.

Johnston began growing vegetables during the Second World War, when victory gardens were allowed on a vacant lot among the foreign embassies in Washington. When he came to Charlotte he found another vacant lot for his garden, and grew vegetables on it for nine years. Then an apartment house was built on it and he was gardenless until Walker offered him space in the country.

I asked Johnston whether he plants by the signs. He says he plants when the ground is right, and when he has time (which is mostly weekends). But he keeps an almanac in his garden notebook, and, if he can manage it, plants all plants that yield above ground in the new of the moon, and all that yield below ground in the old of the moon. He says he spends as much time planning his garden in winter as he does planting it in spring. It provides fresh vegetables from the earliest peas to the latest squash and flowers all summer for Mrs. Johnston to take to Memorial Hospital, where she is chairman of the Gray Ladies.

Johnston has learned in all these years to plant vegetables that do well in the South, but he still experiments with some of his old favorites, such as Burpee's 'Golden Bantam' corn, which doesn't really do very well, and rhubarb, which has grown better than he had expected. Since rhubarb is a perennial, plants grown from roots are ready for use sooner than those grown from seed. The rhubarb and asparagus beds are at one end of the garden, so that they will not be disturbed by spring planting. I did not know before that rhubarb leaves are poisonous, and only the stems can be eaten.

Swiss chard is a vegetable that does do well in the South. It comes from the Mediterranean region, and regardless of heat puts out new leaves all summer and until frost as fast as the old ones are picked for the pot. It is a form of *Beta*, the common beet, but puts its energy into foliage rather than root, and tastes like beet tops. It is called leaf beet.

The summer squashes in the garden are zucchini and the little golden crookneck. Zucchinis grow on little bushes, so they take up less room than the trailing kinds, but that does not matter to Johnston as he can take in more of the field if he needs more garden space.

Mrs. Johnston told me an easy way to cook zucchini: sauté an onion in oil or butter, and add a ripe tomato, skin and all, and the sliced zucchini, skin and all, and steam until tender. I tried it and it is delicious.

Johnston's tomatoes were chosen to ripen over a long period, but he says they come pretty much at the same time. They are 'Early Wonder', 'Earliana', 'Big Boy', and 'Super Marglobe'. Marglobe is the last to ripen.

Rabbits get into the bean patch and eat the tops off the bush beans—all but the limas, they won't touch those. Johnston grows 'Tender Pod', 'Bush Wax', and 'Bush Lima'. The pole beans are limas and 'Kentucky Wonders'. Walker grows pole beans on a wire fence, which makes it much easier to train them but more difficult to disentangle the old vines.

Walker has a patch of cantaloupes, and Johnston grows watermelons. Johnston grows cabbages, eggplant (Burpee's 'Black Beauty'), hot peppers, bell peppers, broccoli, beets, lettuce, carrots, and onions.

For winter vegetables there are salsify and parsnips (which can be left in the ground until spring), rutabagas, and a volunteer 'Hubbard' squash. Johnston even grows his own peanuts. He says all this is more fun than golf, but no less expensive.

August 27, 1967

MRS. HOBBS AND HER HERBS

On a windy and sunny afternoon in mid-March, Paula Patrick and I paid a long-looked-forward-to visit to Mrs. Hobbs and her herbs. Her garden is filled with the old-fashioned shrubs and spring-flowering bulbs that are such congenial herb companions, and it is as remote and as quiet and as fragrant as if it were in the country. When we were there, a peach tree and an oriental magnolia were in bloom with quince and spiraea and daffodils, and there were red tulips under a snowy plum tree. The ten shapely junipers, planted at intervals among the shrubs, are Christmas trees. Their dark foliage makes the spring flowers seem fresher and gayer.

On the shady terraces in front of the house, columbine, coral bells, bleeding heart, and forget-me-nots grow under oaks and dogwoods with the little native *Zephyranthes atamasca*, which Mrs. Hobbs calls marsh lily. And in deep borders that encircle the wide lawns, all the sun-loving things are planted.

The herb garden is a large square with paths running from corner to corner in the form of St. Andrew's cross. There is an enormous oak at one corner. Here we found "herbes of good smell," "herbes to make nosegays and garlands of," and herbs for the pot and salad bowl. The nose herbs are rosemary, costmary, balm, and bergamot, the mints, lavender and thyme and catnip. Beside the catnip was a large, honey-colored cat napping in the sun. I wonder why cats seem so at home in an herb garden, and dogs so out of place. As to catnip, it is well to remember the saying: "If you set it the cats will eat it. If you sow it the cats won't know it."

Mrs. Hobbs believes in another saying: "In pottage without herbs there is neither goodness nor nourishment." She not only grows them, she puts them to use. She uses them for hot teas and cooling drinks, for soups, meats, and breads.

As we walked about the garden we munched crisp little cheese biscuits flavored with sesame seeds, and discussed the herbs and their uses: fennel for fish, mint for lamb, basil with tomatoes, sage for sausage, thyme for meats and soups, sorrel for soups and salads, savory for chicken, and rosemary for veal and garden peas. Mrs. Hobbs grows the gray-leaved French form of *Thymus vulgaris*. This, and not the creeping mother-of-thyme, is the proper one for seasoning. It is as indispensable as parsley.

She has most of the onion tribe: chives, leeks and shallots, giant garlic (or rocambole), dwarf garlic, and the Egyptian multiplying onion, which I read about in the Market Bulletins. And she has the bitter herbs: chamomile, santolina, tansy, rue, hyssop, horehound and wormwood. Paula kept as far away as possible from the wormwood. She says it gives her hay fever. I now have rue in my garden, but it took many trials to get it established. They say it is subject to nematodes. Mrs. Hobbs has green santolina with very fine foliage that is different from the ordinary *Santolina virens*. She says she got it from a garden in Carthage.

The herbs are not confined to the herb garden, but are scattered in the flower borders, and even among the old roses that are planted in front of a covered seat. The seat is one of the most delightful garden shelters I ever saw. It is made of pine that has been stained a mossy green to make it look weathered, and it has a little shuttered window.

There are damask and China roses in the beds in front of the shelter, and a shrub rose called the 'Hon. Lady Lindsay' (1938) that blooms all summer and likes hot weather. Its clusters of pointed buds open into large, fragrant delicate pink flowers, and its shiny, dark green leaves (so the Tillotson catalogue says) are immune to insects and disease. I mean to visit this garden again, and learn more about the rare herbs and old roses.

April 14, 1963

SWEET WOODRUFF

Leon Gutmann asked where he can get sweet woodruff, *Asperula odorata* [*Galium odoratum*]. He said he could not find it in the supermarket. I was not able to give him a source for the dried herb, but plants are available. A number of herbs are grown locally, but so far as I know sweet woodruff is not one of them. Sweet woodruff is an herb with a long history in medicine and folklore.

The earliest quotation in the Oxford Dictionary is for the year 1000—or thereabouts—from a Saxon manuscript: "Herb a astula regia haet is wundurofe." Haet, I take it, means called. There is a quotation from a fourteenth-century lyric: "Away is her wynter when woderove springeth"; and a sixteenth-century treatise on gardening and health lists wood-rowel as a good healer-up of wounds. Coming down to the nineteenth century we have: "Murder will out, although Almighty should lend hearing to the ears of the willow, and speech to the seven tongues of the woodriff."

Through the ages, sweet woodruff has been used in various ways. The Elizabethans kept the dried leaves, which smell like new-mown hay, in little pierced boxes with other sweet-smelling herbs, and the Queen herself is said to have had a way of presenting a sprig as a token of her favor.

It was used like lavender to lay away with the linens; it was "an excellent cordial drink," and a pint of boiling water poured over a large handful of leaves and flowers makes woodruff tea. It was hung in churches along with garlands of roses, lavender and box, to celebrate the feast days of St. Barnabas and St. Peter. It is a wound herb and has other medicinal uses.

"The flowers are of a very sweet smell as is the rest of the herbe," Gerard writes, "which being made up into garlands or bundles, and houses in the heat of summer, doth very well attemper the air, cool and make fresh the place, to the delight and comfort of such as are therein. It is reported to be put into wine to make a man merry, and to be good for the heart and liver."

In Germany, I hope, sweet woodruff is still put into Rhine wine to make the heart merry. In New York we used to go in May to a German restaurant for May wine and caviar sandwiches. The principle that makes the herb refreshing is tannic acid, the same as that in "the cup that cheers," but the recipe in *The Joy of Cooking* calls for a pint of brandy and a quart of champagne. The herb should not be left in more than half an hour. In *The Flowering Plants of Great Britain*, Anne Pratt tells about an Englishman who was so delighted with the May wine that was served to him when he was traveling in Germany that he hired a man to go out and dig plants to take home with him. And then he learned that within a mile of his own house the woods were full of it.

Most of these notes have been gathered from the books of Eleanour Sinclair Rohde. In *Gardens of Delight*, which I sometimes think is almost my favorite, she writes, "Very few grow the humble wild woodruff, *Asperula odorata* [*Galium odoratum*], a delightful carpeting plant for shade parts, where it spreads like a weed. The pretty white flowers and dainty whorls of foliage are the perfect foil for forget-me-nots."

In Connecticut, I find sweet woodruff commonly used as a ground cover for shady places, and it is especially recommended (by Donald Wyman) for planting under rhododendrons. It is neat and green all summer, but it is not evergreen.

Alchemilla vulgar [*A. mollis*], another pretty carpeter, is called lady's mantle, which of course means Our Lady's mantle as the scalloped and delicately serrated leaves are fine enough for a cape for the Virgin. It is said to cover the ground all too well, but a plant from the Merry Gardens has so far shown no tendency to spread or reproduce itself. Just before Christmas when I was cleaning up the border, I cut away the old weather-beaten leaves and found new ones, pale green, silvery and plaited, coming up from the roots.

April 28, 1968

DANDELIONS

When Ann Bridgers and I went to see Mrs. French's garden we found the biggest and most floriferous dandelions we had ever seen. I thought they grew to such a size because they were in fertile soil, but I was wrong. They are cultivated dandelions, grown from Burpee's seed.

I looked them up in the catalogue, which describes them as having large, thick, dark green leaves, whose flavor in salad can be improved if they are tied together so that the hearts are bleached. The plants are vigorous and quick growing, and the foliage can be harvested in ninety-five days. Mrs. French is very fond of boiled dandelion greens, and she has even taught Mr. French to eat them. Dandelions have a long history as pot herbs and salad herbs.

"The French country people eat the roots," John Evelyn wrote in 1699, "and 'twas with this homely sallet the good wife Hecate entertained Theseus."

Theophrastus, who had not thought of Mr. Burpee's trick of tying up the leaves like endives, says the dandelion is unfit for food and bitter. "It flowers early," he writes, "quickly waxes old and the flower turns to pappus, but then another flower forks, and yet another, and this goes right on through the winter and spring up to the summer, and the flower is yellow."

Dandelions are native to Europe and Asia and have been distributed as weeds in all civilized parts of the world. They grew in England before the ice age and were brought from England in the seventeenth century.

In *Old Time Gardens*, Mrs. Earle tells of the dandelion gatherers in New England city parks: "It is always interesting to see, in May, on the closely guarded lawns and field expanses of our city parks, the hundreds of bareheaded, gayly dressed Italian and Portuguese women and children eagerly gathering the young dandelion plants to add to their meager fare as a greatly-loved delicacy. They collect these 'greens' in highly-colored kerchiefs, in baskets, in squares of sheeting; I have seen the women bearing off half a bushel of plants; even their stumpy little children are impressed to increase the welcome harvest, and with a broken knife dig eagerly in the greensward. The thrifty park commissioners, in dandelion time, relax their rigid rule, 'Keep off the Grass,' and turn salad-loving Italians loose to improve the public lawns by freeing them from weeds."

The dandelion is the first flower of St. Bride, protector of early bloom, newborn lambs, and babies. The flat, golden flowers are nearly ever blooming and they are said to follow the sun. I have never noticed this, but they do look up into the sky and are open from before sunrise until after sunset. The English name comes from the French *dent-de-lions*, derived from the tooth—like the lobes of the slender leaves.

Dandelions are called blow-balls, because the feathered seed heads provide material for the child's game of Clocks. You pick a flower that has gone to seed, blow as hard as you can, and then count the seeds that are left. The number will be the hour of the day. It is very convenient when you are far from the house and have forgotten your watch.

The roots of dandelions are roasted and powdered for use as a substitute for coffee; it is something like its near relative chicory. The dried roots are also medicinal, and the juice was once a folk remedy for "intermitting fevers." It was called heart-fever grass.

In *A Garden of Herbs*, Miss Rohde tells how to make dandelion tea and gives a recipe for dandelion wine. The latter yields nine gallons and calls for dandelion pips, "the best Demerara sugar," hops, brown ginger, lemons, Seville oranges, and a little brewer's yeast. It is kept in a barrel for six months before bottling.

July 3, 1960

VINES ARE USEFUL TOOLS

Southern gardeners have the great good fortune of being able to grow a large variety of beautiful and useful vines, particularly those that hold their leaves in winter. Three of these evergreens are common in the woods, but rare in the garden.

One is the Jackson brier, *Smilax lanceolata* [*S. smallii*], with its long bare, prickly stems, and wreaths of shining leaves. Another is our Carolina jessamine, *Gelseminum sempervirens*, that grows as densely as honeysuckle, and is as fragrant when in flower. This time last year (I am writing on the nineteenth of February) the first golden buds were coming out, and it continued to bloom until the middle of April. Even this year, the swollen buds are waiting under the shivering leaves, for the first warm weeks. The third is the cross vine, *Bignonia capreolata*, which sheds most of its leaves before the new ones come out in the spring, but even in this cold winter the branches have never been entirely bare. In late April there are large buff trumpets, powered with brick dust.

Confederate jessamine is another evergreen vine with fragrant flowers. Of the two kinds generally grown, the hardiest is *Trachelospermum divaricatum* [*T. asiaticum*]. It is covered with sweet-smelling, cream-colored flowers in late April and May, and never without a few all summer and in the early fall.

Self-clinging vines are useful for walls. The cross vine makes a pretty pattern as it climbs, especially if some stalks are cut back to the ground in spring, and it is forced to start over in the neat patterns of new growth. The climbing fig, *Ficus repens*, is hardy in Charlotte though the leaves mostly turn brown in winter, and in severe weather some of the stems may be cut back too.

Most kinds of euonymus soon get covered with scale, but a scandent form that is common in gardens is never affected. Mine was collected from various friends, but seems to be all the same thing. It will grow on a wire fence or cling to a wall. Sometimes it gets too heavy for the wall. Then it is a good thing to cut back and let it climb up again. The branches of established plants are covered with yellow and orange fruits in early fall.

Ivy covers a fence more quickly than euonymus. If well-rooted cuttings are planted close together and well watered and fed, they will soon make a thick screen.

For flowers, no vines equal the clematis. It is a pity that it is considered difficult, for many sorts are very easily grown. *Clematis texensis*, with its rose-red urns, blooms—if it is watered—from late April to frost; the enormous white flowers of *C.* 'Henryi' appear at intervals during the summer; and in August there is the creamy froth of the Japanese species, *C. paniculata* [*C. terniflora*].

Annual vines are most important, especially in a new garden. I find that the balloon vine, *Cardiospermum*, is the best one for a quick screen on a fence. The seeds can be planted in March, and if they are close together they will make a ten-foot curtain by midsummer. The balloon vine seeds itself so freely that it will never need to be planted twice, and the pale green balloons are charming.

For a quick tall vine, *Dolichos lablab* [*Lablab purpureus*], the hyacinth bean outgrows them all. The flowers, like sweet peas without their sweetness, are purple or white. For flowers, the prettiest annual vine is *Cobaea scandens*. If the seeds are started indoors in February, and planted out in April, it will climb quickly to the eaves of the house, and bloom until frost. The violet flowers are called cathedral bells.

March 15, 1959

SMILAX

Hannah Withers, who misses nothing, called my attention to the smilax growing over a doorway on Wendover Road. We rang the bell and found that it belongs to Mrs. W. E. Godwin. Knowing that no vine grows so gracefully of its own accord, I asked Mrs. Godwin how she managed to get such a charming effect. She does it by cutting the canes to the ground every year. "It's well you came when you did," she said. "I'm going to cut it down as soon as there is an occasion." The time to cut is before new growth starts, but Mrs. Godwin waits for something like a wedding to come along so that the glittering green can be used for decoration, and not be wasted.

The canes grow from fifteen to twenty feet in a season, and they shoot up very fast, but it takes about two months for the doorway to look as well furnished as it does now. The canes must be kept straight until they reach the lintel. Otherwise the branches will begin to flow sidewise in green cascades, instead of being held back to garland the door frame. The easiest way to fasten a light vine like smilax to a brick wall is with Wayward Vine Guides, little disks that hold flexible wire clasps. The disks come with a small bottle of cement for fastening them to the wall, but there is never enough cement for the number of disks in the box.

Mrs. Godwin's smilax is the Jackson brier, *Smilax lanceolata* [*S. smallii*], the best of the native evergreen species. I have read that it will make a thick screen if grown properly, though what the proper way is was not explained, and I have never figured it out. I think it is at its best over a doorway, or twined around the pillars of a porch, or left to climb into trees as it does in the woods, where it grows to seventy-five feet.

I cannot remember ever having seen berries on the Jackson brier, but I must have seen them at the Brookgreen Gardens, for I have a note in my files of its being in fruit when I was there. The reason for its fruiting seldom in cultivation is that the male and female flowers are on separate plants. The berries are dull red, and of no decorative value, but the coral fruits of *S. walteri* are beautiful. My mother says she used to buy them, when we lived in Hamlet, from an old Negro who brought them in from the swamps. He called them Red Bambro.

The common name of smilax is greenbrier, but it is sometimes called bamboo. It is also called sarsaparilla, because the drug is found in the roots of certain species. It was once a popular tonic. An old medical book says, "We will give him mild aperients, light nutritious diet, and sarsaparilla."

The leaves of the Jackson brier are thin and long pointed, to four inches long. Those of another evergreen native species, *S. laurifolia*, are leathery, oblong, and an inch longer. *Smilax laurifolia* grows in the evergreen shrub bogs of the coastal plain, and I have never seen it in a garden, but I would like to have it in mine.

I saw another native *smilax*, also evergreen, used to advantage on a wall at Brookgreen, though I had been told that it has no horticultural value. In June it was full of bright orange berries. This one is a low-climbing or trailing evergreen, but turning bronze in the winter. It seems a pity that these charming and useful native vines are so seldom grown. The Jackson brier is the only one that I have been able to find in southern nurseries.

March 15, 1959

CLEMATIS HYBRIDS

The clematis hybrids are aristocrats, and they have aristocratic names. Among the English hybrids are many lords and ladies, several duchesses, and at least one monarch, 'King Edward VII'. The French varieties include a countess, 'Comtesse de Bouchaud', and a saint, 'Jeanne d'Arc.' I think the reason that these really spectacular flowers are so little planted is that only a few varieties are generally offered, but more than forty of them are listed by the specialist James I. George.

I don't know how they got the reputation for being so hard to grow. They do have a way of disappearing unexpectedly and unaccountably just when they seem to be at their best, but it is not expensive to replace them, and they grow fast. Most new plants bloom the first season and are well established by the third.

The easiest to grow are *Clematis* 'Henryi' and *C. jackmanii*. These have been listed in the Fruitland catalogue as long as I can remember, and this should be enough to establish them as plants that endure hot summers.

C. 'Henryi' is flourishing in my garden in hard dry soil, with ivy practically on top of it, and where it gets very little sun, though the shade is not dense. I don't recommend this treatment, but it certainly proves that this is no vine for the specialist. The flowers are six inches across, which is large enough for me, but under more favorable circumstances they may be eight. They are white, with a shadowy hint of blue, and a handsome boss of gray-anthered stamens.

Clematis jackmanii is the variety most commonly planted. It grows rapidly and blooms profusely all through the summer and fall. It is a vigorous vine to twelve feet or more. The flowers are five inches across and of an intense purple.

Two hybrids of the *jackmanii* race have done well in these parts. I found 'Mrs. Cholmondeley' growing in a stone jardinière on Tempie Franklin's terrace, trained on a light bamboo trellis tacked to the wall of the house. "Bee Mayer told me I would never be able to grow it in a pot," Tempie said, "but it has been here six or eight years." Gardeners always delight in doing something that another gardener says can't be done. The flowers are of a soft blue-violet, and seven inches across by measurement. The vine was covered with bloom on the sixth of May. Tempie says it begins to bloom in April, blooms through the early summer, and takes up again when the nights are cool. 'Madame Edouard Andre' begins to bloom in late May, and goes on through the summer. The flowers are described as red, but they match the pansy purple of the color chart. It is a strong grower to about seven feet.

The flowers of the white form of *Clematis lanuginosa* 'Candida' are rather like those of *C.* 'Henryi' (only a purer white) and they are almost as large. This is another vigorous vine that gets to be ten feet tall, and already outgrowing the slight bamboo trellis that I made for it.

'Ramona', a popular hybrid with *C. lanuginosa* as one parent, grows as rapidly and blooms well. The flowers are blue-violet with dark anthers. The 'Duchess of Edinburgh' is on my list of clematis to try.

In my experience, which is not great, I have found that clematis is more likely to prosper when it is planted in the spring before new growth starts as new plants may not winter well the first year. The large-flowered varieties do best when they have been grown in pots, but be sure to pull the roots apart gently, when they are taken out, and spread them out so that they have room to grow and won't stay in a ball.

As all clematis like lime, bone meal is the best fertilizer. Dig a hole eighteen inches deep and equally wide, put some stones in the bottom for drainage and fill it with top soil well mixed with a cup of lime and a handful of bone meal. Cover the crown with two inches of soil, with a mulch in summer to keep the roots cool and moist, and in winter to protect them from the freezing and thawing.

June 1, 1958

AKEBIA AND *ROSA BANKSIAE*

One of the most delightful things about gardening is the way people you have never even seen suddenly send you the plants that you most want. Recently the postman left me a square corrugated box, in which I found a bare root carefully wrapped in a still-damp paper towel and a piece of wax paper, with several feet of bare brown stem carefully coiled and tied with bits of string so it would not get broken. On the outside of the package I found a letter from my friend Mrs. Stevens, of Campobello, South Carolina.

"In your article on vines in the Garden Section of the *Charlotte Observer*," she wrote, "you made no mention of one of my favorites, the little akebia, which blooms early in the spring. You must know it. After the chocolate-purple blooms comes the dainty foliage. This is so graceful all summer, and reminds me of the maidenhair fern. I am sending you one, which I hope you will enjoy. I seldom see this vine. In fact it is either almost extinct, or else folks just don't know it."

Akebia [*A. quinata*] has been a favorite with me ever since we found it growing on the south side of the summerhouse when we went to Raleigh to live. Of all of the things that surprised and delighted us that first spring that the garden became ours, the akebia was the most fascinating to a child of twelve. It grew inside the summerhouse as well as out, and late in March the brown stems that twisted themselves around the supports of the roof were hung with clusters of quaint purple flowers on slender bright green stems. The odd thing about the flowers is that there are two kinds to a cluster: several small pale-violet male flowers, and one or two much larger female flowers with three cupped, dark purple sepals. As the flowers fade, the five-fingered, pale green leaves make another charming pattern.

Mrs. Stevens is right about akebia. It is rare in gardens and even rarer in nurseries. When I mentioned it in an article in *Popular Gardening* some time ago, several people wrote to ask where they could get it, and I was put to it to find a source. I did finally track down several in the *Plant Buyer's Guide*.

Akebia is at its best in full sun, but it will grow and bloom in dense shade if the soil is well drained and not too acid. In warm climates it is evergreen and even here it keeps its leaves until late in the fall. As a ground cover it is perfectly evergreen, and makes a neat, close cover for a dark dry place where little else will grow. I found it used this way between a path and the wall of the house in Mrs. A. G. Odell's garden in Concord. It grows well on a wire fence, and can be trained to make a dense cover by keeping the old wood cut out.

In Raleigh the akebia never fruited, though it was well on to forty years old when we left it behind. I think it rarely does fruit in this country unless pollinated by hand. The purple fruits, to three inches long, do not last long enough to be considered decorative, but the Japanese eat them.

Akebia is a fast-growing vine, but not hard to keep in its place. It responds to strong pruning and blooms on new wood. One of its best points is its immunity to insects and disease, a quality shared by Lady Banks's rose, *Rosa banksiae*, which I later planted on the summerhouse. The long, arching branches of the rose became entwined with the akebia, and were covered with pale yellow and dark purple at the same time. I couldn't have thought of a better combination, but I didn't think of it. I planted the rose beside the akebia because it was the only open, sunny spot left in the garden.

The entrance to the summerhouse was not a good place for the rose. In order to get in or out I had to keep chopping it back all through the year. It is a rose that needs a strong support and does well in a tall pine—though keeping it here requires some time spent on a step ladder, tying the branches up so that they can then droop down in their graceful way.

Lady Banks's rose was brought to Great Britain's Kew Gardens from China in 1807, and from there found its way to the garden of her husband, Sir Joseph Banks, who was then Honorary Director of Kew.

The original form was the one with violet-scented, double white flowers. The familiar yellow-flowered variety came later, and this is the one that seems, like magnolia and jessamine, always to have been a part of Southern gardens.

I have been trying to find how soon it was brought to this country. So far, the earliest record that I have is of its growing in Macon, Georgia, in the garden of Mrs. W. G. Solomon in 1860; and Bishop Elliott's description (in an address on horticulture at Macon in 1851) of "Banksias, Ophirie, Bignonias, Wistarias, all intermingling over the sides and roof of the house and crying out for room."

May 11, 1950

GROUND COVERS

There are two difficulties with ground covers: first to get them to grow, and then to get them not to. Even the most rugged must be started in well-prepared soil, and watered and nourished until they are established. All must be weeded until they take over for themselves, and even then they need going over from time to time, though less often in part shade, and still less in deep shade.

Once established the ground cover begins to travel, and then it may travel too far. A plant that is hard to keep in bounds may give the gardener more trouble than it saves.

The perfect ground cover is one that keeps its greenness and freshness all of the months of the year. Periwinkle, *Vinca minor*, does this in the shade. In the sun it is likely to be shabby in mid-winter, though it blooms much more freely. I used to wonder at the unruffled surface of the periwinkle on the steep banks in front of Tempie Franklin's house, but I find that, like everything in her garden, it gets good care. It gets two hundred pounds of sheep manure every spring, and is well watered in dry weather.

When it was first planted it was weeded regularly. Now little comes through the thick, glossy mat except for an occasional wild onion. Perhaps my periwinkle wasn't weeded well enough at first, for I am still pulling out Bermuda grass and sour grass. A light clipping as soon as the blooms have faded keeps it low and dense, but too much clipping does more harm than good. Since it spreads by rooting along the stems it is not as hard to control as plants that spread by underground stolons, such as Japanese spurge and ophiopogon.

Japanese spurge, *Pachysandra*, grows only in the shade; the deeper the shade the better it grows. In his book, *Ground Cover Plants*, Dr. Wyman writes, "Many times it is used to form an evergreen carpet under Norway maple trees, where nothing else will grow." I doubt that, but you can try. He also writes, "Few weeds find it possible to make any start at all in a dense bed of pachysandra."

Few weeds, perhaps, but in my garden it is no match for cow itch and cat briar and seedlings of privet and cherry laurel. It does pretty well choke out my best clump of colchicums, and I would not advise following Dr. Wyman's suggestion of interplanting it with daffodils. One of the good things about Japanese spurge is that it keeps to a fairly uniform height of about a foot. The overlapping rosettes of pale green, coarsely toothed leaves stay fresh even in winters like the last one, and even in summers that are too hot and dry, or too hot and wet.

Bugleweed, *Ajuga*, is nearly always in good condition, especially if *Ajuga brockbank* [*A.* 'Metallica Crispa'], the kind with metallic wine-colored leaves, is planted, but even for that one, last winter was too much. In January flourishing plantings turned brown and shriveled up, though they came out again in the spring. I can't remember its ever happening before, and I hope we are not going to make a habit of winters like the last one. Bugleweed does, occasionally, turn black in patches, but this is easily remedied by taking out the affected plants.

The flowers of the bugleweed are typically blue. There is a very pretty white-flowered form but it is not as vigorous as the blue. These bloom in April. A taller variety, with pale green leaves and large spikes of clear rose-colored flowers, blooms in May and off and on all summer. The books say that bugleweed grows as well in the sun as in shade, but it doesn't do it for me.

For shady places where a coarse turf will do, especially for banks and steep slopes, nothing is as good as the small *Ophiopogon* that is called monkey grass, and is sold as mondo grass (the old name for the genus) by a nursery in Mississippi. It is commonly called lilyturf, but that name really belongs to *Liriope*, a taller, coarser plant with showy spikes of violet flowers. The short and almost colorless flower spikes of the *Ophiopogon* are hidden by the dense tufts of dark green leaves that are a foot or more long, but only an eighth of an inch wide. Unfortunately the beautiful berries, which are like brilliant blue beads, are also completely hidden; but I like to pick them and put them on my desk in the wintertime. In the shade the foliage stays fresh all winter, but in the sun it loses its color, and looks shabby until well into the summer.

August 3, 1958

GROUND COVERS POSE PROBLEMS

When we came to Charlotte sixteen years ago and started a new garden, I decided to let ground covers take the place of grass. A popular gardening magazine led me to believe that this would give me an evergreen carpet, beautiful in all seasons and requiring little or no care. I soon found out that exchanging ground covers for grass just presented a new set of problems.

First there is the difficulty of getting the plants established, and once they cover the ground they are meant to cover, they are apt to be equally hard to restrain. As Brooks Wiggington writes in *Trees and Shrubs for the Southeast*, they should not be used indiscriminately. "In general," Mr. Wiggington writes,

> these plants are difficult to maintain in sunny areas. No matter how poor the soil or how exposed the site, as soon as the ground surface is somewhat sheltered the seedlings of various shrubs and trees begin to invade the planting, following the natural course of ecological succession. Therefore, where the site under study is well lighted, the use of ground covers must be planned with allowance for some weeding. It may be confined to the very steep and difficult spots with slopes steeper than three to one where grass cutting by machine is impractical.
>
> This problem of weeding is not entirely eliminated in shaded areas, but it is much less severe, and the ground covers gain in value here because there are few southern grasses which are very successful in shade. There are of course covers which are suited to either sun or shade, but they cannot be planted thoughtlessly with the impressions that all garden problems will then be solved.

Mr. Wiggington stresses the importance of preparing the ground thoroughly before planting, and getting rid of all roots of Bermuda grass. Bermuda grass is almost impossible to get out once the planting is done. I doubt whether I shall ever get rid of it entirely in a row of *Ophiopogon* on the south side of a *Camellia sasanqua* hedge.

After trying all of the ground covers available, I have decided that the best evergreens for good effect at all seasons are the two most common kinds: periwinkle, *Vinca minor*, and Japanese spurge, *Pachysandra terminalis*. Japanese spurge is more uniform in height, and less invasive, but it prospers only in shade, and periwinkle will also grow in sun.

Periwinkle is almost as invasive as Bermuda grass, though fortunately not quite as difficult to get rid of. Having spent many years planting it, I am now pulling it up as fast as I can. It chokes out bulbs, other plants, and even shrubs, and even in shade it requires a good deal of clipping and weeding. I think periwinkle and spurge should be used only in large areas, and in places between buildings and paths, where no other plants are expected to grow.

Ivy is as troublesome as these two. I planted it to grow on wire fences, and I spend a lot of time keeping it from covering the ground and everything else—especially the paths. Other climbing plants and vines are recommended as ground covers—Carolina jessamine; 'Max Graf', a trailing rugosa rose; *Akebia quinata*; and so on—but I have never found them satisfactory.

In my garden I am keeping a number of low creepers for shady places. One of the best is the partridgeberry, *Mitchella repens*. It lies close to the ground, is always green, and seems to have no troubles. Mine flowers very little and has never fruited, but I hope to find a plant of whichever sex I haven't got, for the red berries in winter are its chief attraction. It is doing well in rather poor dry soil under pine trees, but it likes humus, moisture, and acidity, so I may have to treat it better in order to get it to bloom well.

Mazus reptans is also an excellent flat evergreen creeper. It makes a thick mat, and can even be walked on. At present it is afflicted with something that looks very like red spider mite, but I shall keep it anyway, for the blue violet flowers are charming in spring with the tall blue scillas.

September 20, 1964

TINY CREEPERS

In a small garden it is more important than ever to make use of every inch of space, and there are some plants that can be fitted into a few inches. They are the tiny creepers that grow in cracks and crevices, in steps and pavements. Some of these are difficult alpines, but there are others that will do for a gardener like me, whose one requirement is that a plant will grow without special care or trouble.

I think first of the stonecrops. They are an easy-going race, and the ones I am thinking of are all too easy, though none the less useful for dry hot pavements. Several very flat, creeping species will grow in poor soil in dry sunny places. *Sedum acre* has been grown so long on English walls and roofs that it has acquired a long list of folk names: birdbreak, wall-pepper, treasure-of-love, and welcome-home-husband-though-never-so-drunk. It has neat little evergreen spikelets, and in June there are green-gold flowers. *S. anolicum* [*S. anglicum*] is another little one. Last year I saw it in bloom in May in front of a drugstore in Rock Hill, South Carolina, and I begged a scrap and sent it off to the Stonecrop Nurseries to be identified. Stonecrop has, as the name suggests, an excellent collection of sedums. I get *S. album* var. *murale* from them in the fall; it is a little larger than the other two, and already I find gray-green sprigs rooting themselves several feet from the parent plant.

These little stonecrops are spreaders. You get a few squashed pieces in a letter and, before the year is out, you are grubbing it up by the cartload. Nevertheless it is not very difficult to keep them in check for they come up easily as they take root. Sedum means to sit, and they seem to sit on the ground.

Another little carpeter that came from Stonecrop Nurseries is *Sagina glabra* 'Aurea' [*S. subulata* 'Aurea'], which is called gold moss, but is really grass green. At present it has taken hold and is spreading. It comes from the southern Alps, and it may disappear before the summer is over. Along with it came another alpine, *Globularia cordifolia*, which occurs at high elevations. It is still with me, but barely so, and if I lose it I shall try again, for it likes hot dry places and it is said to make flat lawns of neat dark evergreen rosettes.

The creeping thymes are the best of tiny carpeters, and the best of the creeping thymes is *Thymus serpyllum* 'Coccineus', a flat dense carpet of dark green in all seasons. I can't think where *T. s.* 'Coccineus' got its name for the tiny flowers are not, as so often described, either red or crimson. They are a light red-violet. *T. herba-barona*, the pungent caraway or seed-cake thyme from the hills of Corsica, gets its name from a baron of beef, for which it is the traditional seasoning. These two little creepers give me pleasure every day of the year, and year after year.

The little plant with small round glossy leaves that grows between the bricks in Elizabeth Clarkson's garden is *Hydrocotyle rotundifolia*. Anyone who values one's garden or one's peace will not admit it, but Elizabeth has had it a long time without regret and many people ask where it can be had. It is a tropical plant and is not to be had from northern nurseries.

Another plant that must be watched, for it can be something of a nuisance if it gets established in flowerbeds, is *Veronica filiformis*. It makes thick mats of tiny pale green leaves and has pale blue flowers in early spring. I never like to get rid of it completely, for I like to see the tender green in winter and it grows in sun and shade.

Mazus reptans is an excellent evergreen carpeter for moist shady places, though it may be too much of a spreader for growing between flagstones. It comes into bloom any time between the last of February and the middle of April and is soon thickly dotted with bright violet flowers. It is one of the best low-growing ground covers. Pearl cup, *Nierembergia rivularis*, is not evergreen and is grown only for the white flowers that appear in summer.

August 23, 1964

SIX

Gardeners and Gardens

WING HAVEN

Mrs. McCartney thinks the garden visitors on the spring tours would like to know what to look for in the gardens that are to be open, and how to gather ideas to take home and put to use. I think this can be done by pointing out some of the features of Elizabeth Clarkson's garden.

Look first for a good relationship between house and garden. The connection is direct and intimate with gardens on every side of the house, all seen from within through a door or window. Each of these is a unit, separate and completely enclosed, but connected with the other areas in such a way as to be a part of the general plan. The garden is made up of a number of smaller gardens, each complete in itself, with easy access from one part to another.

Look for vistas. As I walk through this garden I think of Pope: "and ampler vistas open to my view." Each area is enclosed, but a view of something beyond gives a feeling of distance. Elizabeth has made the best use of her space by providing the longest views possible, two of the whole length of her own garden and one that includes the Guinters' garden next door. These vistas are framed by trees, shrubs, hedges, or gates and always there is an adequate termination, a special treatment of the wall, a seat, or a symmetrical tree.

Look for pleasant proportions: the height of the human figure fixes the scale of the garden, and features meant for use like walks, steps, seats, hedges all gauge the size of other features. There is no rule for deciding the relative proportions of things meant only for beauty. This is something that cannot be taught and must be learned from observation.

The pleasure that comes from seeing a well-planned garden depends upon its being arranged in an orderly manner. Directness and simplicity of design are accomplished by restraint, by doing away with meaningless curves, conflicting lines, and indiscriminate colors. Limiting the flowering trees and shrubs to a few kinds, mainly dogwoods, cherries, crabapples, quinces, and azaleas, and the colors to pink, lilac, white, and pale yellow, brings to the garden a feeling of unity. The vitality of the design depends upon the balance of unity and variety, unity strengthened by the repetition and relieved from monotony by the introduction of a new interest.

The things common to all gardens are often those least realized: sun and shadow, green leaves, water, and the songs of birds. There is a great deal of shade to make Elizabeth's garden cool, and no part of it is without the sound of falling water. Water, thickets of wild honeysuckle tangled in privet, and an abundance of wild fruits bring the birds, reminding me of [Joseph] Addison, who wrote, "My garden invites into it all the birds of the country by offering them the convenience of springs and shades, solitude and shelter, and I do not suffer anyone to destroy their nests in spring or drive them from their usual haunts in fruit time . . . by this means I have always the music of the season in its perfection."

Surrounded by woods on all sides is a garden within a garden, a neat square of box-bordered herb beds and brick paths, that reminds me of the inmost one of those little Japanese boxes that fit so snugly one within another. Here I find the seclusion that Dean Hole says must be in every garden, a quiet retreat.

April 17, 1960

IMPORTANCE OF GARDEN DETAILS

Now that my garden begins to emerge from the awkward age, and to take on some character of its own, I can give attention to detail. There is no longer a need to fill space with anything that will grow. The need is to trim, to discard, and to discriminate. The need is to fill odd corners with greenery and to find suitable places for plants that have never seemed at home where they are.

One of the unsuited plants was an *Aspidistra* that Charlotte Trotter gave me some years ago. It never seemed to prosper on the north side of the terrace wall, and the foliage grew even duller when it was moved to a spot with morning sun. Then, in the deep shade under some shrubbery, the leaves became a deeper green and acquired an air of sleek satisfaction. Now that the *Aspidistra* is settled, I must look about for the right kind of companions to share its dark corner between the Japanese flowering apricot and the evergreens beyond.

The ground is covered with periwinkle, *Vinca minor*, which was welcome in the beginning, but has become a nuisance. I have had enough of this evergreen tide, and mean to replace it with things equally green but not so overflowing. I think the bright yellow-green fronds and the graceful curves of holly fern [*Cyrtomium falcatum*] would be a pleasant foil for the stiff dark foliage of the *Aspidistra*. Holly ferns grow very slowly, adding only a few new fronds each season; but in time they make impressive clumps.

For the other side of the *Aspidistra*, I have in mind a small butcher's broom, *Ruscus aculeatus*, which seems insignificant in its present position beside large clumps of Lenten rose. It will benefit by contrast of texture in its new surroundings. Butcher's broom is one of the valuable shrubs, once common in the South, but now discarded to make room for more azaleas. One reason for its disappearance is that we have been growing only one sex (I am not sure which) and there have been no berries. Now I have the hermaphrodite form that berries freely, and I hope in time to be able to distribute seeds and seedlings, but growing them this way will be a slow and tedious process. In Raleigh I valued even the fruitless bushes that had grown, after many seasons, into wide clumps that brought warmth to the garden in winter. Now that I have bright berries over a long season, as they turn from shining green to shining red, I think it one of the best of the slow-growing evergreens.

This winter, for the first time, I saw the berries of *Sarcococca humilis*, a much smaller shrub than butcher's broom, which grows to little more than a foot in height. I am thinking of adding it to the *Aspidistra* community for the sake of its glittering leaves and the February fragrance of the inconspicuous flowers. The small neat berries are sometimes described as blue, sometimes as black. Looking at them closely, I see that they are really black with blue lights. Though small, they are well polished.

Now I am searching for the place where *Liriope muscari* 'Alba' will look its best, perhaps as a border for it already shows signs of spreading fast. This came to me last spring from Mr. Freeland, who says he got it from the Bishop's Garden at the National Cathedral. It is too soon to tell how tall the spikes will be when it is established, or how wide the leaves, but I think the cool white flowers one of the nicest additions to the summer garden.

Another treasure that came to me from Mr. Freeland is a variegated form of *Iris japonica* with crisp white stripes on the fanlike leaves. I grew this species in Raleigh where it bloomed once, in April, but never became established. Now that I have a source for it (I have not seen it offered for some years though it is grown in California), I hope to do better. The little frilly flowers, lightly poised on thin wiry stems, are very like those of our native *Iris cristata* which belongs to the same small group of crested irises.

February 10, 1963

STEPS IN YOUR GARDEN

Whenever I plan a garden, one of the first things I look for is a place to put steps. My own garden happens to be on sloping ground, giving me every excuse for changes of level, but even if it had been perfectly flat I should have created ups and down. Only a slight grade is needed for two or three steps, because they can be very low. At times three inches is not too little for the height of a riser; four or five inches is easy and pleasant and more than six is to be avoided if possible.

The width of the tread is in proportion to the height of the riser. A tread from fourteen to sixteen inches is about right for a riser of five inches. Where the steps are few and there is plenty of room, I like the treads to be even wider. Wider treads take lower risers. For some reason odd numbers have always been satisfying to human beings. Three steps are more pleasing than two, five more pleasing than four. A flight of more than seven steps (or nine at the most) needs to be broken by a landing to rest the climber and to rest the eye. If an even number of steps is unavoidable it may be possible to divide them into two groups of uneven numbers.

Next to a tread that is too shallow or a riser that is too high, the most common fault in garden steps is a flight that is too narrow. There are times, on a steep slope in a woodland or rock garden, when narrow flight lengthens the vista, but in general steps should be broad and inviting. Width emphasizes the beauty of the strong horizontal lines. Steps connected with a path are usually of the same width, certainly not narrower, though they may be wider if they lead to an open place. Steps connecting paths of unequal widths must be progressively widened to make the transition from one to the other.

Material that is beautiful in texture and color is as important as proportion. I think of brick first because its color brings warmth to the garden. If each step slightly overlaps the one below, as it should, two eight-inch bricks laid end to end make fifteen-inch treads. Two bricks laid flat, one on top of the other, make five-inch risers, a comfortable height. Brick steps are expensive because they must be laid in concrete and must have adequate foundation. A row of common bricks laid lengthwise behind them makes the tread wide enough for looks and for comfort. Brick steps go with brick houses, walls, walks, and terraces, with well-trimmed evergreens and close-clipped lawns. Dressed stone has the same architectural finish.

Rough stone, if it has one fairly flat surface and one fairly straight edge, is suitable for less formal places. Stones that are large enough to be stable can be laid without a binder and they look all the better for having small thymes and sedums planted in the interstices. Stone steps require wider treads than those of brick; two feet is not too much. If the stones are not wide enough for the whole step they can be used as risers with treads of gravel or soil carpeted with creeping thyme.

When stones are not at hand, heavy cement blocks can be used in the same way. They are not attractive, but I have found them very useful for a steep bank and now that the ivy has taken them over they are at least less objectionable.

In a Mocksville garden I saw a broad flight of steps, really a series of ramps as the risers were six or eight feet apart, made of old railroad ties and pine needles. It leads between magnificent oak trees down the gentle slope of the lawn to a gap in a low stone wall. The warm browns of creosote and pine needles are delightful and much labor is saved by not allowing grass to grow between the ties.

September 13, 1959

WALKS AND PATHS

After pondering over the difference between a walk and a path, I looked in the dictionary, and found that a path may be a garden walk, but it is primarily a track worn by people (or animals) going from one place to another. A walk is a place or path made for walking: "a broad path in a garden or pleasure ground. A walk must be broad enough for two persons to walk abreast," de La Quintinye, gardener to Louis XIV, wrote, "without which it would no longer be a real walk but a large path." Opinions differ as to how wide a path must be for two people to walk along it together. Some designers consider four feet nine inches the minimum, and some say it must be at least five feet wide. The sidewalks on our street are only four and a half feet, and I see couples strolling along them in comfort. For a path used only to get from one place to another, eighteen inches is wide enough.

With these limits in mind, the width of the path is finally decided by its length and its surroundings, but it is always better for it to be too wide than too narrow, especially in gardens where plants or shrubs are apt to encroach upon the edges. In my garden a width of six feet seemed right for the main path which is over a hundred feet long. It is slightly tapered, with the beginning widened to six feet six inches, and the far end narrowed to five feet six inches. This is supposed to make the vista seem longer than it really is. Longer paths, or even shorter ones, may be even wider. For example in a large garden designed by Gertrude Jekyll there is a path ten feet wide and nearly two hundred feet long. Another of the same width is less than a hundred feet long.

In spite of all its drawbacks the paths in my garden are gravel. I chose it because it is cheap, but also because I like it. The material I used (on the advice of Eddie Clarkson) is the local kind called pit gravel. It has a fine texture, weathers to a warm tan, and to me is pleasant to walk on, though my mother used to say it hurt her feet. The faults of pit gravel are that it gets soft when the ground thaws after freezing, and that, like any gritty material, it sticks to the soles of shoes and is tracked into the house.

Since Elizabeth Clarkson lent me her scuffle hoe I have been able to keep the paths clean very easily. A scuffle hoe is the kind that is pushed instead of being pulled, and this one has a very narrow V-shaped blade that allows the gravel to pass over it instead of piling up.

There are not many weeds anymore. I don't know whether this is due to the borax I have sifted on the paths, or to the frequent use of the scuffle hoe. Borax is said to make the soil completely sterile, but I find that the gravel paths are still pretty good seed beds.

I find gravel more easily raked and pleasanter to walk on when it is not spread more than an inch or two thick. It needs to be edged with stone or brick two or three inches higher than the level of the path to keep it from washing or spreading. I like brick edges set without mortar even though that means that they must be reset occasionally.

I never miss grass in summer when my borders are full of color, but I do miss it in winter; then I think of Elizabeth Clarkson's long green vistas. But grass paths are hard to keep. Pine straw is brown and fragrant for wild gardens or informal places, but I found in my Raleigh garden that it decayed quickly, and had to be renewed constantly. Then the weeds came through it, and it was hard to get rid of them without getting rid of much of the pine straw at the same time. But it did smell so good on a warm winter morning.

Paths are straight or winding according to the lay of the land, the surroundings, or the taste of the times. Modern designers, like those of the eighteenth century, are apt to abhor the straight walk, and delight in the serpentine paths praised by the gardeners and poets of the landscape school.

The Rev. William Mason wrote a poem to the serpentine:

> Smooth, simple path whose
> Undulating line
> With sidelong tufts of flow'ry
> Fragrance crowned.
> Plain in its neatness spans
> My garden ground;
> What though two acres thy
> Brief course confine.

February 6, 1966

TERRACES AND PATIOS

I wish every gardener in town could have heard Edith Henderson talk to the Charlotte Garden Club on terraces and patios and ways of planting them. I went to the meeting well provided with paper for taking notes, as I had heard Mrs. Henderson talk before, and knew that her lecture would be practical and explicit.

She defined a terrace as a definite unit, segregated but not enclosed, that forms a transition from house to garden and is open to a view. A patio, on the other hand, is enclosed on all four sides. *Patio* is a Spanish word which means an inner court, usually a paved area with a fountain.

The exposure of the terrace or patio is the first consideration. Morning sun is wanted, and afternoon shade. A terrace that faces northeast is the first choice, northwest the second, due east the third. A terrace facing due west is not to be tolerated if there is an alternative, and if there is none, all efforts must be bent toward growing a tree, as soon as possible, to shade it from the afternoon sun.

Where a large tree is needed an oak is suitable, and for a small one the golden rain tree, *Koelreuteria paniculata*. The golden rain is a tree, inured to heat and drought, that grows quickly from seed and even volunteers. I always associate the yellow flowers with June in Chapel Hill and Thomas Jefferson's garden at Monticello, but I never see it around Charlotte though it can be found in the nurseries.

After the exposure is settled, the next consideration is the size of the terrace, keeping in mind the windows and doors that open on to it, circulation and furniture. Mrs. Henderson agrees with de La Quintinye that "the terraces adjoining to a house can hardly ever be too broad." He says twelve feet or more might be allowed for width, but she considers fifteen feet the minimum, and twenty to be preferred; she says she has never seen a terrace that is too big. Aside from its usefulness, the large terrace gives the house an adequate platform to rest on. A good rule to follow is to let its width equal the height of the roof line.

As to materials for terraces and patios, many gardeners have learned to their sorrow that old brick is not practical. When this has been learned too late, the damage can be repaired by digging out the crumbled brick, and filling in with dry sand, cement, and color.

Those who want the mellowness of age without its inconvenience can now get new brick that is made to look old. If cement is used between the brick, work it in and let it harden underneath, but don't let it be slick on top.

Colored concrete makes a practical surface that is attractive if a good color is used and if it is scored with a trowel in squares or diamonds. The available colors are tan, a red that fades pleasantly, pale green that fades unpleasantly, and lovely dark boxwood green that is beautiful when waxed. If you have an uncolored cement terrace, do not despair; there is a colored outdoor wax that can be burned into it.

If the old terrace is too small, a brick border can be added to it. Mrs. Henderson says there is an answer to every problem. The shape of the terrace is a matter of taste, but the simplest outlines are best, and no one can improve on the rectangle.

If there are steps, let them be broad and low. Mrs. Henderson's formula is twice the height of the riser plus the tread equals twenty-six inches. This allows five-inch risers to sixteen-inch treads, and six-inch risers to fourteen-inch treads.

November 12, 1961

WATER IN THE GARDEN

Water like fire is a living thing. It dances and sparkles and reflects the changing seasons and the hours of the day; it seems more alive than the green things that grow beside it. From ancient times it has been the central feature of gardens. Civilization began in a garden that grew up around the source of a river: "A river went out of Eden to water the garden; and from thence it was parted, and come into four heads." This pattern of canals coming out from a central fountain in the form of a cross is one of the simplest and earliest designs. It was woven into Persian rugs and was used in the Garden of Fidelity which the Mogul Emperor, Barbar, laid out in Kabul, and it turns up again in the gardens of Tudor England.

For beauty and for use, since the earliest gardens were in dry countries where there could be no plants without irrigation, water has always been essential. When Dr. Donald Wells talked to the Charlotte Garden Club in February, and showed slides of gardens around the world, he stressed the importance of water in all countries. He spoke of woodland streams, waterfalls, of wall fountains and pools, where water reflects the flowers, cools the air and makes a pleasant sound.

He also spoke of the ways that water is used in the Edwin Clarksons' garden (Wing Haven). There are two wall fountains in this garden: in one, water pours from a lion's mouth into a dipping well; in the other it trickles from the center of a circle of doves which represents the sevenfold gifts of the Holy Ghost: the spirit of wisdom, understanding, the spirit of counsel, ghostly strength, knowledge, godliness, and the spirit of holy fear (Isaiah 11:2). "For fountains," Bacon said, "they are a great beauty, and refreshment; but pools mar all, and make the garden unwholesome and full of flies and frogs." In our neighborhood we do not agree as to the pools, but like to hear the frogs by night almost as well as the birds by day.

As you follow the little path in Elizabeth's garden you come to Frog Hollow (or Holler—I was never sure how it is spelled) where water flows from the base of a statue of two wondering children and falls over mossy rocks into a series of little brown fern-edged pools which are crossed by stepping stones.

From Frog Hollow the little paths wind through the woods, where camellias, azaleas, wild flowers, and ferns grow beneath the trees, to the trim box-edged herb garden, and on to the long walk that leads to a brick-paved court. In the court visitors will find a new feature, the duck pool, a great oval tank forty feet long and eighteen feet wide. It is more egg-shaped than oval and is raised higher at one end than the other in order to make the surface perfectly level. By night, the water-mirror reflects the stars, by day the clouds, in winter the green branches of pine trees, in spring the pale flowers of the weeping cherry.

All through the garden, along the little brick paths, there are shallow basins for the birds, always with cool fresh water dripping in and overflowing. In the main garden a formal pool reflects in winter the ivory trunk and branches of a large crape myrtle, and in summer its masses of clear pink flowers.

Wandering through these watery ways, I say to myself:

> still moves delight,
> Like clear springs renewed by flowing,
> Ever perfect, ever in them-
> Selves eternal.

April 9, 1961

MR. KRIPPENDORF'S GARDEN

Everyone who knows me has heard about Mr. Krippendorf and his woods in southern Ohio where he grew thousands of bulbs and wild flowers under his beech trees. I expect that there are a number of Charlotte gardeners who never heard of him who are growing the descendants of his Lenten roses. When I came here to live, he sent me a dozen seedlings that he had potted and grown on for a year or two. When these bloomed and seeded themselves, I passed the seedlings on to other gardeners, and they in turn passed them on to their friends.

When Mr. Krippendorf died, his place was bought by the Cincinnati Nature Center; I have just been out to visit the director Dr. Franklin McCamey and his wife who have an apartment upstairs in the Krippendorfs' house. The first floor is used for offices and classrooms. The times I went to see Mr. Krippendorf were in April; for he always wanted me to come when the daffodils were at their peak. I went to visit the nature center on the second day of November, arriving in a snow storm that seemed to me to be a blizzard. It snowed all day and most of the night, but the next morning the sun came out and the sky was as deeply blue as after a summer storm. The snow clung to the trunks and fine branches of the beech trees, and even the smallest twigs were delicately frosted and sparkling in the sun.

I stood at the window watching the light change and making a list of the birds that come to the feeders. Later I compared it with a list Mr. Krippendorf once sent me and found that the regulars are much the same: cardinals, jays, juncos, the white-breasted nuthatch, woodpeckers, titmice, and the Carolina chickadee.

After lunch, Ginny (Mrs. McCamey) lent me warm boots and a cap, and she and I walked down to the little creek that is called Salt Run. It is nearly a mile from the house, all steeply downhill, with a pause halfway on a little wooden bridge across a ravine. Dr. McCamey calls the bridge a listening post, a place to hear the small voices of the wood. But we heard only silence deep and white. The creek was cold and clear, shallow and swift. The limestone banks on the far side were too deep in snow for even a frond of fern to be seen. I thought of walking along the creekside in April when there was a blue carpet of *Phlox divaricata* under the trees, but even that was no more beautiful than the pattern of the leaves on the new-fallen snow. There were pale yellow maple leaves, and the neatly scalloped green-gold ovals of the chestnut oak were repeated on a smaller scale by those of the chinquapins. The snow was etched with a delicate tracery of the tracks of birds and small animals.

Deep snow the first week of November is most unusual in southern Ohio. I was visiting another garden the day before it fell; and I found *Sedum sieboldii* in bloom and stray flowers of *Campanula poscharskyana* and *Lamium maculatum*. Marion Becker, Mr. Krippendorf's neighbor, had our native witch hazel in full bloom, and on the slopes of her woods there were quantities of the small, pale, rose-colored flowers of two fall-flowering species of cyclamen. Chrysanthemums were in bloom everywhere and the next day their colors showed through the snow as it piled on top of them.

At the turn of the century, when Mr. Krippendorf bought the woods to save them from the axe, the hills around Cincinnati were covered with beech-maple forests, but now his is one of only six stands of climax forest left in Ohio. The nature center has saved it for all time.

The center has already begun its program of nature education, holding classes for school children and scheduling meetings for garden clubs, but it is not yet open to the public. However, Mr. McCamey will welcome visitors from North Carolina if they let him know when to expect them. I hope many will go and enjoy the woods, and realize how important it is for us to start such a project near Charlotte before our forests are all destroyed.

November 20, 1966

PHYSIC GARDEN AT THE COUNTRY DOCTOR MUSEUM

Linda Lamm and I have been working on a list of trees, shrubs, and herbaceous plants for the Physic Garden at the Country Doctor Museum in Bailey, North Carolina. The trees and shrubs will be in the background, with native medicinal plants in their shade. The herbs will be in concentric circular beds in a square plot of ground, a design taken from a section of the Botanic Garden in Padua, which was established in 1493.

The Physic Garden is also a flower garden: roses and violets, anemones, poppies, peonies, Madonna lilies and lily-of-the-valley, hollyhocks, foxgloves, irises, and calendulas will bloom in it along with other ancient plants of healing. Many old roses have been grown for medicinal use: Culpeper mentions the dog rose [*Rosa canina*], the damask, *Rosa rubra*, and *R. alba*, but the apothecary rose is *Rosa gallica* 'Officinalis', known to cultivation since 1300 and celebrated for its fragrance and beauty as well as for its medicinal properties. It was a favorite in the Middle Ages and is supposed to have been the Rose of Miletus that Pliny tells about, and it is generally considered to be the red rose of Lancaster. Since it was grown in the earliest American gardens, it seems particularly appropriate for the Country Doctor Museum. *Rosa gallica* has an alarming habit of suckering when grown on its own roots, so I have written to Dorothy Stemler to ask where budded plants can be found, in case she doesn't provide them herself, for it would not do to have suckers coming up through the bricks of the paths that divide the beds.

In the history of medicine the peony goes as far back as the rose. Pliny called it the oldest plant of all. It was named for Paeon, the physician of the gods, who by means of its roots healed the wound inflicted upon Pluto by Hercules. Dioscorides recognized two species: the male peony, *Paeonia mascula*, and the female, *P. officinalis*. *Officinalis* as a specific name means that the plant is adopted by the *Pharmacopoeia* and used in medicine. *P. officinalis* was common in England in the sixteenth century, and probably came to this country in the early days, though there is no record of peonies in American gardens before the nineteenth century. There are single and double forms in both red and white.

The iris, like the rose and the peony, is one of the most ancient garden plants, particularly *Iris florentina* [*Iris* × *germanica* var. *florentina*, orris root]. Perhaps this species will grow in Bailey on the coastal plain, though I have never been able to keep it for more than a year or two. If not, the Physic Garden will have to fall back on our old white dooryard iris and nothing could be lovelier. The southern Indians and the mountain people have long known the medicinal properties of the roots of our native species, *Iris verna*, and the blue flag, *I. versicolor*. Mrs. M. Grieve says the root of the blue flag is an official drug of the *United States Pharmacopoeia*, and is the source of the Iridin of commerce.

The Madonna lily, *Lilium candidum*, also has a claim to being the oldest of garden plants, and its uses in medicine are numerous as set forth by the herbalists. "The root of the garden lily stamped with honey gleweth together sinews that be cut asunder," Gerard says. "It bringeth the hairs again upon places which have been burned or scalded . . . stamped and stained with wine, and given to drink for two or three days together, it expelleth the poison of the pestilence." Parkinson says, "This lily above all the rest hath a mollifying, digesting, and cleansing quality, helping to suppurate tumours and to digest them, for which purpose the roote is much used. Divers other properties are in these lilies, which my purpose is not to declare in this place."

March 21, 1971

MR. BUSBEE'S GARDEN

Jacques Busbee's Raleigh garden was the first one I ever knew that was all walks and flowerbeds. The house was set forward on the narrow lot so that there was only a scrap of lawn between the front steps and the street; and the space behind the house was devoted entirely to plants, the rarer the better. The garden was all in blue and gold, blue the color of his wife's eyes and gold the color of her hair. There were cornflowers and forget-me-nots, ageratum, anchusa, and Nigella, bellflower and veronica, and bluest of all, *Delphinium belladonna.* At that time, before the First World War, nobody in the South thought of growing delphiniums but that made Mr. Busbee want them all the more. There were blue irises: the Dalmatian iris, *Pallida dalmatica* [*Iris pallida* var. *dalmatica*], 'Princess Beatrice', and 'Lord of June' in delicate tints long since discarded in favor of large, coarse, and gaudy flowers. There was the gold of alyssum, anthemis, and lemon lilies. There were primroses and daffodils and golden pansies.

Rosa 'Gardenia', a charming old rose with a creamy bud, grew on the garden fence and 'Lady Banks' rose spilled itself over the little rustic summerhouse. When a 'Dr. Van Fleet' was in bloom at the corner of the porch, I used to think that the pale pink flowers represented Mrs. Busbee's blushes.

"But Jacques couldn't resist the wonderful red of *Sprekelia*," Isabelle Henderson said when I asked her what she remembered about the garden, "so he planted the bulbs at the back of the beds so the flowers couldn't be seen." There were a few white things too: a Cherokee rose over the garden gate, the Peruvian daffodil, and the satin hyacinth. Mr. Busbee remembered the satin hyacinth in his great-grandmother's borders, but he didn't know its Latin name, which proved to be *Ornithogalum nutans*.

Isabelle says she first saw the Busbees' garden by lamplight. She had gone with her mother to pay a call on their new neighbors, and although it was a very dark night, they were taken into the garden, Mr. Busbee going ahead with a lantern. "I thought it must be an enormous place," Isabelle said, "but when I saw it by daylight I found it was tiny; we had been walking round and round a circular path."

The plants were remarkable for their rarity, but even more so for their size and quality. "And no wonder!" Isabelle said. "They had a yearly dressing of elephant manure." In those days the circus used to come to Raleigh every fall, and pitch its tents in Cameron Field. When it left, the Busbees would go down to the field with a cotton picker's basket, which they would fill and carry home between them, trudging uphill for nearly a mile.

When we went to Raleigh to live, the Busbees were gone, and, except through their garden, it was not until they settled at Jugtown that I knew them. At Jugtown, Mr. Busbee started his large and systematic collections. He had the first Louisiana irises in these parts; the new daffodils as they came along ("Don't tell Juliana what I paid for 'Fortune'," he whispered when I saw it in bloom for the first time); the new daylilies and the new bearded irises. *Iris pallida dalmatica* [*Iris pallida* var. *dalmatica*], 'Princess Beatrice', and 'Lord of June' were left to bloom in Raleigh.

Mr. Busbee was a true gardener. He wanted some of everything that grows. He didn't wait to find out from someone else what a plant would do in North Carolina. He ordered everything he saw or heard about or found in the catalogues. He was not in the least discouraged by failure. "Is *Lycoris aurea* hardy?" he asked in a letter dated "Second day of spring." "Mine had all the foliage frozen off this winter. *Amaryllis belladonna* came up in January and was badly damaged by frost. *Nerine bowdenii* and *N.* 'Fothegillii Major' [*Nerine samiensis* var. *curvifolia* f. *fothergillii*] were both frozen to the ground but are showing signs of life. We had a nasty freeze two or three days ago that killed all the buds on the dwarf irises and spoiled several of my hybrid daffodils."

This is what the true gardener expects. He knows that "gardening is eleven months of hard work and one month of disappointment."

January 15, 1961

A VISIT TO ITALY'S OLDEST BOTANIC GARDEN

When I was in Italy many years ago, I stumbled by chance into the oldest botanic garden in the country, and I think in the world. It was laid out in 1545 by Professor Francesco Bonafede for the benefit of students from all over the world who came to study medicine at the University of Padua. It became a model for all others. I had gone to Padua because I wanted to see Giotto's frescoes in the Arena Chapel. As so often happened in those days, even in the midst of the tourist season, I was alone in the little church when I went to see them. There was no one in attendance, and all the while I was there no one came in. It was cool and the light was dim. The delicately colored walls were like a garden full of pale flowers. There is something of the peace of the garden in Giotto's paintings. It was after I left the chapel that I came upon the botanic garden, not knowing it was there. But that day it was closed.

I have no idea now how I managed to get in. Perhaps there was an unlocked gate. However, I did get in and wandered along a path in the shadowy twilight beneath ancient trees, and found myself at the entrance to a circular garden surrounded by an old brick wall with a marble balustrade on which there were urns, busts, and statues. "The original scheme of the old part is still to be seen," Marie Gothlen writes in her *History of Garden Art*. "There are four squares enclosed in a great circle, which has on the outside high barriers and balustrades.

"Two of the squares are laid out in concentric circular beds, a plan that seems to have been thought convenient for a survey of medicinal herbs and has so often been imitated. Many of the fountains which are there now are of a later date, but there were certainly some in the middle and probably some in the sidewalks from the beginning. The statues of Theophrastus and King Solomon behind the fountains must have been erected very early." I wish I had known when I was there that I was looking at a statue of Theophrastus, but at the time I did not even know who Theophrastus was. I can't remember the beds of herbs, or even the fountains, but I do remember the tall crape myrtles which I afterward learned are the finest in Europe. Crape myrtles were introduced into Europe in 1747. I wonder if those at Padua were among the first.

I had wandered about the garden for a long time, still in a daze, still in the peace of Giotto, when I heard angry shouts, and, turning around, saw two fierce Italian guards bearing down on me. I was so frightened I ran back to the wire fence that surrounds the whole garden, and threw my pocketbook and notebook over, and followed in haste, snagging my skirt but getting safely on the other side. I did not stop running until I was sure I wasn't being followed.

In my haste I missed the Prato della Valle, a sort of common or public park, which had "served as a playground before the time of Christ." It is also an open-air Hall of Fame, containing statues of all the great men who have made this university city famous. Only a short distance from the Orto Botanico, it is a pleasant spot for the weary sightseer to seek repose.

Edith Wharton, who wrote so delightfully of Italian gardens, considered Padua one of the most picturesque cities of northern Italy. Those looking for gardens, she writes, "will find many charming bits along the narrow canals or by the sluggish river skirting the city walls." I hope someone who is going to Padua will read this and will go to see all of those things that I missed.

October 5, 1967

COLETTE'S MOTHER'S GARDEN

In *My Mother's House* Colette describes the French garden she grew up in in Puisaye. I always think of her as standing on the gravel path, like Renoir's dreamy little girl, with the green watering pot in one hand and daisies in the other. In 1876 Colette would have been about the age of that little girl, or a year or two younger. Her mother's garden must have been like the country gardens that the Impressionists liked to paint.

It was on a steep hillside above the Rue des Vignes, with an upper garden overlooking the lower one where aubergines and pimentos grew, and the scent of tomato leaves was mixed with the scent of apricots ripening on the garden wall. In the upper garden some old rose bushes were the only flowers that had survived in the shade of two fir trees and a Persian walnut, which we would call an English walnut. The soft unripe fruits fell on the shabby grass, and Colette's mother picked them up and pocketed them; perhaps she made them into pickles.

The house smiled on the side garden, a suntrap, where a bignonia and an ancient wisteria on a sagging iron trellis shaded a paved terrace outside the living room door. There were ancient lilacs "blue in the shade and purple in the sunshine." They shaded the broad top of the wall between the kitchen garden and the farmyard, where the little girl had her hideout, her secret garden of pebbles and colored glass and beheaded flowers. She called it "the presbytery'," a mysterious word some grownup had used in describing the priest's house.

Madonna lilies and scarlet poppies grew in the kitchen garden with tarragon, sorrel, garlic, carrots, and lettuce. Colette was allowed to cut armfuls of lilies to lay on the altar for the Hail Mary celebration. Before the green parakeets could peck the fine black seed from the little pepper pots of the poppies, the children poured them into their palms, and ate them. Poppy seeds lose their bitter taste when they are nearly ripe, Colette says, and have "the agreeable taste of opiated almonds."

Colette, who wrote so vividly and so passionately about flowers, was not a gardener, not even—I think—a real flower lover. Flowers were only a part of the bright world she held so close to her, and consumed with all her senses. And it was not enough to see them and smell them, she must also taste and feel and be dusted with pollen and even—her husband and biographer says—lick the poisonous berries.

It was Sido, Colette's mother, who worked in the flowers, and whose clothes were scented with them, with violets, lavender, crushed bay leaves and the lemon verbena that she stuffed in her pocket, and her shawl held the scent of orris root. The palms of her small slender hands were calloused by the dibble, clippers, and the rake; her wide-brimmed garden hat was weathered by wind and rain; a packet of seed of love-in-a-mist rattled in one pocket of her garden apron, and her clippers made a hole in the other.

On summer nights the garden expanded in the warm and fragrant shadows, and waves of perfume from the white flower of nicotine mingled with "the bitter cool smell of the little worm-eaten walnuts that fell on the grass." But in the winter twilight, when her playmates had grown tired of their games and gone home, and the light from the window turned the green garden to blue, the little girl shivered. She was frightened by the cold leaves of the laurels, the sharp spines of the yuccas, and the spiky caterpillars on the monkey puzzle tree.

Years later, in Paris, when she was old and bedridden, a friend brought Colette a branch of the wisteria that spilled over the wall onto the sidewalk of the Rue des Vignes, and bloomed so freely in May and again, less freely, in late summer. It brought back to her all the sensations of the garden of her childhood and she felt again "a vehement need to touch fleeces and leaves, warm feathers and the exciting dewiness of flowers."

March 7, 1971

THE SPLENDOR OF ROYAL GARDENS

If I were going to England this year (and I wish I were), I would plan to see the Royal Gardens in Windsor Great Park. They are at the far end of the park, three miles or more from the castle, and to the north of Virginia Water, a large meandering artificial lake more than a mile and a half long. The oldest section is the Savill Gardens, begun in 1932 by Eric Savill. In the spring of 1934 the planting was considered far enough along to risk a visit from King George V and Queen Mary. As the fate of the gardens depended on their approval, Eric Savill and his staff were horrified when, at the entrance, the Queen's hat was put askew by a low-hanging branch, and she was obviously annoyed. She was silent as she walked through the garden, and it was not until the end of the tour that she turned to Sir Eric with a smile and said, "It's very nice, Mr. Savill, but isn't it rather small?" This faint praise was taken as complete approval, and Eric Savill knew that he would be allowed to go ahead with his plans for the present and the future.

The spot that Savill had chosen for the Savill Gardens is almost level in some places, steeply sloping in others. He first cut away the bracken and scrub, clearing long vistas but leaving the fine old oaks, birches, and mixed hardwoods. Then he cut drainage ditches which later became clear slow streams running through meadowland and connecting the new Upper Pond with the old crescent of water called the Obelisk Pond.

The first flowers planted were native kingcups, which I take to be *Caltha palustris*, the marsh marigold, though buttercups are also called kingcups. They were planted along the margins of the streams and ponds and have been on the increase ever since. In April their gold is reflected in the water, along with the gold of wild daffodils and forsythia.

The wild daffodil of England is, of course, the small trumpet that is naturalized everywhere in the south. When I drove through eastern Carolina, early in March, they were blooming by the thousand in all the old gardens and in ditches along the roadside. They all came from

England many years ago. Our wild flowers are blooming in Windsor Great Park: trillium, Solomon's seal, bloodroot, dogtooth violets, shooting stars, lilies and foam flowers and Virginia bluebells. The Virginia bluebells that bloom on the wooded slopes of Windsor were grown from seed sent to English plantsman Clarence Elliott by my old friend Carl Krippendorf, who told me that he collected a quarter of a pound of seeds for that purpose.

During the war the Savill Garden became a wilderness, but a very beautiful one. Some visitors thought it even more beautiful than when it is kept in its usual neat perfection. After the war the garden was restored and new sections were added. One of these is the great wall, eighteen feet tall, and more than 200 feet long with buttresses twenty feet apart. It was built with bricks from the bomb sites of London. On the south side, between the buttresses, tender shrubs are planted: 'Lady Banks' rose, *Erythrina crista-galli* (which is root hardy in Charlotte), *Ceanothus* 'Cascade', *Carpenteria californica*, and *Hypericum* 'Rowallane', the most beautiful by far of all the St. John's worts. At the foot of the wall alpines grow in screes raised above the paths and supported by low rock walls. In the screes are rare plants and particular treasures.

When King George VI came to the throne he took great interest in the gardens and was particularly enthusiastic about the rhododendrons. After the death of Mr. J. B. Stevenson, the King decided to acquire the comprehensive collection of species that he had gathered together at Tower Court Ascot and now the collection at Windsor is the largest in the world.

I gathered all this from Lanning Roper's book, *The Gardens in the Royal Park at Windsor*. There is a copy in the public library. Reading it and studying the excellent photographs will be a great help to anyone who plans to go to Windsor and for those who cannot go, the book is almost as good as a visit, perhaps better, for the reader need not hurry.

April 3, 1966

GOTELLI'S COLLECTION OF DWARF CONIFERS

For some years I have been reading about the Gotelli collection of dwarf and slow-growing conifers, and this summer when I was in Washington, I had a chance to see them in the National Arboretum. When I first heard of the collection it was still in William Gotelli's garden in South Orange, New Jersey, but in 1962 he gave it to the arboretum.

When 1,500 specimens arrived in forty truck loads, there was a great scurrying to get them placed on a four-acre hillside, open to sun and air, but now, after four years, they look as if they had always been there. The skillfully placed outcrops of rock look as if they too belonged to the setting.

In spite of all I had read, and the specimens I had seen in nurseries, I was unprepared for the charm and variety of the miniature plants. There was so much color in the grays, greens, blues, gold, and silver bronze; such variation in the shapes—the weeping, the globe, the pyramid, and the cushion, and those that lie as flat as a carpet; such fine texture and such delicate lace in the foliage. At first I ran from one to another, and then I realized that I could not really see them in all directions and so I started at the entrance and went along slowly taking notes on as many as I had time for.

A little boy who was progressing slowly with a camera must have had the same idea, for I heard his mother say impatiently, "Come along, John, you can't take pictures of all of them in one afternoon." The plants are skillfully arranged, each in an ample area of clean gravel with plenty of room to develop its characteristic form and able to stretch out in all directions, gradually increase in circumference or reach up for some feet, and then allow its branches to tumble and trail.

In the spaces between there are some rock plants, such as *Alyssum saxatile* [*Aurinia saxatilis*], pinks, succulents, and spring-flowering bulbs. There are a few other low-growing shrubs, among them some interesting prostrate forms of the willow-leaf cotoneaster and a dwarf pomegranate. The flowers of the pomegranate are a cheerful scarlet among all those grays and greens.

The taller dwarfs are scattered among the miniatures, with the tallest in the background. The small forms of the Hinoki cypress are charming bits of bright green lace. *Chamaecyparis obtusa compressa* is no more than a few inches tall after ten years and the variety *minima* is said to reach a height of only four inches in twenty-five years. Another tiny one, *C. obtusa* 'Tetragona Minima' is called the tennis ball cypress.

All these are mutations of a forest tree that grow to a height of over a hundred feet. In an article in the *Rock Garden Bulletin* for April 1966, Joel Spingarn lists some dwarf forms of the Hinoki cypress according to their annual rates of growth. The very slow ones grow less than half an inch a year, and *C. obtusa* 'Intermedia' will be about six inches tall in twelve years. Mr. Springarn distinguishes between dwarf and pygmy conifers. The pygmies, I gather, are smaller than the dwarfs. Some dwarfs grow in time to be rather big shrubs. *Pinus strobus* 'Nana' [*P. s.* 'Radiata'], for example, may reach a height of six feet in fifty years, but the tallest of a row of eight-year-old plants I once saw at Tingles was only eighteen inches.

I am thinking of planting a few dwarf conifers in pots for the terrace. I have had great success with a moss cypress, *Chamaecyparis pisifera* 'Squarrosa Cyano-viridis' [*C. p.* 'Boulevard'], that I got from Mr. Coleman four years ago and planted in a fifteen-inch pot. It is now four feet tall, a beautiful blue-green, soft and fluffy. It suffers cold without changing color and seems to stand any amount of drought, followed by any amount of rain.

October 2, 1966

THE SCENTED GARDEN

On the fifth of May I went to see (and smell) the scented garden that Mrs. Philip Howerton made for her daughter, Jane Keesler. It is a small walled garden entered through a wooden door, and full of plants with scented flowers and scented leaves. There are scents from all seasons, the sweets of spring, summer, autumn and winter.

Daphne odora comes into bloom some time in February, filling the garden with fragrance for a month or more no matter how bad the weather. For summer there is the creeping gardenia, and from November through the New Year, if the weather holds, a vanilla-like fragrance comes from a loquat outside the wall. The sweet olive blooms in the fall, and again in spring, and sometimes at intervals throughout the year.

The small and fragrant enclosure (with the house and terrace on two sides) is only about thirty feet square. It reminds me of Reginald Farrer's saying: "A little garden, the littler the better, is your richest chance of happiness and success."

When I went through the gate, the garden looked as if it had been worked in and enjoyed only a moment before. A wicker basket left on the terrace was well stocked with snippers and forks and trowels. There was a pair of well-worn garden gloves, and, I am sorry to say, a large can of weed killer. Empty pots showed that planting had been going on. Clove pinks and sweet scented geraniums (apple, rose, peppermint, nutmeg, and lime) had been set out in the raised, bricked-edged borders to take the place of primroses just going out of bloom.

There is an anise tree, *Illicium anisatum*, in the garden, but the refreshing aroma of its leaves is noticeable only when they are crushed. I always think of it as a winter smell, and I like to go out on a very cold day to pick a few leaves and crush them and sniff them. It makes me feel warm, just the way the smell of mint makes me feel cool in summer. The scented-leaved sages are even more fragrant than the geraniums.

Each spring I try to remember to order (and writing this has reminded me to do it) the wonderfully fragrant *Salvia dorisiana*, and *Salvia rutilans* [*S. elegans*], the pineapple sage. The large velvety leaves of *S. dorisiana* smell like a basket of ripe fruit. These sages come in very small pots, but they grow very fast and by the end of the summer they are handsome bushes three or four feet tall. They do not live over the winter. The pineapple sage begins to bloom in late September and blooms on until heavy frost, sometimes even into November. Its flowers are carmine. I have never found a source for *Salvia clevelandii*, but perhaps some day I shall. They say it is the sweetest of all herbs.

At night, especially on dark ones when nothing is seen, and the sense of smell is keener, the scents of flowers seem stronger and more delightful.

> Then with the falling of
> The dusk
> The scent of Mignonette
> And Musk
> Will all the air enshroud.

I think the idea that mignonette is more fragrant at night is poetic license—I have never heard that it is—but anyway it sounds well with musk. Summer nights are fragrant, especially in the South where the scent of the moon lily [*Datura*] (as poisonous as it is beautiful) is almost overpowering.

Honeysuckle and privet are always with us, and nicotine [*Nicotiana*], once planted, renews itself forever. Nicotine looks so dejected in the daytime, I sometimes think I will dig it up and sometimes I do, but it comes again, and I am glad it does: "When darkness falls and . . . The dumb white nicotine awakes and utters her fragrance in a garden sleeping."

Edna St. Vincent Millay also knew that the nights of soft rain are the most fragrant when she wrote in *The Buck in the Snow*:

> Now comes night, smelling of box and privet,
> And the rain falls fine.

June 6, 1966

THE GARDENS OF A SOLDIER'S WIFE

I suppose I am the only one who still reads Mrs. [Juliana Horatia] Ewing, but I read her books over and over, especially the parts about gardens. Mrs. Ewing was a soldier's wife, so she never had a chance to garden in one place very long, but each time she went to a new post she started to make a new garden, and to do it thoroughly.

In *The Story of a Short Life*, the colonel's wife (obviously the author), set O'Reilly, her gardener, to trenching the sandy soil as soon as she arrived at Asholt (obviously Aldershot). O'Reilly said it was a waste of time to trench what would be "a poor patch when all's done to it." He said she had better take an old soldier's advice and stick to runner beans: "They're growing while you're on duty. The flowers are the right soldier's colour, and when it comes to beans, ye may put your hand out of the window and gather them." The colonel's wife said she must have more than runner beans, and if she were not there long enough to enjoy her flowers, they would give pleasure to her successors.

Wherever she went, the colonel's wife planted her favorite rose, one that had grown over her bedroom window at home. The colonel called it 'Marching Orders', for whenever it grew enough to flower well, the regiment was sure to "get the route."

"It shall be called 'Standing Orders' now," O'Reilly said, "if soap and water can make it blossom, and I'm spared to attend to it." O'Reilly had great faith in soapy water because he was once officer's servant to a captain who had him put his bath water on the roses every morning. The captain used very highly scented soap—not for himself, he said, but "the roses will be the sweeter for it."

For the last two years of her life, Mrs. Ewing had a house of her own, and set out at once to make a garden of an old potato patch. "Things grow fast here," she said. All of her friends contributed plants. She got into her new house the first of June, and in December she wrote to a friend:

> A rose-growing admirer of "Laetus" from *The Story of a Short Life* made a pilgrimage to see me and brought nineteen grand climbing roses. On a wall that faces quite nearly south, grow 'Marechal Niel', a 'Cloth of Gold' ['Chromatella'], and 'Charles LeFebvre', and 'Triomphe de Rennes', and a Banksia and 'Souvenir de la Malmaison', and Chestnut Hybrid, and a bit of the old Ecclesfield white rose—sent by Undine—and some Passion Flowers from dear old Miss Child in Derbyshire, and a Wistaria which the old lady of the lodgings we were in when we first came, tore up and gave to me, with various other oddments from her garden. And a very lovely rose, 'Fortune's Yellow', given to me by a friend, Miss Sullivan; before she went abroad, sent me a farewell memorial of sweet things: Lavender, Rosemary, Cabbage Rose, Moss Rose, and Jessamine.

Here again, the Army provided her with a rose-loving Irish gardener. On the third of December, weak and ill and swathed in furs and shawls, she was feebly tramping on some newly planted rose bushes (fortunately the border was ready; she had "only to dig holes in very soft stuff"), when a magnificent individual, over six feet, with a coal-black melodramatic moustache appeared in full dress. He looked down on her with a twinkle in his eye and a conscientiousness of maids at the kitchen windows and began "toeing and heeling the roses into their places . . . he trod them in very nicely."

July 18, 1965

PIONEER SEEDSMEN

Some of my winter reading has been about David Landreth, founder of the oldest seedhouse in America, and his son David who went into business with his father and later succeeded him. David, the father, was an Englishman who came to Philadelphia in the latter part of the eighteenth century as a gardener at The Hills, a country place on the Schuylkill River, where Robert Morris, financier of the Revolution, had created a spot "as beautiful as any in the world." There he planted wild flowers from the woods, walnuts and hawthorns from England, and "all manner of trees, shrubbery and flowering vegetation." The hot houses were filled with oranges, pineapples, and a collection of tropical plants.

In 1784 David Landreth established his seedhouse in Philadelphia. Washington, Adams, Jefferson, James Monroe, and Joseph Bonaparte patronized it. He developed the fine vegetables that Philadelphia was famous for, and became one of the leading seedsmen, not only in this country but also in the world.

Early in the nineteenth century he introduced a new vegetable, the tomato, which until that time had been grown only as an ornamental plant called the love apple. The Mexicans, who got the tomato from Peru, had cultivated it for food long before the conquest, but the Europeans considered it poisonous until the Italians discovered its usefulness as a vegetable. In *The American Gardener*, William Cobbett describes the "Tomatum" as a plant from countries bordering on the Mediterranean, and says that "it bears a sort of apple about as big as a black walnut with its green husk on. This fruit is used to thicken stews and soups, and great quantities are sold in London."

When Thomas Jefferson sent Lewis and Clark to explore the West they brought back seeds that were distributed by David Landreth and Bernard M'Mahon, among them the osage orange, a valuable hedge plant for farmers in the prairie states. Among the shrubs they collected was a western barberry that Nuttall named *Mahonia* for M'Mahon. M'Mahon was an Irishman who settled in Philadelphia and engaged in the seed business and, in 1804, listed a thousand species in his catalogue.

His seed store was a meeting place for gardeners, botanists, and the plant explorers: Thomas Nuttall, William Baldwin, student of botany and medicine, and Baldwin's neighbor and biographer, Dr. William

Darlington. When M'Mahon published his *American Gardener's Calendar* in 1806, he sent a copy to his customer and correspondent Thomas Jefferson. "I have growing the fine tulips, hyacinths, tuberoses and amaryllis you formerly sent me," Jefferson wrote. "My wants are anemones, auriculas, ranunculus, crown imperial and carnations . . . and some handsome lilies."

Until the Civil War, the Landreths carried on a flourishing business in their Charleston branch, but this came "to a sudden end by act of the Confederated States District Court, which confiscated the real estate and merchandise alike, on April 22, 1863." The younger David had managed the South Carolina business until he became head of the firm in 1828. In 1832 he began to publish the *Floral Magazine*, one of the very early American horticultural periodicals. The firm continued to introduce new plants, among them the zinnia in 1898 and one of the first of the improved varieties of garden peas, Landreth's 'Extra Early', in 1823.

In 1853 when Commodore Perry opened up trade with Japan, the Landreths sent with him a box of seed for Japanese gardeners, and received one of Japanese seed when he returned. They specialized in camellias, roses, rhododendrons, azaleas, and magnolias and became the leading seedsmen in America and among the foremost in the world.

Along with their serious undertakings the Landreths had their fun. They once advertised the Baron Munchausen cabbage, "guaranteed to resist heat, cold, sun, and drought; will grow equally well in summer and winter; will kill any bug or worm that gets in the leaves." When customers ordered seed of this remarkable cabbage, they were reminded that Baron Munchausen was the world's greatest liar.

December 29, 1963

YOUNG BELGIAN GUIDED SOUTHERN HORTICULTURE

A few years before the War Between the States, a young Belgian came to this country and started a nursery in Augusta, Georgia. Fruitland was not an ordinary nursery. It was also an experimental station and a botanical garden for which seeds, cuttings, and plants were collected from all over the world. The young man was Prosper Julius Alphonse Berckmans, scholar, botanist, horticulturist and nurseryman, who for the next fifty years was the leading spirit of horticulture in the

South. It was to him that Dr. Henry Nehrling turned when he began to lay out his celebrated Palm Cottage Gardens in the high pinelands of Orange County, Florida.

"The plants he recommended to me, and added to my collection, form today a most important part of my garden," Dr. Nehrling wrote. "Almost all were of Japanese and Chinese origin. He distributed the most beautiful Chinese and Japanese evergreens, and the camellia was one of his special favorites. He largely propagated them, and his importations from Japan, China and Europe ran into many thousands. In 1894 he sent me a collection of such beautiful [*japonica*] hybrids as *Camellia* 'Donckelaeri', *C. Chandleri* 'Elegans', 'Contessa Lavinia Maggi', 'Lavinia Maggi Rosea', 'Lady Hume's Blush', 'C. M. Hovey', 'Alba plena', 'Countess of Derby', 'Jenny Lind', 'La Maestosa', 'Madame Ambroise Verschaffelt', 'Marchioness of Exeter', 'Rubens', 'Thomas Moore' and others."

In his catalogue for 1861 Mr. Berckmans listed a hundred camellias. When Dr. Nehrling asked him about getting some large camellias for a friend in Orlando, Mr. Berckmans replied that specimens from six to eight feet high could not be dug anywhere in Georgia for less than two hundred and fifty to five hundred dollars. And anyway, he added, no one wanted to part with them for any price.

Other broad-leaved evergreens sent to Dr. Nehrling were the banana shrub, the camphor tree, *Ligustrum japonicum*, *Osmanthus fragrans*, and *O. ilicifolium* [*heterophyllus*], the tea plant, *Photinia serrulata*, *Ilex integra* and *Elaeagnus*. Dr. Nehrling called *Elaeagnus* the silver shrub. About a dozen kinds came to him from Fruitland, among them *Elaeagnus macrophylla*, the finest of the evergreen species. Unfortunately, this one is no longer available probably because it is considered hard to propagate. *E. pungens* and its varieties, some of them with variegated leaves are still being grown along with the fine variety *E. fruitlandii* [*Elaeagnus pungens* 'Fruitlandii'].

Mr. Berckmans also sent all of the coniferous trees that he thought would do well at Palm Cottage. The cedar of Lebanon did not thrive but the deodar did. So did the Chinese fir, *Cunninghamia lanceolata*, which grew to a height of thirty feet. It was extremely rare at that time, and Dr. Nehrling thought it great fun when some of his friends who were overproud of their knowledge mistook it for an *Araucaria* [monkey puzzle tree].

Mr. Berckmans was one of the first gardeners to appreciate the oriental magnolias. He sent Dr. Nehrling *Magnolia denudata* and *M. liliiflora*. Once when I was at Fruitland in mid-January, *M. denudata* was in full bloom, though it usually blooms there, as in my garden, the first half of March.

The nursery was called Fruitland because Mr. Berckmans was the foremost pomologist of the South. His 1860 catalogue listed 1,300 varieties of pears, 900 of apples, 300 of grapes, and 300 of peaches. He originated twelve varieties of peaches, seven pears and a plum. His house at Fruitland is the clubhouse of the Augusta National Golf Club. The avenue of magnolias that he planted still leads to it and his azaleas and camellias still bloom by the spring.

January 17, 1960

MEET CAROLINE DORMON

In October, when I went to Louisiana to lecture, I went to see Miss Caroline Dormon, who wrote and illustrated *Flowers Native to the Deep South*, and who is coming to Junaluska next April to be the main speaker at the meeting of the Garden Club of North Carolina. We have been writing to each other ever since she read a copy of *A Southern Garden* (nearly fifteen years ago), but I saw her for the first time when I found her waiting on her doorstep in the warm October twilight.

Miss Dormon is the kind of gardener who wants to plant everything that grows, and she corresponds with her kind in England, Japan, New Zealand, and Australia, exchanging seeds as well as letters. "A good many of our native plants are now flourishing around the world," she writes, "and I must admit that the things I have sent have done better than those I have received. I blame that on our blistering summers." She says that a New Zealand lily, from Marlin Ross, is one of the best things that she has gotten from foreign gardens. "It is a lovely clear yellow, with a few tiny brown spots, and like our native *Lilium catesbaei* it is upward-facing."

Miss Dormon says that her landscaping is largely a problem of deciding what to eliminate: "I wanted to leave as many trees as possible, so I have very little space for planting. It seems absurd with a hundred and twenty acres to say that I have for no room for shrubs, but it is true. I keep taking out trees, but others soon fill the gaps. Now I am confronted with the need to take out some big shrubs, things do grow so outrageously!"

Some of Briarwood's visitors give nature all of the credit for its beauty, never guessing how much thought goes into planting around the house so cleverly that it seems as much a part of the forest as the birds' nests in the trees. Even the cenizo against the stone chimney and the exotic Australian bottlebrush seem to have grown there naturally. Cenizo is the local name (the Spanish word for ashes) for *Leucophyllum frutescens*, a low shrub with ashen leaves that covers the hillsides along the Rio Grande. It is also called barometer bush because it bursts into bloom after summer rains; and purple sage because the violet flowers hide the gray foliage. Elizabeth Clarkson sent me a twig from Texas, in full bloom on September 22. As it will stand zero temperatures, Elizabeth thinks that it will grow any place where rosemary prospers, that is in full sun in light, well-drained soil with some lime in it. If I can persuade a Texas nursery to send it to me, you can look for a cenizo in front of our house next spring.

A bottlebrush survived in Dr. Mayer's garden for three or four years. This, too, has stood zero weather in Louisiana, but the species at Briarwood is *Callistemon viminalis*, not the more commonly grown *C. rigidus*. There was a good display of bright red flowers in mid-October. This is a shrub for dry soil and sun.

Miss Dormon and I spent a morning of "October's bright blue weather" (her quotation and I don't know where it came from) roaming the wooded hillside between her house and the dark waters of her pond. There I found the white, summer-flowering Azalea serrulata [*Rhododendron viscosum*] that Mr. Morrison told me about, and the ever-rarer *A. prinifolia* [*Rhododendron prunifolium*]. Along the water's edge *Pinckneya* is planted where its reflection will double its beauty. "I would give you seeds, but it wouldn't grow in your garden," Miss Dormon said, and was amazed when I told her that it is already growing there in spite of the dry soil. This is only the beginning of what I have to say about Miss Dormon and her woods and her plants.

December 14, 1958

SHE TALKS TO THE BIRDS

A copy of Caroline Dormon's *Bird Talk* has just come to me from the publisher. Instructions from Caroline came ahead of it. "Be sure to point out that it is not intended to be a bird guide . . . there are already plenty of good ones . . . It just tells little things I have learned about birds throughout a long life. It will probably arouse controversy —hope it does."

Caroline Dormon lives at Briarwood, all alone in a Louisiana forest. People wonder at her living so far from anyone else and think she must be lonely. But she asks, "How could anyone be lonely with birds and squirrels for company, and the sound of the wind in the pine trees?" She talks to the birds and they talk too.

She says the mockingbird needs encouragement. When he sings a few tentative notes, she tells him, "How sweet! But sing some more." Then he sings several bars and she praises him again while he sings on and on.

The kinglet is so little, he is afraid of every other bird; so Caroline watches for him and calls, "Come on, flitter-wing, while I keep the other birds away." Then he lights at her feet and pecks at the cornbread she puts out for him. You can always identify the kinglet, she says, by the way he twitches his wings.

Then she calls, "Come on, titmouse, before the big birds get here," and down he comes and eats out of her hand. The pine warbler will eat out of her hand and so will the nuthatch. The chickadee never does, but when he hears her voice, he answers and follows her about the place.

Caroline says the towhee never comes to her feeding stations, but I think I have seen him at my sister's, and he eats out of Elizabeth Clarkson's hand. Almost every time I go into the garden, mine calls "Towhee?" and I say, "Yes, I know." He is very companionable, and when I am working in the garden, he hides nearby and calls out every little bit to remind me that he is there.

Birds like to watch people and to see them do the same thing at the same time of day. Once when we had a long stretch of Indian summer, my mother and I had elevenses under a pine tree every morning. Our mockingbird would fly to the tree as soon as he saw us coming and sing to us as long as we sat there. One winter a redbird spent each night in the bamboo outside the living room window. Every evening when we lighted the fire, we would hear his call and see him peering in. When we lighted the candles for dinner, on a table by the window, we could see him perched on a slender branch fast asleep. Once when we lighted the candles for breakfast before dawn, he was still asleep.

September 28, 1969

THE HUNT ARBORETUM

In November, Chancellor W. B. Aycock announced William Lanier Hunt's gift of Laurel Hill to the University of North Carolina. Laurel Hill joins the university's research farm, arboretum, and the Mason Farm which is also owned by the university. Altogether, there are now 240 acres to be developed as a laboratory for students of the Department of Botany and as a botanical garden for all of the native and exotic plants that can be grown there.

Ever since I can remember, Bill Hunt has been talking about Laurel Hill. Years ago he had the foresight to begin to acquire the property bit by bit with the idea of giving it to the university. All these years he has been preserving the native growth and natural beauty and adding new plants. When Billy first took me there on a warm, bright autumn day about twenty-five years ago, I was amazed that such a place could be found as far east as Chapel Hill.

As we stood at the top of a steep, wooded slope looking down on the clear waters and lichened rocks of Morgan's Creek with the banks of laurel and rhododendron on the other side, there was not a sound except the music of the water as it chattered "over stony ways in little sharps and trebles." I could not believe we were not in the mountains.

Billy grew up in the Lindley Nurseries in Greensboro. He says he cannot remember a time when he was not begging space for his plants in the field and in the greenhouses. At Chapel Hill he has been growing plants and talking about plants ever since he came there as a student and rented a lot for his iris collection. Before he had Laurel Hill, he used to park things in his friends' gardens. I remember going to somebody's yard on a gray winter day to pick a bouquet of Algerian irises.

At Laurel Hill, in addition to the wild flowers and native trees and shrubs along the lovely reaches of the creek, the plant collection on the hillside has grown so that there is no time of the year when there is not something in bloom. In the fall there are crocuses, sternbergias, and nerines. Hoop petticoat daffodils bloom through the winter and then there are daffodils until late in April. I can't think what blooms in May or June, but I am sure there is something—brodiaeas perhaps and lilies, and then in July the lycoris comes into bloom.

"I wonder what goes on over there," Billy wrote on the fourth of September, "and I must tell you what goes on here. *Lycoris cinnabarina* turns out to be an amazingly beautiful light brown spider lily. Late July and early August is the time. I wish to report wonderful success with *Cyclamen repandum*. When you are here, I will show you the many, many forms in color plates in the rare *Jordan and Fourreau*, *Icones ad Forum Europaeum*. I have ten scapes of the pink and sky-blue *Lycoris sprengeri*. What a flower! They are somewhat like *L. squamigera* but tougher, more heat resistant, and of course, more than a month later. The early red spider lily has gone now, and the early *Colchicums*, *Rhodophialas* (pink and red), and *Zephyranthes candida* are coming in. No *Sternbergias* yet."

Years ago, Billy gave me my first oxblood lilies. They were called amaryllis then but now they are *Rhodophiala*. Dr. [Hamilton P.] Traub has named a new hybrid, *Rhodophiala* × *huntiana* in honor of him. It is described in the *Amaryllis Year Book* for 1961 as a cross between *R. bifida* and *R. spathaceum* [now regarded as a subspecies of *R. bifida*].

Billy is well known in Charlotte as a garden consultant and lecturer. "We want him every year," Claire McKay said to me once when she was on the program committee of the Charlotte Garden Club. Everyone who has seen the beautiful slides of Billy's woods will want to see Laurel Hill. I feel as if it is a personal gift to you and me.

January 14, 1962

SEVEN

Gods, Legends, and Rituals

THE GODS OF THE GARDEN

In ancient times it was the custom for some figure to preside over the garden. In Greece it was apt to be Priapus, the god of fruitfulness. He is represented as carrying a cloak filled with fruits of all kinds, or with a horn of plenty, and always carries a wooden scythe to scare away thieves and birds. Even the peasant's garden had its crude image of Priapus, cut from wood or stone. The Romans adopted him, and Virgil, writing about bees, says, "Let there be gardens fragrant with saffron flowers to invite them, and let the watchman against thieves and birds, guardian Priapus, Lord of Hellespont, protect them with his willow hook."

Pan, the Arcadian god of shepherds, later became the guardian of bees, and was at times worshipped as the god of all nature, "pan" meaning all. The Arcadians called him Lord of the Wood. Represented as half man, half beast, he is said to be the child of Heaven and Earth. His horns, pointed ears, cloven hooves, his fawn-skin crook and reed pipe are all familiar.

> His river-reed that's pierced for singing;
> The crooked stick he keeps for flinging
> At hares; his javelin sharp and slender;
> His fawn-skin tawny gray and tender
> Whose fur the faintest pattern dapples:
> His little scrip that smells of apples.
> (Elinor Wylie)

Pan also appears in Roman literature. In the opening verses of the *Georgics*, Virgil calls on Pan, guardian of the sheep, bounteous Ceres, and "Thou, O Silvanus, with a young uprooted cypress in thy hand; and ye, O gods and goddesses all, whose love guards our fields—both ye who nurse the young fruits, springing up unsown, and ye who on the seedlings send down from heaven plenteous rain!"

But Horace calls on Faunus, the Roman rural deity, who was also god of poets. When Horace narrowly escaped a falling tree, he wrote that he would have been killed "had not Faunus, protector of poets, with his right hand warded off the stroke."

Groves were sacred to Silvanus, and cattle, field, and boundaries were under his care. He was represented as an old man, and Horace calls him shaggy. "When Autumn in the fields has reared his head crowned with ripened fruits, the countryman delights to pluck the grafted pears and purple grapes, with which to honour thee, Priapus and thee, Father Silvanus, guardian of boundaries."

Terminus, a minor deity, at one time presided over boundaries. He is represented as a bust without feet or arms, because he never moves. A figure called a term, a bust on a post or pillar, was placed at each corner of the property. On the shoulders of the term there were knobs to hang garlands on at the festival of the Terminalia, in February. The peasants crowned the landmarks with flowers and made sacrifices, pouring libations of milk and wine.

The Terminalia must have been the origin of the Rogation Days, the three days before Ascension, set aside by the church in 511, for chanting litanies in procession (rogations). In England they are still celebrated by processions along the parish boundaries.

January is named for Janus, the Roman god of the New Year. He has two faces, one looking back on the old year and one looking forward to the new. He also opens the day, looking to the East and the West and is therefore in charge of the gates of heaven and of all gates and doors on earth. He holds a key in his left hand, and in his right a staff. Sir James Fraser considers Janus the same as the older god, Jupiter, and going back further, the same as Zeus. Sometimes his term has four heads representing the seasons. As god of the beginning of all things, I have always thought I would like to have him in my garden.

For those who prefer female statues in the garden, there are Flora and Pomona, and Ceres the goddess of grain and the harvest who is the same as Juno, the wife of Jupiter, and is the Greek Demeter. She is represented with poppies in her hands and hair, and sometimes with the torch that she held when she went in search of Persephone.

August 18, 1963

THE ASH, A SYMBOL IN HISTORY

When men first tried to explain to themselves where they had come from and where they were going, they thought of the forest tree as the greatest and most lasting thing in their world. To them it stood for all things created, as well as the life to come. They called it the World Tree and made a symbol to represent it. As early as the sixteenth century BC, the symbol of the sacred tree was carved on Nestor's ring; it appeared again in the mosaics of Roman basilicas and in the carvings of church portals.

In Oriental countries, the sacred tree was the date palm or the fig, but as civilization crept northward, it became a tree of the northern forests.

In Scandinavian mythology, the ash Yggdrasil was the World Tree; it was the symbol of existence, the origin of fate, and the source of knowledge. The tree, they said, supports the universe; its branches cover the whole world, and reach up into the clouds; it drips honeydew, and its flowers are stars. Its three great roots penetrate the three regions of the world: the land of the dead, the realm of the frost giants, and Asgard, the home of the gods.

The fountain in the realm of the giants is the source of all wisdom; in the white waters of the well of Urda the fate of men and god takes shape; Urda holds the past in her hands, and her sisters hold the present and the future. An eagle sits on the top of the ash tree, and a dragon in the realm of death is ever gnawing at its root. A squirrel runs up and down, from the eagle to the dragon, bearing tales and causing trouble. In the shade of the tree the gods sit and judge the deeds of men.

One of the oldest theories of the creation is that men descended from trees. In the Greek legend a fierce and strong race of warriors were created by Zeus from the cloud ash. The Scandinavians believed that Odin and his brothers made the first man from the trunk of an ash tree that was washed up on the shore.

The great European ash is *Fraxinus excelsior*. It grows fast but lives long, taking a hundred years to mature, and sometimes reaching a height of a hundred feet. Because of its height it is said to attract lightning: "Avoid an ash, it courts the flash." It grows on higher ground than most trees and is strong in its resistance to the elements, as Virgil observed:

> Nature seems to ordain
> The rocky cliff for the wild ash's reign.

The strength of its roots is proverbial. "May your footfall be by the root of an ash," is a saying that invokes a sure footing.

For its strength in storms and its ability to grow in exposed places, the Saxons chose the ash as their guardian tree, and planted it around their remote thorps and granges. From the wood the husbandman made his implements, the Viking his ships. The wood of the American ash is still used for the handles of farm implements and for baseball bats.

From early times the ash has been considered the bane of snakes. Pliny recommended an extract of ash for snakebite, and said no serpent would cross a ring of ash leaves. Belief in the virtues of the ash is ancient and widespread. Spencer said it was "for nothing ill," and a Finnish poet found magic in the smallest fragment of its boughs.

> He who took a branch from off it
> Took prosperity unceasing . . .
> He who broke a leafy branchlet,
> Gathered with it love unending.

Yet pain and sorrow have a place in the traditions of the World Tree. There is a mysterious similarity between the Christian symbol of the cross and the ash Yggdrasil, on which Odin sacrificed himself. In the Elder Edda, Odin tells how he hung

> Nine whole nights on a wind-rocked tree,
> Wounded with a spear.
> I was offered to Odin, myself to myself
> On that tree of which no man knows.

Perhaps there is an echo of this in the lines of the twelfth-century Welsh poet:

Bright is the top of the ash,
Long, and white,
When it grow by the dell,
Long is the sickness of the sad heart.

August 26, 1962

THE TALE OF THE MAGICAL HAWTHORN TREE

And forth goeth all the court,
Both most and least,
To fetch the flours fresh and
Branch and bloom,
And namely hauthorn brought
Both page and groom.

The custom of gathering hawthorn branches on May Day stems from an even earlier time than the age of Chaucer, and is a relic of the days when men worshipped trees, and believed that the freshly cut branches brought the blessing of the tree spirit to the household, making the crops grow and the cattle increase.

The church could not do away with the old beliefs, and the celebration of the renewal of nature survived. On mid-Lent Sunday, death and winter, in the form of a straw effigy, were carried out and thrown into the water. On May Day, life and summer were brought back in the budding branches of the thorn tree that would be taken from door to door by revelers, who sang:

We have carried Death away,
And brought the Spring to stay,
With Summer and the May,
And all the flowers gay.

A curious tale told by the brothers Grimm seems to connect the hawthorn with the sacred bird of the Egyptians, an even more remote symbol of death and resurrection. It is the story of a thorn tree that stood in the garden of a lady who loved to gather the sweet white blossoms in the spring, and the bright red berries in fall. When she died she begged to be buried under its branches. Soon after her death her little boy acquired a stepmother who slew him and hid his bones, but his half sister found them, and laid them on his mother's grave. Immediately, the tree moved and tossed its branches so that the little girl thought it looked like a person clapping her hands for joy. Then a flame sprang from the tree, and out of the flame flew a singing bird. When the bird flew away the little girl saw that her brother's bones had disappeared, and she knew that he was alive and happy.

January 14, 1962

THE HOLY THORN BLOOMS FOR ROYALTY

As the time drew near for Queen Elizabeth's visit, everyone at the Washington Cathedral was anxiously waiting to see whether the Holy Thorn in the Cathedral Close would be in bloom for her, as it was when she came to this country as Princess Elizabeth, in November 1951, and as it always does—they say—at the approach of royalty. When the Queen Mother was here, also in November, one blossom, high up in the tree, was picked for her. When the Prince of Wales was here in November 1919, two or three flowers were found and presented to him in a silver box, by the Bishop of Washington, according to the custom of Glastonbury Abbey.

The Washington Thorn is a scion of the English hawthorn, *Crataegus monogyna* var. *praecox* [*C. m.* 'Biflora'], which is said to have grown from the staff of Joseph of Arimathea, who went to Britain soon after the Ascension of Our Lord, and made his way to Glastonbury. One day, during the Christmas season, he stuck his staff in the ground, and when he tried to pick it up again, he found that it had taken root and burst into bloom. From then on, until the Reformation, when some fanatic cut it down, it bloomed at odd times during the year, but especially at Christmas and Easter. New growth sprang up from the roots of the original tree, and this blooms at Glastonbury still. From it a cutting was sent to the Washington Cathedral in 1901. The Washington Thorn is now about twenty-five feet tall, with a thirty-foot spread.

Some time ago I wrote Nancy Hawkins, a member of the Cathedral Altar Guild, asking her to let me know if there were any hawthorn blossoms on October the twentieth, when Queen Elizabeth came to the dedication of the War Memorial Chapel. It was a most appropriate occasion for the Queen's visit, as her father, George VI, gave the hand wrought silver cross, candlesticks, and vases for the chapel altar, and the Queen Mother was one of the eighty British women who made the needlepoint for the cushions.

Nancy wrote that the twentieth was a day of brilliant sunshine after the rain of the day before. "I had a seat in the chapel," she said, "and the Queen walked up the aisle on my side. She had a deep blue coat and a little hat, and her eyes are the bluest things I've ever seen."

After the service Nancy walked through the cathedral grounds to look at the thorn tree. "Sure enough, it had quite a few blooms scattered here and there. It has been blooming a little all fall." She picked a small cluster to put in her letter for proof. The blossoms are small creamy ones, and not very pretty in themselves, but effective when the tree is in full bloom.

I was interested to find an Ohio nurseryman advertising the Holy Thorn in a recent number of one of the popular garden magazines. He offers an eight to ten foot tree, complete with the legend on a parchment scroll, for ten dollars. However, the English hawthorn is not an easy tree to grow in this country, and the one at the cathedral requires a good deal of care to keep it in good health.

A number of trees have autumn- and winter-blooming forms, or produce an occasional blossom out of season. There was a flower of *Magnolia grandiflora* at the Fall Flower Show, and the almost ever-blooming *Magnolia* × *soulangiana* 'Lennei' in my garden has had flowers until very recently.

Mrs. Huffman wrote of a dogwood in full bloom in September, and at the same time there was a picture in the *Observer* of a pear tree in blossom at the Dilworth Methodist Church. There are several autumnal cherries in town, but the one I watch for is at the back of Mrs. Church's garden. I have found it in bloom in November and in January, and sometimes there is a scattering of blossoms all winter. Then it blooms at the usual time in the spring, as freely as if it had not bloomed before.

November 3, 1957

THE CHRISTIAN YEAR PARALLELS THE GARDEN YEAR

The Christian year follows the garden year so closely that I seldom think of one without being reminded of the other. As the days begin to lengthen, and the Lenten lilies come into bloom, it seems appropriate for the gospel of the day to be a parable of seed time.

On the fifth Sunday after Epiphany we hear about the parable of the wheat and tares and the man who sowed good seed. In the night his enemy came and scattered tares among the wheat; and on the Second Sunday before Lent we hear another parable of the soils about the sower who went out to sow his seed on fertile soils along with rocky soils.

In England, when the Book of Common Prayer was new, the congregation must have been made up of sowers who went out to sow the Lenten grains: barley, peas, oats, and corn.

I seem to remember that Mammy, who came from Georgia, always planted her vegetables on Good Friday, and I am told that in South Carolina this is still the custom. I have always heard that parsley should be planted on Good Friday only, and under a rising moon. In *A Witch's Guide to Gardening*, Dorothy Jacob says four times as many seeds as are needed must be sown, for parsley is the devil's plant, and he will claim his share. The seed will be slow in coming up; it must go to the devil nine times before it germinates.

The ancient custom of lighting bonfires on the first Sunday in Lent, and on Easter Eve, was handed down to the Christians by the pagans, who believed that the fire made the land fertile, the crops abundant, and man and beast free from all evil. When I am driving through the country in late winter and early spring, burnt-over fields make me wonder whether the Lenten fires may not have been a very good practice.

The peasants who ran through the orchards waving their flaming torches under the branches of the fruit trees, and through the fields, exorcising mice, darnel, and smut, must have accomplished much the same thing as the modern farmers who found that burning over the alfalfa fields destroys weevil eggs. The ashes from the Easter Eve fires were scattered over the fields on Easter Monday, and some were mixed with the seed corn.

The Lenten lily is the English daffodil, the little early yellow trumpet that came over with the colonists and has become naturalized in parts of the South, where it is often called buttercup. The other day Laura Braswell told me she had some buttercups to bring me, and when she came she had a bunch of daffodils. She said the bulbs came from Lincolnton. I should have known better, for the bulbs are often advertised in the market bulletins as buttercups.

A. E. Housman wrote a poem about the Lenten lily and its brief flowering:

> And there's the Lenten lily
> That has not long to stay
> And dies on Easter day.

Tennyson wrote of the Lenten lily, but the earlier poets Spenser, Shakespeare, and Herrick called the trumpet narcissus the daffodil. It was also called the Lent rose. Lenten rose is a name for *Helleborus orientalis* and its hybrids must have been an invention of the Victorians.

The first three days in March, the Rev. Hilderic Friend writes in *Flowers and Flower Lore*, "were formerly called blind days, and, being unlucky, the farmers would never sow any seed on these days."

There is still a belief in Devonshire and in other places that if seeds, flowers, and plants be put in the ground on Good Friday, they will grow all the better for it; but strange to say, exactly the reverse is believed by some people.

In Sussex the peasants used to look forward to Good Friday as a regular day for working in their cottage gardens, and I find the same belief in the neighborhood where I am now living.

When I was a child I wondered why Good Friday was called good. Spending the day in the garden was the only relief I knew for the overwhelming sadness that weighed upon me. The child is close to the savage, and the yearly recognition of the cycle of life and death, in the festival of the dead and risen god, is as old as the history of man.

March 19, 1967

HOLIDAY WREATHS

Just before Thanksgiving I wrote to Mr. Starker to ask him to lend me a photograph of one of his wreaths. I thought that it would be of particular interest after his talk here in the fall, and I was afraid that mine wouldn't come from Oregon in time to have its picture taken before Christmas. When he sent the picture, he wrote that he was already gathering material for this year's wreaths: "Right now we are starting on the pine wreaths. They keep wonderfully if left out of doors on the grass. We expect the juniper to arrive any day from southern Oregon. It is lovely this year, with fine big blue frosty berries. The first holly will come next week."

Mr. Starker uses the English holly, which grows so well in Oregon. We can get the same effect with the foliage of Chinese holly, and if it hasn't berries, berries of *Pyracantha formosana* [*P. koidzumii*] are as bright and red and glossy as those of the English holly.

Our juniper has berries as blue and frosty as Mr. Starker's and leaves as fragrant, but we have nothing that smells as good as balsam, though the Chinese fir (*Cunninghamia*) might substitute for form and texture. Last year I did a wreath of the fronds of Chinese fir with bunches of pyracantha berries. I don't know the name of the evergreen with small oval leaves that Mr. Starker is so found of using, but I think yaupon holly could take its place.

Holly and ivy, mistletoe, rosemary, and bay are the traditional Christmas greens. I was startled to read in one of the popular garden magazines that English ivy is a "newcomer to holiday decorative material." The writer must have been deaf not to have heard one of the oldest of the English carols, "The Holly and the Ivy," or "When Christmastide comes in like a bride, with holly and ivy clad."

It is a pity that rosemary and bay have been forgotten. If nothing else, they should be used for their fragrance. Rosemary is all the better for being pinched, and my green bay tree, which has grown to twelve feet in nine years, in spite of its frequent contributions to the kitchen, can still furnish Mrs. Broward with clippings for her arrangements of plants from the Bible.

Box is sometimes used in Christmas decorations, but it is not in the tradition. Box belongs to Lent. It is supposed to go up on Candlemas

Day, the second of February, when the Christmas greens come down (I suppose the foliage and berries lasted longer in unheated houses and churches), and to stay until the dawn of Easter Day.

In our family we consider galax leaves as a part of Christmas. They grow in our garden, but not freely enough to allow much picking. Sometimes they can be had from the florist. A galax wreath is made by coating the leaves with shellac and laying them one by one on a padded form, winding a string over the stems as you go. They are a lot easier on the hands than juniper and holly, and there is something very satisfying in the roundness of the wreath and the roundness of the wine-stained leaves.

Mr. Starker also makes cone and pod wreaths that keep from year to year. He uses a wide variety of materials: some from the woods and fields around him, and some from far and wide. Mrs. Broward has made a beautiful one of materials collected right here, among them some small snuff-colored cones that she says are cones for the sugar pine.

I never heard of a sugar pine (if anyone has, please enlighten me) but I shall keep my eyes open from now on. Cone collecting can become as absorbing as shell collecting. The unopened cones of the pond pine are shaped like toys. If they don't get wet they stay round and glossy for years. I brought some home from Lake Phelps, and used them with sycamore balls to decorate a wreath of sea oats. Mrs. Broward's small brown wreath of sugar-pine cones, sweet gum balls, acorns large and small, small smooth pecans, felted magnolia seed pods for contrast in texture and size, and—at the other end of the scale—the tiny cones of the deodar is kept from year to year as a center for a larger wreath of fresh evergreens.

Now I must begin a search for acorns with a variety of cups; the small saucers of the water oak; the deep, fringed cups of the mossy cup oak, and those of the overcup oak which almost cover the acorn. But to get back to Mr. Starker: "We don't know yet, what we will do for Christmas." He wrote, "We hope we will be invited out—but can't depend on it. The family always seems to think our house fits a gathering best."

December 22, 1957

THE ADVENT WREATH

The Christian year and the garden year begin before the end of the calendar year, at the time when the growing season is over, the harvest in and new green already springing from the earth. The first season of the Christian year is Advent, the fourth Sunday before Christmas, a period of repentance and preparation for the coming of Christ. The lily of the valley is the season's emblem.

An old custom of making a wreath of evergreens for Advent has recently been revived. The wreath itself is a symbol of eternity, as it has no beginning and no end, and the evergreens, never leafless, have the same significance. Four candles, one to be lighted each Sunday before Christmas, stand for Christ, the Light of the World. Sometimes a fifth, in the center, is lighted on Christmas Day. In church the candles are lighted at the morning services, and at home at the evening meal.

The wreath is a survival of pagan customs, older than Christianity, when on the short days of the winter solstice men brought evergreen boughs in their houses, and lighted bonfires on the long nights to remind themselves that winter would end and warmth and light and green leaves would come again in spring.

The Advent wreath is made of seven evergreens representing the seven-fold gifts of the Holy Spirit, which Isaiah names as wisdom and understanding, counsel and ghostly strength, knowledge and true godliness and holy fear. The choice of evergreens will depend upon the supply, but the following are recommended as of particular significance: ivy as a reminder of human weakness and dependence upon God; cypress for eternal life; bay (or laurel) for victory over death; rosemary, sacred to the Virgin; holly for the crown of thorns; juniper (or cedar) for incense; and mistletoe, green in winter on the leafless tree, as a sign of eternal life in the face of death. There is no substitute for mistletoe.

In *A Merry Christmas Herbal*, Adelma Simmons writes of festivities that begin on the first Sunday in Advent at Caprilands, her Connecticut farm, and last until Epiphany. She tells the legends of the Advent saints, gives directions for the decorations she makes, gives the receipts she uses for holiday food and drinks, and describes folk customs she observes on each occasion. She also describes the culture of thirty-six herbs for the Christmas garden and tells how to make herbal gifts from kitchen and garden.

At Caprilands the Advent wreath is made of juniper and trimmed with herbs. The herbs chosen for it are: lavender for the purity of the Virgin; sage for immortality; horehound because it comes from Palestine and is nice with sage; rue, the herb of grace; santolina because it lasts well; thyme, a manger herb; wild strawberries, dedicated to the Virgin; rosemary; gallium, Our Lady's bedstraw; pennyroyal, an aromatic herb supposed to bloom at midnight on Christmas Eve; and costmary, or bible leaf, the herb used by Mary Magdalene to make the precious ointment.

Early in December Mrs. Simmons celebrates the festivals of Saint Barbara, Saint Nicholas, and Saint Lucy. Saint Barbara's Day is December 4. Her symbol is the tower in which her father imprisoned her to keep her unspotted from the world. Her flower is herb Saint Barbara, *Barbarea vulgaris*, a small crucifer called wintercress and used for winter salads. It was once considered a wound herb. In paintings, Saint Barbara is often shown with the martyr's palm in her hand for victory over death. December 6 is the feast of Saint Nicholas, archbishop of Myra. His flower is a South African heath, *Erica nudiflora*. He is a legendary figure and patron of children and sailors. Saint Lucy's day is December 13. She is a Sicilian saint who traveled to Sweden, where the thirteenth is celebrated as a feast of lights, a survival of the pagan bonfires of the winter solstice. Lucy comes from *lux*, meaning light, and she carries a flame or a lamp. The arborvitae is dedicated to her.

November 24, 1968

LEGEND AND LORE OF THE CHRISTMAS TREE

For years I have been collecting lore and legend of the Christmas season, and now I find that I might have saved myself the trouble, for all that I have, and much more, has been gathered together in *The Christmas Tree* by Daniel J. Foley.

The early Christians, Mr. Foley writes, took their symbols from the Old Testament: the Tree of Jesse (with the Cross at the top, and the Star of David at the base) had the family of the Jews as its root, Mary as its stem, and Christ as its flower; the Tree of Life reminded men that "out of the ground made the Lord God to grow every tree that is pleasant to the sight, and good for food"; and the Tree of Knowledge reminded them that "in Adam's fall, we sinned all."

In the Middle Ages, the church celebrated Advent by giving plays that told the story of the Garden of Eden. On the stage was a fir tree hung with apples, and Eve picked one of these to give to Adam.

When, at the end of the fifteenth century, the performances became too hilarious, they were no longer allowed, but Mr. Foley says that people continued to celebrate the holiday season at home by setting up little evergreens, the symbol of immortality, and decorating them with apples, the symbol of sin. Later they added small round wafers, as a symbol of the Sacred Host, the fruit of redemption. Later still, cookies cut in the shape of stars, flowers, bells, angels, hearts, and animals, took the place of the wafers.

The custom of putting tapers on the tree came from the lighting of a candle on Christmas Eve to remind men that Christ is the Light of the World. "In Germany, instead of a single candle many small ones were placed on a light stock or pyramid made of shelves of graduated widths. When lighted the effect was that of an elaborate candelabra gleaming with cheerful flames on several levels. The name *Lichstock* clearly defines the purpose of this candle stand which was decorated with baubles and tinsel to give it a truly festive appearance. The paradise tree and the lighted stand or pyramid with its candles when combined produced what we know today as the Christmas tree."

In parts of Germany a tree was trimmed for each child, or member of the family, a custom described by Elizabeth in the story of her German Garden. "Every time the three babies go into the garden they expect to meet the Christ Child with His arms full of gifts," she wrote. "They firmly believe that it is thus that their presents are brought, and it is such a charming idea that Christmas would be worth celebrating for its sake alone. The library is uninhabitable for several days before and after, as it is there that we have the trees and presents. All down one side are the trees, and the other sides are lined with tables and presents, a separate one for each person in the house. When the trees are lighted, and stand in their radiance shining down on the happy faces, I forget all the trouble it has been."

Mr. Foley says that "in most European countries it was the Child Jesus who brought the gifts at Christmas. The children were told the legend that on the eve of His birth, a little child came with His angels to trim their trees and place their presents under it . . . The gifts were given on the basis of good behavior, and so as this custom developed there arose the idea of a reward for good children and punishment for the bad."

December 4, 1960

INTERNATIONAL CHRISTMAS TREES

The nicest thing that happens at Christmastime is the trimming of the trees for the Mint Museum. They are done by the Charlotte Garden Club, one for each gallery, showing all aspects of the season—the solemn, the gay, the holiday feasting—in all parts of the world.

The ornaments on the Chrismon tree are all symbols of Christ. They were made of white styrofoam and gold beads, by the Lutheran women of Christ's Church. A Chrismon is a monogram made from X and P (Chi and Rho), the first two letters of the Greek word for Christ. The first and last letters of the Greek alphabet, Alpha and Omega, also stand for Christ. "I am Alpha and Omega, the beginning and the end." The cross stands for Christ the Redeemer, and the cross over a circle (the world) is a reminder of His command "Go ye into all the world." Other symbols are the Sun of Righteousness, the Crown of Victory, the butterfly (which stands for the resurrection), the fish (an early Christian mystical symbol of Christ), and the rose, which stands for the nativity of our Lord.

I know a rose-tree springing
Forth from an ancient root,
As men of old were singing,
From Jesse came the shoot
That bore a blossom bright
Amid the cold of winter,
When half-spent was the night.

In Italy a pyramidal stand, called a *ceppo*, takes the place of the tree. The one the museum uses is red lacquer trimmed in gold. On the lowest shelf are the gaily wrapped presents, above this a crèche, then fruit, then a compotier filled with colored balls, and above it another filled with candy. On each corner of each shelf there is a candle in a red glass tumbler and at the very top a large golden star.

The English tree—with its real candles, candy lanterns and coins and chubby chocolate angels done up in red and gold tinfoil and at the top a fairylike angel with real hair and gauzy wings—will remind those of my generation of their childhood. It is a modest counterpart of the one featured in the *Illustrated London News* in 1848, showing Prince Albert, Queen Victoria, and the royal family gathered around it at Windsor: "On each tier, or branch, are arranged a dozen wax tapers. Pendent from the branches are elegant trays, baskets, bonbonniers, and other receptacles for sweetmeats, of the most varied and expensive kind; and of all forms, colours, and degrees of beauty. Fancy cakes, gilt gingerbread and eggs filled with sweetmeats, are also suspended by variously-colored ribbons from the branches."

The kindergarten tree is hung with ornaments that a child could make: painted pinecones and sweet-gum balls, plastic beads and paper ornaments.

The Danish tree is done in red and white, the colors of the Danish flag, with strings and strings of tiny bright red pennants bearing the white cross. There are enchanting dolls in peasant costumes and delicate scissor cuts of stars and swans that are like illustrations for Andersen's fairy tales. The heart-shaped baskets of red and white paper woven in a checkered pattern are traditional.

In Austria, children are allowed to eat all the candy they want at Christmas, so the trees are hung with sweets. This one has white candles, candies in twists of shredded white tissue paper, and round cookies with holes in the middle.

The Japanese tree is for the New Year. It is of silvered bamboo, and is trimmed with toys and paper lanterns.

In the main gallery there is a big tree, reaching to the ceiling. Fourteen gossamer angels flit through branches hung with crystal icicles and snowflakes, and golden balls and bows of gold ribbon, bringing the Christmas tradition up to date in a modern interpretation.

December 23, 1962

THE FLOWERS OF THE TRINITY

While I was browsing in *Flowers and Flower Lore*, trying to find what Rev. Hilderic Friend has to say about the passion flower, I came across several references to trinity, and as it is now that season, I thought it a good time to look further. Two flowers are called herb trinity: the pansy and the hepatica, the pansy because there are three colors (violet, yellow and white) in one flower, and the hepatica, *Hepatica triloba* [*H. americana*] because the leaf has three lobes.

In *Saints and Their Flowers*, Gladys Taylor quotes an herbal (1562) by William Bulletin, *Dr. of Phisicke:* "I read in an old Monkish written Herball, wherein the author writeth, that this herb did signify the Holy Trinitie; and therefore was called the Herbe of the Trinity, and thus he made his allegorie. This flower is but one in which said he, are three sundry colours, and yet but one sweet savour. So God is three distinct persones, in one Undivided Trinity. United in one eternall glory . . . God send thee hartes-ease. For it is much better with poverty to have the same, than to be a Kyng with a miserable mynde. Pray God give thee but one handful of heavenly hartes-ease, which passeth all the pleasaunt flowers that grow in this world."

Trilliums are called trinity flowers, and *Trillium grandiflorum* is the trinity lily. Mrs. Juliana Ewing wrote a story about it, *The Blind Hermit and the Trinity Flower*. The species she had in mind was *Trillium undulatum*, the painted trillium.

The hermit in the story had spent his life healing sick people with the herbs he grew, and when he became blind he prayed to find an herb to give him back his sight. He had a vision of the flower that would make him see, and he told his little serving boy about it: "it was about the size of Herb Paris, but instead of being fourfold every way, it numbered the mystic Three. Every part was threefold. The leaves were three, the petals three, the sepals three. The flower was snow-white, but on each of the three parts it was stained with crimson stripes, like garments dyed in blood."

A root of the plant was brought by a heavenly messenger, and the boy watched over it. They thought that when it bloomed the old man would see again. And he did, "but his vision opened on eternal day." Trinity grass is one of the trefoils, perhaps the shamrock, though that cannot be positively identified, as "shamrock" is a generic name for any three-leaved plant.

St. Patrick is supposed to have won over his hostile audience, when he returned to Ireland in 433, by picking a shamrock, and saying, "Is it not as possible for the Father, Son, and Holy Ghost, to be one as for these three leaves to grow upon a single stalk?" The three leaves stand for Faith, Hope, and Charity. The story is apocryphal, for it is not in any biography of St. Patrick. He was not the first to use the trefoil as a sacred symbol, for it was held as such by the ancient Persians, and the Arabic name for it is *shamrakh*. It was used in the festivals of the ancient Greeks, and Pliny says no serpent would go near it. So it is easy to see how it would become associated with St. Patrick who is supposed to have driven the snakes from Ireland.

The trefoil was long held to be a protection against witches and magic:

> Woe, woe to the wight,
> Who meets the green knight,
> Except on his faulchion arm,
> Spell-proof, he bear, like the brave St. Clair,
> The holy trefoil's charm.

The blessed herb, *Geum urbanum*, is called herb Bennet, a corruption of *Herba Benedicta*, or perhaps from its connection with St. Benedict. Though an inconspicuous and lowly roadside weed, it was considered a cure for all ills, and a protection against all evil: "Where the root is in the house, Satan can do nothing and flies from it, wherefore it is blessed before all other herbs, and if a man carries the root about him no venomous beast can harm him" (Ortus Sanitalis, 1491).

From the thirteenth century onward, the three-parted leaf, as a symbol of the Holy Trinity, and the five-petalled flower, for the five wounds of our Lord, were painted on church walls, and carved on the capitals of the columns.

August 1, 1965

THE FLOWERS OF PASSIONTIDE

For Lenten reading I have been browsing in *Flower Lore* by Hilderic Friend, *Flowering Plants* by Anne Pratt, and *Modern Herbal* by Maude Grieve, collecting notes on the customs and beliefs of Passiontide, the season which begins with the Fifth Sunday in Lent, "when the Church begins her public grief," and ends with Holy Week and Easter.

Like all the Church seasons, Passiontide has its flowers, and "the cross of our blessed Lord may be said to fling its shadow over the whole vegetable world. From this time the trees and flowers which had been associated with heathen rites and deities began to be connected with holier names, and not infrequently with the Crucifixion itself" (R. J. King).

The passion flower, "with symbol holy," is the first to come to mind. It has, the old monks said, "the Marks of the Passion, Nailes, Pillar, Whippes, Thornes, Wounds." The *Passifloras* belong to the New World, and so they were not known until the sixteenth century, but in the Middle Ages plants of the Old World were associated with Gethsemane and Golgotha.

The crown imperial was said to have grown in the garden of Gethsemane. When all the other flowers bowed low before Christ, it stood proudly erect, and was rebuked; ever since the flowers have been drooping.

Two potherbs were eaten at Passiontide. Young leaves of *Rumex patientia*, called passions (a corruption of patience), were cooked as a vegetable, and the tops of passion-dock, *Polygonum bistorta* (also called patience), went into puddings that were in some places a special dish for Good Friday or Easter.

Parsign-dock was also called Easter giant or mangiant (a corruption of the French *mangeant*); both leaves and roots, Culpeper says, "have a powerful faculty to resist all poison. The root in powder, taken in drink, expelleth the venom of the plague, the small-pox, measles, purples, or any other infectious disease."

Tansy, in particular, is associated with Easter as a survival of the bitter herbs of the Passover. Tansy teas were brewed in Lent, tansy puddings stirred up for Easter Day, and tansy cakes were baked. Even in this country receipts for tansies are sometimes advertised in garden papers.

In Palestine, Friend says, wallflowers are called "blood drops of Christ," and certain plants supposed to have been growing at the foot of the cross were forever after marked with dark spots.

Among these were *Arum maculatum* (called Gethsemane in parts of England), the purple orchis (*Orchis mascula*), and *Polygonum persicaria*, the spotted persicaria:

> Those deep unwrought marks
> The Villager will tell you
> Are the flower's portion
> From the stoning blood
> On Calvary shed.

A dwarf birch native to Scotland was thought to have provided the scourges, but a more general belief is that they were taken from the willow, which has wept ever since.

Any number of plants have been assigned by tradition to the crown of thorns: *Ziziphus spina-christi*, *Paliurus spina-christi*, *Euphorbia splendens*, the briar rose, the buckthorn, the black thorn, and the white thorn. In Italy the barberry is called the Holy Thorn.

The Judas tree, not our native species, but *Cercis siliquastrum*, is generally believed to be the tree on which Judas hanged himself, but some say it was the elder. There is also a tradition that the cross was made from the elder. Ben Jonson and Gerard, and other poets and herbalists, held to this belief, but others believed the tree to have been the aspen (and that is why the leaves tremble), mistletoe (once a forest tree but condemned thereafter to be a parasite), ash, oak, pine, dogwood, and so on. And some say the cross was made of four kinds of wood.

> Nailed were his feet to
> Cedar, to Palm his hands
> Cypress His body bore,
> Title on Olive stands.

March 27, 1966

THE STORY OF THE PASSION FLOWER

The Passion-floure long has blowed.
To becken us signs of the Holy Roode.
—Dr. Foster's Perennial Calendar 1824

In the seventeenth century, the Spanish missionaries took *Passiflora caerulea* to explain the Crucifixion, just as St. Patrick picked a shamrock to explain the Trinity. Since then, the parts of the flower have been interpreted in various ways, but in *Saints and Their Flowers*, Gladys Taylor gives a comprehensive list: the five-lobed leaves stand for the hands of Christ's persecutors; the seed pod, the sponge dipped in vinegar; the tendrils, the whips and cords with which our Lord was scourged; the five petals and five sepals, the ten disciples, leaving out Peter who denied and Judas who betrayed; the pistil, the column where Christ was scourged (or some say the cross itself); the triple style, the three nails; the five stamens, the five wounds; the filaments, the Crown of Thorns; the fringed corona, the halo; the color (blue), Heaven; and the three days that the flower lasts, the time between the Crucifixion and the Resurrection. The last is pure fancy. The flowers last only a day.

The flower became the emblem of Passion Sunday (the Fifth Sunday in Lent) and Holy Cross Day (the fourteenth of September). Holy Cross (or Holy Rood, being the earlier name for cross) is the feast of the Elevation of the Cross, celebrating the consecration of the Church of the Holy Sepulcher at Jerusalem in 335 AD.

In the decoration of churches the flower takes a place beside the rose and the trefoil, especially in the rood screen (surmounted by the cross) of carved wood or stone or wrought iron, which separates the nave from the chancel.

The passion flower is one of the flowers of the dead. The Reverend Hilderic Friend says the Queen had a wreath of white roses and camellias and passion flowers placed on the coffin of young Prince Waldemar, and that more recently they were on the coffin "of the lamented President of the United States." (Lincoln?)

Passiflora caerulea is but one of the some three hundred species of passion flower, most of them native to our hemisphere, and a dozen of them native to the United States. In *Passifloras for Your Garden*, Florence

Knock, who has the largest private collection in this country, describes twenty-five of the species she has grown. She has been many years in collecting them, and growing them from seed, some coming from correspondents in Australia and New Zealand. In the book she gives specific and detailed directions for propagating them and for growing them indoors and outdoors; she tells where to get seeds and plants. As Mrs. Knock lives in Minneapolis, Minnesota, and the passion flowers are mostly tropical plants, she grows them in the garden in summer, and pots them before frost and brings them into the house to winter in a sunny window.

Though none of the species is absolutely hardy in Minnesota, several have survived a number of winters, and I think we should do some experimenting in this climate. *Passiflora caerulea*, the best known and one of the most beautiful kinds, is said to be hardy with protection as far north as New York.

P. coccinea is grown in gardens in Shreveport, Louisiana, and I think it would certainly be worth trying here. *P.* × *violacea* is the one that Mrs. Knock has found hardiest, but unfortunately she can give no commercial source for it at present. And of course, there is our own delightful Maypop, *Passiflora incarnata*. The Maypop has taken up in my garden, and my only problem is to keep it from taking over. At present I have *P. trifasciata*, which I got this spring from the Merry Gardens. It has not grown very fast, and probably won't bloom this season, but that doesn't matter, as the variegated leaves are more ornamental than the flowers.

July 25, 1965

RITUALS OF THE PALMS

Wearing palms on Palm Sunday, and carrying them in procession, is a survival of an ancient custom handed down to Christians from earlier ages. I suppose its origin was already lost in time when the Greeks went about singing and wearing garlands to welcome the spring, a custom that still lingers in parts of Europe.

In Rome, *Palma nobilis* was the prize at chariot races and the token of victory in battle. It became the symbol of Christ's victory over death and the emblem of martyrdom. As Christianity spread in Europe, real palms brought by pilgrims from the Holy Land were used in the processions, but when these were not available, evergreens (the symbol of immortality) such as yew, holly, juniper, and especially box, were substituted.

The Boxwood Society has recently published in their bulletin an English résumé of Dr. A. J. Kemper's book, *A Humble Bush That Became a Symbol*, in which he writes that the consecrated box sprigs, called palms, were a Christian version of the green bough of earlier spring festivals.

"To primitive peoples those trees and bushes which kept their evergreen appearance during the winter season when the whole of Nature seemed dead were highly convincing proof of an everlasting vitality and energy. What happened in Nature was another manifestation of the divine life, holiness, truth and reality, which is the spiritual background of this natural and human world. Green boughs consequently are not merely symbols of a natural life but even more so of supernatural values. With their help Man can be in direct contact with that higher world."

As a symbol, Dr. Kemper writes, the green bough has much in common with the golden bough that admitted Aeneas into the world of the dead, and the golden-leaved staff of Hermes, who led the dead to the lower world.

The consecrated palms or box branches, like the green boughs, were instruments of vitality and fertility and a protection from evil and misfortune. They were hung in houses to bring a blessing. At the end of the year they were burned, and scattered over the fields, or mixed with seed before sowing. Sometimes the branches were planted as a protection against hail and lightning. They were also hung on trees to bring rain in dry weather. There is an old saying that if it rains on the palms on Palm Sunday, it will rain on gardens on Corpus Christi (the Thursday after Trinity Sunday).

In the Netherlands bunches of box are tied on poles, and often at the top there is a little cock (made of bread) with a sprig of box stuck on his head. I find in *The Golden Bough* that the cock stands for the corn spirit, and it is killed at harvest, but is represented as rising to new life at seed time. The poles with cocks on them were seldom consecrated, and sometimes they are decorated with oranges and candies. Children carried them from door to door, and are given little presents—something like a trick-or-treat.

When Christ entered Jerusalem palms and olive branches were thrown before him because they were growing by the wayside, but also as symbols of victory and peace, and for their significance to the Jews. At the Feast of the Tabernacles, after the fruit of the land was gathered, they were to take "boughs of trees, branches of palm trees, and branches of thick trees, and willows of the brook" and to rejoice before the Lord for seven days.

In England and in Russia budding branches of willow take the place of palms. A writer in *The Gentleman's Magazine* (1779) says, "With us in the North the children go out into the fields apalmsoning, as they call it, and gather the flowering buds of the sallow." In some churchyards a monumental palm cross was decorated on Palm Sunday with palms or palm substitutes. In England the yew was frequently used for this purpose and that may be the reason that there are yews in most old churchyards.

April 7, 1968

ROGATION DAYS—THE BLESSING OF THE CROPS

In the spring there were editorials in two of the *Southern Market Bulletins* about the revival of the old custom of setting aside the Rogation Days to ask a blessing on the fruits of the earth, and to give thanks for the Lord's bounty. This year Rogation Sunday (the fifth Sunday after Easter) fell on the eleventh of May. Gov. Lester Maddox of Georgia proclaimed May 11–18 as Soil Stewardship Week, a special time for giving thanks for soil, water, and natural resources and for stressing the importance of using them wisely and preserving them for the future. "We must be ever mindful that the earth is the Lord's," Maddox said.

In proclaiming May 11–18 as Soil Stewardship Week in Mississippi, Gov. John Bell Williams spoke of "the infinite variety in the quality and capabilities of the land that the Lord has entrusted to us" and asked for support of the State Soil and Water Committee.

Rogation comes from the Latin *rogare*, to ask. Asking a blessing on the crops is a survival of pagan customs. On the twenty-fifth of April the Romans celebrated the Robigalia, carrying garlands in processions and beseeching the god Robigus to protect the young corn from blight.

In the early Church the Rogation Days replaced this festival, and the custom spread to Gaul. St. Gregory of Tours described the Rogations order by Mamertus, the Bishop of Vienne, for the three days before Ascension in 477. From Gaul, St. Augustine took the custom to England. Strype, the English historian, tells about the processions in Queen Mary's reign. In 1554, "Rogation Week being come, May 3 being Holy Thursday, at the court of St. James's, the Queen went in procession within St. James's, with heralds and sergeants of arms, and four bishops mitered. And all three days there went her chapel about the fields." Masses were said at St. Giles's, St. Martin in the Fields, and Westminster.

In Queen Elizabeth's reign the religion changed, but the Rogation Days were still observed with processions, garlands, and singing. They sang the 103rd Psalm, "Praise the Lord, O my soul, and forget not all his benefits," and the Benedicite Omnia Opera, "O all ye Green Things upon the earth, bless ye the Lord: praise him and magnify him forever."

After the Reformation the processions were no longer public affairs, but the Rogation Days were celebrated by walking the boundaries of the parish and praying for the crops. The priest or curate led the procession, and stopped under some large tree, usually an oak and therefore called the holy oak, to read psalms and passages from the gospels. Robert Herrick wrote a poem about it: "Dearest, bury me / Under that holy oke or Gospel Tree; / Where though thou see'st not, thou may'st yet think upon / Me when you yearly go'st Procession."

All sorts of flowers were woven into garlands to carry in the processions, but one in particular, the milkwort, *Polygala vulgaris*, was called the Rogation flower. Milkwort, John Gerard said in his Herbal, "is called by Dodonaeus, *Flos Ambervalis*, because it doth especially flower in the Cross or Gang week, or Rogation week: of which flowers the maidens which use in the countries to walk in the Procession do make themselves garland and nosegaies: in English we may call it Cross-flower or Procession-flower, Gang-flower, and Milkwort, of their virtues in procuring milk in the brests of nurses."

The Ambervalia was another Roman festival. It was known as *Lustratio Agrorum*, and took place on the twenty-ninth of May. One of the meanings of *lustration* is "a going about." The flowers of the milkwort are purple, pale blue, or lilac. "Our milkwort is little heeded now," Anne Pratt says. "But few lovers of wild flowers would pass it without a thought of praise for its beauty, as they see it among the short grass of the hillside, where 'it purples all the ground with vernal flowers.' "

The collect for the Rogation Days is: "Almighty God, Lord of heaven and earth; we beseech thee to pour forth thy blessing upon this land, and to give us a fruitful season; that we, constantly receiving thy bounty, may evermore give thanks unto thee in thy holy Church. Through Jesus Christ our Lord. Amen."

July 27, 1969

EIGHT

Bits and Pieces

ASAFETIDA

In "Things I Remember" (a feature in the Sunday edition of *The State and Columbia Record*), Zan Heyward mentions the asafetida bags that school children used to wear around their neck "to keep off the onslaught of various and sundry diseases to which the human body is heir." To get at the facts about their use is difficult, he writes, so I have been doing a little research myself.

I asked Hannah Withers if she ever heard of asafetida, and she said she had not only heard of it, she had worn it. She said Uncle Charles used to hang a bag around her neck before she left for school. Then I asked Mary Harris and she said she wore one too. "It must have worked," she said, "because none of us ever caught anything."

Then I wondered what asafetida is. I find that it is a fetid gum that comes from the roots of several plants of the carrot family, but as far as I can tell no one grows the plant. The gum comes from the drug store. I called the Charlotte Drug Company, which never fails me, and asked if they carry it. They do. I asked if people still buy it. They do. I asked what they buy it for. "They wear it and eat it," the pharmacist said. "Do you wear it or eat it?" I asked. He said, "No, M'am!" I asked Hannah and Mary Harris whether they had ever taken asafetida internally, and neither of them had.

So I asked my South Carolina authority on plant lore, Elizabeth Russell, whether she had ever heard of its use as a food or medicine, and she said that the gum steeped in whiskey is good for indigestion, and that they give it to babies for colic. In the old days people wore asafetida bags to funerals. (That was before the custom of embalming.) She had never heard of using it to flavor food. That is a French custom, I think, although Goldsmith's *The Citizen of the World* says, "I am for sauce strong with asafetida or fuming with garlic." In India and Persia asafetida is used as a condiment.

I asked Elizabeth Russell if she ever heard that asafetida has magic properties. She says she has not, but I have read somewhere, and made a note of it in my files, that it is sometimes used in conjure bags. It must be dug when "blood is in the moon."

Mrs. Grieve in *A Modern Herbal* says asafetida is good for colic, asthma, bronchitis and whooping cough. It is also supposed to be useful for hysteria and malingering, as its bitter and acrid taste, and its odor (stronger and more unpleasant than garlic), are so nasty that a second dose is sure to be avoided. "Some stynkinge thynges ben put in medycynes," John de Trevisa wrote in 1298, such "as Brymstoon and Asaafedida."

But one man's meat is another man's poison and it is possible, in a short time, not only to get used to an unpleasant taste or smell, but to find it acceptable or even pleasant. So some call asafetida "Devil's Dung" and others call it "Food of the Gods."

The chief source of the drug is *Ferula assa-foetida*, the giant fennel of southwestern Asia. It doesn't seem to be in the American trade, at least I have never come across it, and no source is given in the *Plant Buyer's Guide*. But it is recommended as a handsome foliage plant for the herbaceous border (though it would have to be a large border, for the giant fennels grow to eight feet and more), or to plant with shrubs or near water. Mrs. Grieve says it grows on the high plains of Afghanistan, and the great heads are eaten raw by the natives.

Ferula communis is considered the most handsome of the giant fennels for the garden. It is called *ferula*, from *ferire*—to strike, and was used as a rod, Loudon says, because the stalk makes a loud noise without much hurting the palm of the schoolboy.

Sophocles says Prometheus brought fire from heaven in a stalk of fennel. The plant he had in mind is supposed to be *Ferula communis*, because the pith in the stem will take fire and burn slowly, and primitive peoples used it to carry fire from place to place.

June 28, 1964

FEEDING THE BIRDS

I wonder whether anyone has written a history of bird feeding, and how far back the practice goes. All the way, I suppose, but the earliest description I have come across is Miss Mitford's in *Our Village*: "We used, before we lived in a street, to fix a little board outside the parlour window, and cover it with bread crumbs in the hard weather. It was quite delightful to see the pretty things come and feed, to conquer their shyness, and do away with their mistrust.

"First came the more social tribes, 'the robin redbreast and the wren', cautiously, suspiciously, picking up a crumb on the wing, with the little keen bright eye on the window; then they would stop for two pecks; then stay till they were satisfied. The shyer birds, tamed by their example came next; and at last one saucy fellow of a black bird used to tap his yellow bill against the window for more."

But a table for the birds must have been unusual in the early part of the nineteenth century, for Miss Mitford says, "I wonder that the practice is not more general."

In *Natives Preferred*, Caroline Dormon says, "the simplest way to feed birds is to plant their food." She lists native plants to provide for them the year around, but she says that a supplement of nuts, suet, and cornbread is needed in winter. Mulberry, wild cherry, and elder fruit in summer, and pokeberries last until late in the year.

Birds like the native beautyberry, *Callicarpus americana*, but Caroline says they prefer the white-fruited form to the common purple. As soon as the leaves fall, she says, robins strip the berries from the dogwoods. We don't seem to have many robins around my garden, but the dogwood berries certainly disappear very quickly.

Caroline says the winter huckleberry, *Vaccinium arboreum* (which we call sparkleberry), is a standby for winter, as the fruits hang on until spring. But they don't do that in my garden. They are gone before the leaves fall. And so are those of the blackhaw, *Viburnum prunifolium*.

Caroline mentions some trees I had not thought of as providing food for birds. One is the hackberry. Its berries are small and dry, but very sweet and much appreciated (I think she must eat them herself); and another is the black gum. There used to be a black gum beside our front porch when we lived in Raleigh. I don't remember its fruit or visiting birds, but I do remember that the bright and shining red leaves used to begin to fall in August. Then my grandmother, who hated the cold, would pick them up, saying sorrowfully, "Summer is over already."

In January and February, Caroline says, bird watchers would stand under a sweetgum. "At this time the prickly burrs open, spilling out the seeds, and flocks of tiny finches cling upside-down and feast. They constantly give out a little long-drawn 'swe-e-et.' "

Berried evergreens offer shelter as well as food. Yaupon, *Ilex vomitoria*, is one of the best of these, for as Caroline says it provides both board and lodging. "Once," she wrote, "I saw a thing that delighted me. Freezing rain had sheathed a Yaupon in ice, but the little birds had found a way inside. The next morning cat tracks in the snow went round and round the bush, but they did not find the door. The small occupants were snug inside."

It is just as well to keep some insects on hand for a varied diet. I hope it is borers that a pair of hairy woodpeckers is industriously digging out of the trunks of my standard cherry laurel. Whatever it is the myrtle warbler is after it too, and pecks it on the wing. The warbler gets its name from its fondness for the bayberry, *Myrica cerifera*—also called myrtle.

The woodpeckers have been working on the trunks of the firethorns. Firethorns are excellent for food and shelter, but I don't think the birds will benefit from this year's crop of berries. Before Christmas, squirrels began to strip the bright red berries from the heavily laden branches of *Pyracantha koidsumii* and now they are starting on the orange-berried kinds. I am afraid the cedar waxwings will go hungry.

January 30, 1966

HONEY

My friend Jack Mitchell, who keeps bees in his garden in Fairmont, North Carolina, says the epicure can always tell where the bees take the nectar. He thinks the most beautiful and delicious honey of all is taken in early spring when the woodland flowers are in bloom, or later when the fruit trees are at their height. If the honey is dark and syrupy, with a flavor of nicotine, he knows that the farmers are not the only ones who have been at work in the tobacco fields. Mr. Mitchell sent me the catalogue of the S & L Honey Center, which offers honey from all over the world, but I doubt whether any of their wares can equal Robeson County honey, fresh from the hive.

Mr. Cook, a mountain beekeeper, doesn't think any honey fit to eat unless it comes straight from the bees. Mr. Cook brought me some of his sourwood honey when I was at Beech Mountain this summer. I asked him why it is so rare, and he said it is because the sourwood trees are being destroyed. No sourwood honey from North Carolina appears on the Honey Center's list, but they offer one from South Carolina. Their North Carolina honeys are pine honeydew ("often recommended by local doctors for the rare sugar it contains") and sparkleberry, *Vaccinium arboretum*, a major honey plant in the Sandhills. They also stock a gall berry honey from Georgia. Gall berry, *Ilex glabra*, is one of the most valuable bee plants of North Carolina.

Among the imported honeys I found several from Australia, made from the nectar of eucalyptus flowers. According to the catalogue these are frequently used for medicinal purposes, and "the belief in the anti-tuberculotic effect of eucalyptus honey is worldwide." If it tastes like the foliage of eucalyptus, I don't think I would like that kind of honey.

Honey is good for the throat. Mixed with Jamaica rum it is as soothing as rock-and-rye for a cough. The center says that Caruso always made it a point before singing to take a spoonful of Abrossoli's Ulmo, "a satiny, creamy, golden honey from Chile."

Bees are partial to blue flowers, especially borage and rosemary. Honey derived entirely from borage has a poor taste, but the rosemary honey of Narbonne, France, is the most celebrated of all, and is said to have been Caesar's favorite. Many other herbs are bee plants, but especially those of the mint family: the giant hyssop (*Agastache foeniculum*), catnip, balm and bergamot, horehound, hyssop and germander, lavender, the mints, sage, and thyme.

All summer there is a murmur of innumerable bees when the thyme is in bloom between the stone of my garden steps, but no one has ever been stung in spite of the number of small, bare feet that go up and down. I wonder what becomes of my honey. It is probably stored somewhere in a hollow tree.

The Honey Center lists two items from the Mediterranean that have long been famous. One is a honey harvested from the bee-alluring thyme of Mt. Hymettus, called food for the gods, the other from the nectar of the strawberry tree.

The strawberry tree is the *Arbutus* of the *Georgics*, which Virgil says should be brought from the mountains and planted near the hives. I grow *Arbutus* in my garden because the flowers are like little pearls, and they bloom in November; but I don't think that the bees have ever found them. *Arbutus*, sparkleberry, and heather are all fine bee plants, but honey harvested from some members of the heath family is more or less poisonous. Mountain laurel, *rhododendron*, and some sorts of *Pieris* must be kept away from the hives, and recently it has been reported that people have been poisoned by honey harvest from the flowers of yellow jessamine [*Gelsemium sempervirens*].

Virgil warned beekeepers against planting yew near the hives, and the ancients believed that honey from box flowers would drive men mad. But a poison plant does not always produce poisoned nectar. One of the rarities of the Honey Center is a poison-oak honey from Oregon.

August 23, 1959

ORGANIC GARDENING

My friend Ellen Flood, who lives in Connecticut, likes to take trips with the Organic Garden Club. Not long ago she went with them to visit the Brookside Nurseries where she found such a fascinating collection of compost heaps that she was moved to write me a lyrical letter about them.

"One of them, only a year old," Ellen wrote, "looked like velvet. I've seen nothing to compare with it outside of England. I was made to feel that I could have one just like it, if I fed it twice a year with natural fertilizer, and went back to a hand mower."

When the tour was over Ellen asked for a catalogue for me. The nurseryman said, "Is she an organic gardener?" Ellen said, "Yes, but she's not a fanatic."

"Whereupon he smiled and said, 'Then I'll give you a brochure for her. I like to deal with middle-of-the-roaders.' "

The brochure arrived at the same time as the *New Yorker* (June 16) with "The Silent Spring," the first of three articles by Rachel Carson. After reading about the "Silent Spring," and I wish every man, woman and child would read it, I was even more organically inclined than usual.

The brochure begins with a quotation, "As civilized man marches across the face of the earth a desert is left in his footprints," and continues with sentiments that would please Miss Carson: "In medicine, present day miracle cures are from the fungi of the soil. But in the raising of food, farmers sterilize and poison this same soil life as undesirable. In so-called sanitation, public health authorities demand costly incineration of organic wastes, while gardeners and home builders find it increasingly difficult and expensive to purchase organic matter diversified enough to build the soil's fertility."

In his zeal for restoring fertility to the earth, Brookside is trying "to alert health authorities to better sanitation of our garbage disposal and to demonstrate to the taxpayer the possibilities of making salable commodities of mulches and composts from almost all of the city or town waste and garbage collections. Make these municipal plants self-supporting instead of a tax burden."

When the State Health Department of Connecticut challenged the Brookside statement, that garbage ground up by a machine of the Somat type (whatever that is) loses its odor almost immediately, does not attract animals or support vermin, and makes fertile soil after a few weeks in the compost pile, their test compost passed the test at the state laboratories, and a committee was appointed to investigate Brookside methods.

The committee consisted of "State Health Department personnel, sanitation engineers, and three members of the town's Board of Selectmen." After their investigation the compost was approved. Brookside now hopes "to be instrumental in introducing an amendment to Connecticut's State Sanitary Code Regulation No. 104. This amendment will recognize composting by aerobic bacterial action for towns and cities to follow.

"If this story serves to help you create interest in your town, we feel this page will have contributed much toward conservation and organic gardening." In spite of the findings of the health department, Ellen says the garbage compost piles smelled awful; but it seems to me that instead of hauling off our garden trash the city might give it back. After their machines (Somat or whatever) have chewed it up, I would dearly love to keep all those branches of climbing rose, trees, and shrubs that I put out this summer. I would then have room for it.

If you still have any doubts about the Brookside method, maybe you will remember the lawns that they made for the 1938 World's Fair from the salt water muck of Flushing Meadows, with only the addition of humus and sand; or their exhibit, at the 1957 International Flower Show, of a garden and lawn growing "on man-made soil from city dump wastes."

August 5, 1962

PRUNING

Pruning is an art and a science. The rules are simple, but putting them into practice requires skill and judgment. Looking around, I gather that almost everyone leaves the job to an unskilled yardman with years of inexperience. The purposes of pruning are to encourage new growth by cutting out old wood, to open the center of the plant to light and air, to make it more compact and shapely by heading back the ends of the branches, and to make it flower and fruit more freely.

Old wood is thinned by cutting a small branch back to its base, or a large one back to the main stem or trunk. Hold the blade next to the part that is being left, and make a close, clean cut parallel to the stem or branch, leaving no stub, split, or torn bark. When heading back the end of a branch, cut just above a bud, cutting as close as possible without injuring it. Let the cut slope away from the bud, or cut above a twig that turns outward.

Sometimes shrubs that have become crowded need to have a few main stems cut out all the way to ground. It is better to take them out completely than to cut them partway, leaving new growth to come out from old stubs. Some shrubs will grow again from the roots after all of the top has been cut off. Box, privet, lilac, and forsythia are said to do this, and there is a good chance that rhododendron will recover.

Last summer, Laurustinus [*Viburnum tinus*] and pineapple guava [*Acca sellowiana*] that had been killed to the ground came up again and grew to about five feet. Nandina and mahonia will grow back, but it is better to take out a few stems each spring. Every year, when the freezes are over, lespedeza and butterfly bush [*Buddleia*] should be cut back to within a foot of the ground.

In late winter or early spring prune other summer-flowering shrubs: crape myrtle, althea, vitex, hydrangea, and the late flowering spiraeas. Prune spring-flowering shrubs as soon as they have bloomed: January jessamine, flowering almond, Japanese quince, forsythia, pearl bush, mock orange, *Viburnum carlesii*, deutzia, spring flowering spiraeas, and weigela. There is disagreement as to the pruning of lilacs, but I believe the best advice is to take out a few suckers each spring, and cut out some of the oldest stems in order to give the new wood room to grow.

Prune broad-leaved evergreens in spring just before growth starts. If they are allowed to grow naturally they need only enough cutting to keep them full and shapely. In summer, after the new wood hardens it may need further clipping. Some gardeners prune broad-leaved evergreens in summer, and this is all right if a light trimming is all that they need. The main point is to leave the lower branches longer than those above them so that the shrub will be well furnished all the way to the ground.

The books say that a shrub that needs cutting back to keep it in bounds is in the wrong place. Nevertheless, it is not always possible to find one of the exact size and shape for every spot, and if a plant is likely to get too big, control should begin when it is young.

Dead or diseased wood can be cut out at any season. When the leaves are down it is easier to see where to prune, and when new growth begins it is easier to tell live wood from dead.

Some say that no trees should be cut into when the sap is rising, but the general opinion at present seems to be that very early spring is the best time for pruning most trees and shrubs, as wounds heal more quickly then than at any other time. Maples, birches, yellow wood, and other trees that bleed freely should be pruned in early summer as soon as the leaves are fully out.

January 15, 1961

PRUNING SHOULD BE DONE EVERY DAY

I think of pruning as an art, and it is one that I have never mastered or even made much progress in, though I have been studying and practicing it for many years. Whatever tree, shrub, or rose bush I take in hand seems to have no resemblance to the diagrams in the manuals. The trouble, I think, is that my heart is not in it. I do not really like to prune.

In order to reduce pruning to a minimum, I have tried to put each plant in a place where its ultimate size will be suitable. I have not had much success. For example, having read that *Prunus incisa* is a tree up to twenty feet tall, or more often a bush six to eighteen feet, I thought I had given it plenty of room. I did not know that it would have a spread of thirty feet, and even more, I am sure, if I had not begun at a late date to cut it back severely. Fortunately it is one cherry that will tolerate drastic pruning.

I have now come to the conclusion that in a garden, especially a small one, pruning is the most important chore of all. Mr. John Baumgardt, who has written a manual, *How to Prune Almost Everything*, seems to agree with me. He writes there is pruning to be done every day in the year, even if it is just cutting off spent flowers, and that no one should ever go into the garden without first picking up the clippers.

We learn from the Japanese, he writes, the importance of careful grooming: "In their gardens pruning is continuous, carried on with thumbnail and fingernail. Every shoot is nipped at just the proper time to give plants the well groomed look so seldom seen in our western gardens. Perhaps the term 'green thumb' came from the color of the pinching fingers of a good gardener. His thumb is indeed green, stained from plant juices as he frequently interrupts his other chores to nip back or pinch off a spent blossom.

"You can avoid a lot of sawing, looping, and hand-pruning if you practice pinching. When a bud breaks, it makes a stem with leaves along it. You can wait until it is tough and woody to cut it back and induce branching, or you can pinch out the tip when the shoot has expanded to two or three leaves, and thus alter growth at that point.

"Pinching involves tender, rapidly growing tissues that can heal quickly with never a stub or scar. Nobody is going to pinch a barberry hedge rather than shear it, but surely nobody should shear a rhododendron when growth is so easily controlled by pinching out terminal buds as shoots reach desired length. By all means become a pincher. Save your cutting tools for old wood and big jobs like hedges. As you walk about the garden, pinch out new growth here and there to control the development and shape your plants. And this applies not only to woodies but to your perennials and annuals as well."

All gardeners learn sooner or later the importance of early and constant pruning; but there must be few gardens in which some fast-growing shrubs do not, at some time, get out of hand, especially pyracanthas. Prune them hard when young, Mr. Baumgardt writes, and heavily when older. If old bushes get tall and scraggly, cut the trunks back to the ground, one trunk each season. The ice, I think I have said before, settled this for me. The pyracantha that has taken nearly twenty years to hide a telephone pole is now about to start from the beginning.

In addition to instruction on routine pruning, and special techniques such as root pruning, and training plants as espaliers, topiaries, and bonsai, Mr. Baumgardt gives specific directions for pruning 300 species: trees, shrubs, vines, and perennials. As this includes plants for the whole country, both warm and cold climates, 300 is not "almost everything." Even so I am amazed, as I check various plants as the season advances, to find how many it does cover. So far, *Raphiolepis* is the only one I didn't find. I suppose not even Mr. Baumgardt knows how to prune *Raphiolepis*.

I have put this book on the shelf (and I have come to the point of having to take a book off every time I put one on), and I shall be referring to it again.

February 25, 1968

HISTORIC FLOWER ARRANGEMENTS

I should think that all gardeners and all Americans, whether flower arrangers or not, would be interested in *Flowers at the White House* by Ruth Montgomery. It is a picture book with entertaining captions and an introduction that gives glimpses of the history of flower arrangement.

Thomas Jefferson did the arranging himself. His idea of house decorations was filling the windows with rare plants. Mrs. Pierce ordered formal bouquets "as big around as a breakfast plate, and invariably composed of half a dozen wired japonicas ornamented with a pretentious cape of marvelously wrought lace-paper." At every plate, at every state dinner, one of these was laid. Decorations were lavish when the Lincolns came to the White House, but after the death of her little boy, Mrs. Lincoln would not allow any flowers at all.

President Buchanan built an "elegant conservatory," and more greenhouses were added. The Marine band played sentimental music while guests wandered among hothouse flowers. After the Civil War the flowers became more elaborate and more expensive. President Arthur is said to have spent $1,500 from his own pocket on flowers for a single state dinner.

When President Cleveland was married at the White House, "floral national shields were fastened to every column in the East Room, the fireplaces in all state rooms were solidly banked with flowers, mirrors were wreathed, and mantles were banked with floral monograms of the bride and groom."

In contrast to the Polks who would not even use flowers from the government greenhouses, Mrs. Harrison had florists fill the White House with orchids, and for one party they crammed into the East Room 5,000 plants: "2,000 azaleas, 800 carnations, 300 roses, 300 tulips, 900 hyacinths, 400 lilies-of-the-valley, 200 bouvardias, 100 sprays of asparagus fern, 40 poinsettias, and 200 small ferns." After the turn of the century the display of flowers was less lavish, but the potted palms remained and the decorations were conventional.

It was Mrs. Kennedy who brought order and simplicity to the flower room. Vases were assigned to each room, plans were made for the whole year, and color photographs made of arrangements for state occasions. The photographs were made as models for the future. They are used to illustrate the book. Mrs. Kennedy wanted fresh flowers in every room at all times, but she did not want many, and she did not allow them on the mantelpiece. She liked garden flowers arranged in a loose natural manner, suitable for a large country house, but simple enough for any establishment. In the photographs there are lilies, lilacs and roses, daisies, stocks, sweet Williams, dahlias, tulips and cornflowers, and lots and lots of chrysanthemums. The flowers in the White House are what anyone might have, but the vases are not. Treasures long locked in cupboards are now filled with flowers: President Monroe's bronze-doré basket; a Roman marble urn of the eighteenth century, acquired by Mrs. Theodore Roosevelt; a tureen, an urn, a bowl, and a compotier of the Biddle vermeil; a pair of Sèvres cachepots; lovely Chinese bowls and a tole monteith.

One of the most delightful arrangements is a handful of white daisies in a Chinese mug. I like to think of President Kennedy's stopping in the flower shop to ask the names of the flowers, and being amazed to learn that cyclamens are not orchids. The staff always kept a supply of blue bachelor's buttons for the lapel of his dinner jacket.

There are two photographs of Mrs. Kennedy's garden behind the East Wing. At one end, under what seems to be a large magnolia, there is a graceful white pergola paved with brick, and furnished with comfortable wicker chairs. In the square beds bordering the lawn there are small trees clipped as standards. The beds are edged with low evergreen hedges, and filled with flowers for cutting, and herbs for the kitchen. It is a garden anyone could have.

May 4, 1969

BOUQUET CARRIED MESSAGES

In the nineteenth century no young lady could afford to be without a dictionary for interpreting the language of flowers because a simple bouquet might carry a significant message. Every bud, every leaf had its meaning, and by a combination of blossoms love was declared, vows were exchanged and sometimes hearts were broken.

I like to mull over these sentimental volumes and to imagine the romances they brought to happy endings, but I never thought, until a murder story called *The Estate of the Beckoning Lady* [by Margery Allingham] came my way, of their being connected with the annals of crime.

The Beckoning Lady, a pub in an English village, is the scene of three murders that take place in a short space of time. The bouquet which seems to be connected with them is given to a small boy who takes it to his father, Mr. Campion.

"For you," he says.

"A curious collection," his father observes. "Who sent it?"

"A man," the little boy answers, and that is all they can get out of him.

Amanda, the boy's mother, thinks it must be a message. "Cypress means death," she says. Charles Luke, the divisional detective chief inspector who happens to be present, corrects her. Cypress does not mean death, it means mourning. The chief says he is an expert in this sort of thing, and taking over the greenery, he explains that the California poppy means "do not refuse me." And the pink means "make haste."

"Mourning, do not refuse me, make haste . . . it sounds like the old story. Someone is broke again." But there are other sprigs in the bunch, and he does not know their meaning.

Amanda goes to the bookshelf and takes down a volume belonging to her aunt. It is white, with gold lettering: *The Language and Sentiment of Flowers*, published by Ballantyne and Hanson, London, 1863. She finds that the rhododendron means "danger, beware!" and that the monkshood's message is "a deadly foe is here."

The sender of the bouquet proves to be an insurance agent. Since he requires an answer, Mr. Campion gathers from field and garden a snapdragon, a sprig of mint, a bulb of meadow saffron (it is not the season for flowers), a twig of elder, and a petunia. He asks the chief inspector to deliver these for him, and as he hands them over, he murmurs, "I should have added a red red rose."

"Which means love," the chief inspector says, and reads the message that he has been given to deliver: "No. I declare against you. Beware of excess zeal. Keep your promise. That's a funny message to an insurance company."

"Not at all," Mr. Campion says. He explains that what his correspondent wanted to know is whether one of the deaths is a suicide, in which case his company will not have to pay the benefit. Mr. Campion is sure that it is murder, so he is telling the agent that his company will have to pay up.

Flower messages are clever, and may serve a purpose if sender and receiver consult the same authority. There were many dictionaries of the language of flowers, however, and they did not always agree. In *Flora's Dictionary, by A Lady*, Fielding Lucas, Baltimore, 1861, I find that the petunia means "keep your promise," but the snapdragon does not mean "no." It stands for presumption. And it is the oleander, not the rhododendron, that means "beware."

It might be a very serious matter if correspondents consulted different dictionaries and their authorities were not in agreement; if, for example, a lover sent his lady a branch of ivy under the impression that it was a token of lasting friendship and she accepted it as a proposal of marriage.

June 23, 1963

POMANDERS

I had almost forgotten about pomanders when Mary Hobbs asked me how to make one. We always made them at Christmas, but when I looked them up in Rosetta Clarkson's invaluable *Herb Journal* I found that the proper time to present them is on New Year's Day.

The original pomanders were scented balls or beads made of rare and costly perfumes, and worn on chains or bracelets—Queen Elizabeth wore a pomander girdle. Men wore them, too, and Julia sent one to Herrick:

> To me my Julia lately sent
> A Bracelet richly Redolent;
> The beads I kist, but most
> Lov'd her
> That did perfume the
> Pomander.

The name comes from the French *pomme d'ambre*. Pomanders were called amber apples because the balls were shaped like apples, and the chief ingredient was ambergris. The kinds that Queen Elizabeth and Herrick wore were expensive and complicated to make, but Mary Hobbs had in mind pomanders made by sticking cloves in some fruit—an apple, an orange, or a quince. Mrs. Clarkson says she used limes and lemons too, for variety in shape and size and scent.

Apples are much easier to stick, but oranges are more aromatic and more symmetrical. You must choose a thin-skinned orange, and it had better be small unless you have infinite time, patience, and plenty of cloves.

You begin at the end away from the stem, and stick the cloves in as closely as you can, going round and round until the whole orange is covered. Mrs. Clarkson first made holes with a darning needle, but I should think this would take more time, though you might have the needle handy to help out with some of the cloves with dull points. Mary Hobbs says she gets on better by making the holes first with a toothpick.

When there is no room for another clove, you can consider the pomander finished, or you can make it even more fragrant by dusting it with orris powder, or powdered cinnamon or nutmeg or a combination of these. We used to add enough cinnamon to the orris root to make it a pale café au lait, and then add a little mace. The cloves preserve the orange, so that it never decays, though it shrinks and grows lighter. The perfume lasts for several years.

Elizabeth and Herrick used their pomanders when they had to go among crowds to cover up odors and to ward off infections. We put ours on the shelves to scent the sheets and pillowcases. Or they can be hung in closets to make clothes smell good and keep the moths away. They are nice to keep in a bowl just for their fragrance or supplied with a ribbon to hang them up. The ribbon was always red and I think we attached it to a small nail that we stuck in the stem end of the orange.

January 11, 1959

CREATURES ADD TO A GARDEN

No one brought up on Benjamin Bunny, Squirrel Nutkin, Timmie Willie, Mr. Jeremy Fisher, and Mr. Alderman Ptolemy Tortoise could possibly be indifferent to the creatures of the garden. I think of them all as personal friends, even though I have had to acknowledge that some are very destructive.

Mr. Jeremy Fisher and the Alderman are on the gardener's side—at least it is said that a toad is worth twenty dollars a year, and I suppose a frog helps, too. In my garden there are more frogs than toads, as we have a pool, and their evening chorus is such a din I have been expecting the neighbors to complain, but all I have heard them say is they like it.

Last summer I never saw my toad—or toads. I have never been sure whether it is the same or several. He usually startles me by hopping out from under a plant when I am weeding the border, and I think he lives in the rock wall. If toads are really so valuable I think something should be done to attract them, but I have never known what they like.

Turtles eat insects though the Alderman brought a salad with him in a string bag when he came to dinner with Mr. Jeremy Fisher. Some seasons a great many turtles wander through our garden. Last year I didn't see a single one. I wish they would stay, but they never do unless they fall into the pool and can't get out. They always pass through in the same direction, coming from the West, going to the East, and I have never seen the same one twice, though I have clearly marked their backs with paint. Lafcadio Hearn says that in Japan turtles are marked "servant of Kompira" when caught. Then they are given a drink of sake, which they are supposed to like, and sent on their way.

Last year two rabbits made their home with me. They toured the garden twice a day, once early in the morning, and again in mid-afternoon. They ate a great many petunias and some things much more valuable. Still, they did no permanent damage, and when one disappeared I was very sad. The other stayed all winter and when it snowed I put out lettuce leaves and carrots, but he wouldn't eat them and by spring he was gone as well. This year I have a new one. I have read that rabbits are so fond of soybeans that they are not likely to bother other things when a patch of their favorite food is planted for them. I have also read that they avoid plants dusted with powdered aloes.

In my garden chipmunks are the most serious raiders. They have almost annihilated the collection of winter crocus that I have spent ten years building up. This spring they ate my only two corms of a very rare and beautiful white one that cannot be replaced. I am afraid I am going to have to make a choice between chipmunks and crocus.

None of the books I have tell how to discourage these little animals. I certainly wish them no harm for they are so gay as they chase each other, or the birds, up and down the gravel paths, or scurry in and out of their holes in the rock walls.

February 5, 1961

Index

Abeliophyllum distichum (white forsythia), 112
Abies (fir)
  A. nordmanniana (caucasian fir), 108
Acca sellowiana (pineapple guava), 218
Acer
  A. davidii, 91
  A. floridanum (southern sugar maple), 28
  A. grosseri var. *hersii*, 91
  A. pennsylvanicum, 91
  A. saccharum, 89
Aesculus (buckeye)
  A. × *carnea*, 99
  A. hippocastanum, 99
  A. parviflora, 35, 99, 115–16
  A. pavia, 99
Agastache foeniculum (giant hyssop), 215
Ageratum, 41, 42
Ajuga, 145
  A. 'Metallica Crispa' (syn. *A. brockbank*), 145
Akebia quinata, 142–43, 147
Albizia julibrissin, 102
Alchemilla mollis (syn. *Alchemilla vulgar*), 135
Allium
  A. christophii (syn. *A. albopilosum*), 22
  A. gigantum, 22
Alstroemeria psittacina, 26
Alyssum, 41–42, 60
  A. saxatile, 24, 171
× *Amarcrinum memoria-corsii* (syn. *Amarcrinum howardii*), 19, 82
Amaryllis
  A. belladonna, 165
  A. johnsonii, 67
Amelanchier (serviceberry)
  A. alnifolia var. *semi-integrifolia* (syn. *A. cusickii*), 96
  A. asiatica, 96
  A. canadensis, 95
  A. × *grandiflora* (apple serviceberry), 95
  A. laevis, 95, 96
  A. ovalis, 96
  A. stolonifera, 96
  A. vulgaris, 96

Anchusa myosotidiflora, 60
Anemone
A. blanda, 69
A. coronaria, 66
Animals, 181–82, 213–14, 226–27
Apricot, Japanese, 3, 6, 13
Aquilegia vulgaris, 23
Arabis, 60
Arbutus, 10, 216
Argyreia speciosa (woolly morning glory), 40
Aronia arbutifolia (chokecherry), 62
Arum maculatum, 204
Asafetida, 211–12
Asarina barclaiana, 41
Ash, 187–89
Asparagus virgatus, 63
Asperula odorata, 134–35
Aspidistra, 152–53
Asteromoea indica, 51, 52
Aurinia saxatilis (syn. *Alyssum saxatile*), 24, 171
Azalea vittata, 13

Bamboo, 11–13
Banana shrub, 13, 69
Begonia grandis (hardy begonia), 19, 21
Berckmans, Prosper Julius Alphonse, 177–79
Betula
B. alleghaniensis (syn. *B. lutea*), 90
B. lenta, 90
B. nigra (river birch), 90
Birds, feeding of, 213–14
Black-eyed Susan, 18
Bletilla striata (syn. *B. hyacinthoides*), 57
Boltonia asteroids, 80
Bowles, E. A., 43, 54, 125–27
Boxwood, 207–8
Braswell, Laura, 103, 104, 193
Brunnera macrophylla (syn. *Amchusa myosotidiflora*), 60
Buddleia, 218
Bulbs, planting of, 65–66
Busbee, Jacques, 23, 164–65

Calliandra tweedii, 40
Callicarpus americana, 213
Calliopsis. See *Coreopsis tinctoria*
Callistemon
C. rigidus, 180
C. viminalis, 180
Calocedrus decurrens (syn. *Libocedrus decurrens*), 109
Caltha palustris, 169
Camellia, 178
C. 'Berenice Boddy', 3, 124
C. 'Dawn', 7, 9
C. × *hiemalis*, 125
C. japonica, 125, 178
C. oleifera, 123
C. saluenensis, 3, 124–25
C. sasanqua, 9, 122–23
C. × 'Williamsii' (*C. salunenensis* × *C. japonica*), 124
Campanula poscharskyana, 38, 162
C. divaricata, 38
Cardiospermum (balloon vine), 138
Carex fraseri (syn. *C. cymophyllus*), 39
Carolina jessamine, 6, 137, 147, 216
Catharanthus rosea, 17
Cedar, 109, 190
Cedrus deodara, 109
Cenizo (syn. *Leucophyllum frutescens* and *L. texanum*), 1, 180
Cercis siliquastrum, 204
Cereus, 58–59
Chaenomeles
'Apple Blossom', 110
'Pink Lady', 4

Chamaecyparis
C. obtusa, 172
C. pisifera 'Boulevard', 172
C. thyoides (white cedar), 62
Chimonanthus (wintersweet), 83
C. praecox (wintersweet), 7
C. p. 'Lutea', 84
Chinese fir, 109, 194
Christianity
Christian year, 192–93
Passiontide, flowers of, 203–4
Rogation days, 208–10
Trinity, flowers of, 201–2
Christmas rose, 9, 54–55
Christmas trees
legend and lore of, 197–99
with international themes, 199–200
Cichorium intybus (chicory), 33
Clarkson, Elizabeth, 3, 24, 26, 83, 98, 149, 151, 156–57, 180–81
Clematis, 48–50, 140–42
C. alpina, 48
C. armandii, 49
C. cirrhosa, 8, 49
C. *cirrhosa* var. *balearica*, 49
C. 'Henryi', 30, 138, 141
C. × *jackmanii*, 30, 141
C. lanuginosa, 48, 141
C. montana var. *rubens*, 31, 48
C. patens, 48
C. tangutica, 31
C. terniflora (syn. *C. paniculata*), 50, 138
C. texensis, 49, 138
C. vitacella, 48
Cleome hassleriana (syn. *C. spinosa*), 42–43
Clerodendrum trichotomum, 19–20
Clethra acuminata (summersweet), 20
Cleyera, 13
Cobaea scandens (cup-and-saucer vine), 10, 139
Colchicum autumnale, 68, 183
Colette (Sidonie-Gabrielle Colette), garden of mother of , 167–69
Coreopsis 'Baby Sun', 21
C. tinctoria (syn. *Calliopsis*), 25, 41
Corms, planting of, 65–66
Cornus
C. alba 'Atrosanguinea', 91
C. florida, 97
C. sanguinea, 97
Corylus avellana 'Contorta', 125–26
Cotoneaster, 1
C. bullatus, 86
C. lacteus, 1, 11
C. mairei (syn. *C. wardii*), 11
C. microphyllus, 11
C. salicifolius, 86
Crape myrtle, 86–87
Crataegus monogyma 'Biflora' (syn. *C. m.* var. *praecox*), 190
Crinum 'Herald', 1, 72
C. 'Cecil Houdyshel', 34
C. moorei 'Frank Leach', 77
C. moorei var. *Schmidtii*, 82
Crocosmia 'Rheingold', 66, 72
Crocus
C. imperati, 9, 67
C. laevigatus 'Fontenayi', 8
C. ochroleucus, 27
C. sieberi, 67
C. speciosus, 81
C. speciosus 'Albus', 81
Crown imperial, 73–75, 203
Cunninghamia lanceolata, 109, 194
Cyclamen
C. hederifolium (syn. *C. neopolitanum*), 28, 68
C. repandum, 183
Cytomium falcatum, 153

Daffodil. See *Narcissus*
Danae racemosa (Alexandrian laurel), 35
Dandelion, 136–37
Daphne odora, 7
Delphinium belladonna, 164
Dianthus deltoids (maiden pinks), 60
Dogwood, 91, 97
Dolichos lablab (hyacinth bean), 138
Dormon, Caroline, 28, 76–81, 84–85, 88, 96, 179–82, 213
Dusty miller
  'Diamond', 22
  'Silver Queen', 22
Dwarf conifers, 171–72

Elaeagnus pungens, 20
  E. p. 'Fruitlandii', 20
Elizabeth II, 60, 190–91
Erica carnea (winter heath), 5
Erythrina crista-galli, 39, 170
Eschscholzia (California poppy), 23
Eucalyptus, 215
  E. camaldulensis (syn. *E. rostrata*), 1, 69
  E. pulverulenta, 100, 101
Eucomis bicolor, 72
  E. punctata, 72
Euphorbia splendens, 204
Exochorda (pearl bush)
  E. giraldi var. *wilsonii*, 111
  E. racemosa, 111, 112

Farrer, Reginald, 3, 111–12, 173
Fern, holly, 153
Ferula
  F. assa-foetida, 212
  F. communis, 212
Ficus repens, 138
Fir, 108
Firethorn. See *Pyracantha*
Flower arrangement, in White House, 221–22
Forsythia, 3
Foster, Lincoln, 38–39
Fothergilla major, 35
Fountains, 159–60
Fritillaria imperialis, 73–75, 203
Fruitland Nursery, 6, 20, 100, 101, 107, 109, 118, 124, 141, 177–79

Galanthus elwesii, 67
Galium odoratum (syn. *Aserula odorata*), 134–35
Gelsemium sempervirens 'Pride of Augusta', 6, 137, 147, 216
Geum urbanum, 202
Ginkgo biloba, 88
Giridlian, J. N., 1, 56–58, 63–64
Gladiolus, 73
  G. tristis, 57
Gleditsia triacanthos (locust)
  G. t. 'Morain', 89, 102–3
  G. t. 'Sunburst', 103
Globularia cordifolia, 148
Gotelli, William, dwarf conifer collection of, 171–72
Groundcovers, 144–49
Guava, 218

Habranthus brachyandrus, 82
Hackberry, 213
Halesia monticola, 89
Hamamelis (witch hazel)
  H. mollis, 5, 92
  H. virginiana, 84
Hawthorn, 16, 189–90
  English, 190
Hayward, Wyndham, 2, 77–78
Hechenbleikner, Herbert, 61, 62, 86, 87
Hedychium coronarium, 82

Hellebore (Lenten roses), 6, 13–14, 55
H. argutifolius (syn. *H. corsicus*), 54
H. atrorubens (syn. *H. atropurpureus*), 54
H. foetidus, 53, 55–56
H. × *hybridus* (syn. *H. orientalis*)
H. lividus, 54
H. niger (Christmas rose), 9, 54–55
H. viridis (green hellebore), 53
Hemerocallis 'Sonata', 34
Hepatica Americana (syn. *H. triloba*), 201
Herbs, 132–34
dandelion, 136–37
tansy, 203
of Trinity, 201–2
winter, 8–10
Heuchera × *brizoides*, 21
Hippeastrum × *johnsonii*, 67
Holly. See *Ilex*
Holly fern, 153
Honey, 214–16
Hosta
H. lancifolia (syn. *H. lanceolata*), 19
H. plantaginea (August lilies), 21
H. tardiflora, 19
Hunt, William Lanier, 22, 28, 182–83
Hydrangea, 121–22
H. × *anthoneura* 'Thomas Hogg', 115, 121
H. aspera macrophylla (syn. *H. a.* ssp. *strigosa*), 121
H. macrophylla, 114, 121
H. paniculata 'Grandiflora', 122
H. quercifolia, 114, 121
H. villosa (syn. *H. aspera*,), 121
Hydrocotyle rotundifolia, 149
Hylocereus undatus, 59
Hymenocallis, 77

Ilex (holly)
I. cassine, 105, 106
I. cornuta, 86, 106
I. crenata, 106
I. decidua, 105
I. glabra, 215
I. latifolia, 105
I. opaca, 105
I. pernyi, 105
Illicium anisatum, 173
Impatiens sultani (syn. *I. walleriana*), 17
Ipheion (syn. *Triteleia iniflora*), 67
Iris
I. albicans, 32
I. cristata, 154
I. × *germanica* var. *florentina* (syn. *I. florentina*), 163
I. japonica, 154
I. pallida var. *dalmatica*, 164, 165
I. unquicularis (Algerian iris), 4, 8, 182
I. versicolor, 163
Ismene, 77
Ivy, 37, 147
'Canary Cream', 37
'Glacier', 37

Jacobinia carnea (syn. *Justica carnea*), 40
Japanese apricot, 3, 6, 13
Jekyll, Gertrude, 7, 23, 42, 119–20, 156
Juniperus (juniper), 107–8
J. chinensis 'Fruitlandii', 107
J. chinensis 'Pfitzeriana', 107
J. conferta, 107
J. horizontalis 'Plumossa', 107
J. procumbens 'Nana', 107

Juniperus (*continued*)
J. sabina 'Tamariscifolia' (syn. *J. s.* var. *tamariscifolia*), 108;
J. squamata 'Prostrata', 107
J. virginiana, 107
Justica carnea, 40

Kalimeris pinnatifida (syn. *Asteromoea indica* and *A. mongolica*), 51, 52
Koelreuteria paniculata, 88, 158
Krippendorf, Carl, 33, 161–62, 170

Lablab purpureus, 138
Lagerstroemia, 86–87
Lamium maculatum, 162
Lamm, Linda, 53, 123, 162
Landreth, David, 176–77
Language of flowers, 223–24
Lantana, 17
Larkspur, 24–25, 41
Lathyrus (sweet pea), 43–44
Laurus nobilis (bay tree), 13
Lenten roses, 6, 13–14, 55, 69, 193
Leucojum
L. aestivum, 67, 68, 69
L. a. 'Gravetye', 69
L. var. *pulchellum*, 68
L. vernum, 69
Leucophyllum frutescens, 1, 180
Lilium (lily), 50–51
L. auratum, 78, 80
L. candidum (Madonna lily), 80, 81, 163
L. catesbaei, 179
L. formosanum, 51, 79, 81
L. henryi, 33–34, 80
L. longiflorum, 81
L. regale, 80
L. speciosum, 80
L. tigrinum, 80
Lily of the valley, 15
Lilyturf. See *Liriope*
Limnanthes douglasii, 22
Liriope, 89, 145–46
L. muscari 'Alba', 153
L. m. 'White Giant', 64
Lobelia, 42
Locust. See *Gleditsia triacanthos*
Lonicera fragrantissima, 93
Lophospermum erubescens, 41
Loquat, 13
Lycopodium alopecuroides (running pine), 61
Lycoris
L. albiflora, 78
L. aurea, 78, 165
L. caldwellii, 77
L. cinnabarina, 183
L. incarnata, 77
L. × *jacksoniana* (syn. *L. radiata* × *L. sprengeri*), 76
L. radiata, 75–76
L. radiata var. *pumila* (syn. *L. morrowi*), 75
L. sanguinea, 78
L. sprengeri, 77, 183
L. squamigera, 77, 78–79, 183
Lygodium japonicum (Japanese climbing fern), 8

Magnolia, 3
M. acuminata (cucumber tree), 37, 89
M. denudate, 89–90, 179
M. grandiflora, 89, 105, 191
M. liliiflora, 179
M . × *soulangiana* 'Lennei', 1, 14, 191
M. stellata (syn. *M. halleana*), 78
Malus
M. × *micromalus*, 86
M. sargentii (Sargent's crab), 110

Malvaviscus arboreus var. *drummondii*, 18
Marigold, 30
Maurandya
M. barclayana (syn. *Asarina barclaiana*), 41
M. ereubescens (syn. *Lophospermum erubescens*), 41
Mayer, Walter B. and Helen, 39, 83, 84, 101, 109, 115, 118, 121, 124, 141, 180
Mazus reptans, 147, 149
Michelia figo (banana shrub), 13, 69
Mitchella repens (partridgeberry), 147
M'Mahon, Bernard, 176–77
Montbretia, 66, 72
Myrica cerifera, 214
Myrrus communis, 13
Mythology
Greek and Roman, 185–87
Scandinavian, 187–88

Nandina, 119–20
N. domestica 'Harbour Dwarf', 35
Narcissus, 4, 66, 69–72
N. bulboscodium (hoop petticoat), 4, 6
paperwhite, 6
Nehrling, Henry, 109, 122, 178–79
Nemophila, 24
Nerine
N. bowdenii, 165
N. samiensis var. *curvifolia* (syn. *N.* 'Fothergillii')
Nichols, Beverley, 5–6, 62–63
Nierembergia rivularis, 149
Nigella damascena (love-in-a-mist), 23
Nyctocereus serpentines (syn. *Peniocereus serpentinus*), 59
Ophiopogon jaburan, 56, 63, 145, 147
O. planiscapus 'Nigrescens' (syn. *O. arabicum*) 56, 126–27
Orchis mascula, 204
Organic gardening, 216–18
Osmanthus
O. × *burkwoodii* (syn. *Osmarea*), 70
O. delavayi, 104
O. × *fortunei*, 13
O. fragrans, 3, 20, 104
O. fragans f. *aurantiacus*, 103–4
O. heterophyllus (syn. *O. ilicifolius*), 20, 104
Osmarea, 70

Pachysandra terminalis, 145, 147
Padua Botanical Garden, 166–67
Paeonia, 45–48
P. mascula, 163
P. officinalis, 163
Tree peonies, 47
Paliurus spina-christi, 204
Palmus (palm), 206–8
P. nobilis, 206
Passionflower. See *Passiflora*
Passiflora, 203, 205–6
P. × *alato-caerulea*, 40
P. caerulea, 205
P. coccinea, 206
P. trifasciata, 206
P. × *violacea*, 206
Paths and walks, design and maintenance of, 156–57
Patios, design and construction of, 158–59
Peniocereus serpentines, *59*
Pentas lanceolata, 16
Peony. See *Paeonia*
Petasites fragrans, 63
Petunia, 30
Phlox divaricata, 161

Physic Garden at Country Doctor Museum (Bailey, North Carolina), 162–63
Physostegia (false dragonhead), 19, 61
Pinckneya, 180
Pinguicula (blue butterwort), 61
Pinus (pine)
P. bungeana (lacebark pine), 91
P. strobus, 172
Platycodon (Chinese bellflowers), 21
Polygonum bistorta, 203
Pomanders, 224–26
Porana paniculata, 40
Potter, Beatrix, characters of, 226
Pruning, 1, 51, 218–21
Prunus
P. glandulosa, 110
P. humilis, 94
P. incisa, 83, 94, 219
P. lannesiana, 94
P. mume (Japanese apricot), 3, 6, 13
P. sargentii, 85, 87, 89, 94
P. serrula, 91
P. serrulata, 91,
P. serrulata 'Shirotae', 94
P. subhirtella, 83, 93
P. tomentosa, 93
P. triloba, 110, 113, 114
P. umbellata, 96
P. × yedoensis ('Yoshino' cherry), 89, 94
Pyracantha, 1, 118–19
P. coccinea 'Lalandei', 119
P. crenato-serria (syn. *P. yunnanensis*), 118
P. koidzumi (syn. *P.* 'Formosana'), 86, 118, 194, 214
Pyrus calleryana, 85, 88
Quercus (oak), 89
Q. coccinea, 89
Q. palustris, 89
Q. phellos, 89
Q. rubra, 89
Quince, 4, 10

Rhododendrum
R. prunifolium, 180
R. simsii 'Vittatum', 13
R. viscosum, 180
Rhodophiala
R. bifida, 183
R × huntiana, 183
R. spathaceum, 183
Rosa (rose)
R. alba, 163
R. banksiae 'Lady Banks', 31–32, 143–44, 164, 170
R. canina, 163
R. gallica, 163
R. rubra, 163
Rudbeckia 'Gloriosa', 25
Rumex patientia, 203
Ruscus aculeatus (butcher's broom), 35, 57, 153
R. hypoglossum, *57*

Sagina subulata 'Aurea' (syn. *S. glabra* 'Aurea'), 148
Salvia
S. clevelandii, 173
S. dorisiana, 173
S. dorrii, 17
S. leucantha, 29, 82
S. rutilans (syn. *S. elegans*), 29, 173
Sarcococca humilis, *153*
Sarracenia flava, 61
S. purpurea, 61
S. rubra, 61
Scented plants and gardens, 172–74

Schoenocaulon drummondii, 26
Scilla mischtschenkoana (syn. *S. tubergiana*), 67
S. peruviana, 57
S. siberica 'Spring Beauty', 67
Sedum
S. acre, 148
S. alboroseum, 19
S. album var. *murale*, 148
S. anglicum (syn. *S. anolicum*), 148
S. sieboldii, 162
S. spectabile, 19, 21
Selenicereus grandiflorus (syn. *S. macdonaldiaes*), 59
Semele androgyna (climbing *Ruscus*), 57
Serissa foetida, 10
Silene pendula, 24
Silverbell, 89
Smilax
S. laurifolia, 62, 140
S. smallii (syn. *S. lanceolata*), 137, 139
S. walteri, 140
Snapdragon, 30
Solanum seaforthianum, 40
Sorbaria tomentosa var. *angustifolia*, 3
Spirea
Spirea angustifolia (syn. *Sorbaria tomentosa* var. *angustifolia*), 3
S. grandiflora, 112
Spirea × arguta, 111
Sprekelia, 164
Starker, Carl, 34, 54, 194–95
Steps, design and construction of, 154–55
Sternbergia fischeriana, 4
Stigmaphyllon, 40
Syringa × persica (Persian lilac), 114
Sweet William, 21
Sweet woodruff, 134–35

Tanacetum coccineum (painted daisy), 60
Tansy, 203
Tecoma stans (yellow elder), 2
Terraces, design and construction of, 158–59
Tetrapanax papyrifer (paper plant), 40
Thalictrum flavum ssp. *glaucum*, 21
Thomas, Graham Stuart, 90–91
Thunbergia grandiflora, 40
Thymus
T. herba-barona, 149
T. serpyllum 'Coccineus', 148–49
T. vulgaris, 133
Torenia, 42
Trachelospermum asiaticum (syn. *T. divaricatum*), 138
Trillium
T. grandiflorum, 201
T. undulatum, 201
Tubers, planting of, 65–66
Tulipa clusiana, 67

Vaccinium
V. arboretum, 213, 215
V. crassifolium, 62
Vegetables, 129–32
Verbena pinnatifida (syn. *V. pulcella*), 32
Veronica filiformis, 149
Viburnum, 116–17
V. × carlcephalum, 113
V. carlesii, 9, 113, 219
V. fragrans (syn. *V. farreri*), 3, 8, 9
V. japonicum, 13, 14, 117
V. macrocephalum, 113
V. opulus, 126

Viburnum (*continued*)
V. plicatum var. *tomentosum* 'Mariesii', 113
V. × *pragense*, 116–17
V. prunifolium, 213
V. rhytidophyllum, 116–17
V. tinus, 13, 218
V. utile, 116–17
Vinca minor, 144, 147, 153
Vinca rosea, 17
Viola patrinii (Chinese violet), 26–27
V. striata, 4, 27
V. tricolor (Johnny-jump-up), 24

Washington Cathedral, 190–91
Water features, 159–60
White House, flowers and gardens at, 221–23
Windsor Great Park, Royal Gardens at, 169–70
Wing Haven, 151–52, 160
Winter heliotrope (syn. *Petasites fragrans*), 9, 62–63
Wintersweet (syn. *Chimonanthus praecox*), 7, 9
Withers, Ben, 59
Withers, Hannah, 58, 118, 139, 211
World tree, 187–89
Wreaths
Advent, 196–97
holiday, 194–95

Zelkova serrata, 88
Zephyranthes atamasca, 67, 132
Ziziphus spina-christi, 204

Elizabeth Lawrence (1904–85) was the author of *A Southern Garden*, *The Little Bulbs: A Tale of Two Gardens* (also published by Duke University Press), *Gardens in Winter*, and *Lob's Wood*, as well as many other writings for newspapers, magazines, and gardening bulletins, some of which were collected in posthumous books including *A Rock Garden in the South* and *Gardening for Love: The Market Bulletins*, both also published by Duke University Press. A graduate of Barnard College, she was the first woman to receive a degree in landscape architecture from North Carolina State College (now North Carolina State University). Lawrence received the Herbert Medal of the American Plant Life Society in 1943 and was honored by the American Horticultural Society and the National Council of State Garden Clubs for her writing.

Ann L. Armstrong is a garden lecturer and writer in Charlotte, North Carolina. She wrote the *Wing Haven Garden Journal*, a garden planning and maintenance calendar. Lindie Wilson has for twenty years lived in Elizabeth Lawrence's house in Charlotte, where she maintains the garden that Lawrence began in 1948.

Figures 1 and 7 by permission of Elizabeth Rogers and Warren Way. Figures 3, 5, and 6 by permission of The Friends of Elizabeth Lawrence. Figure 10 by permission of Wing Haven Gardens and Bird Sanctuary.

Library of Congress Cataloging-in-Publication Data

Lawrence, Elizabeth, 1904–1985.

Beautiful at all seasons : southern gardening and beyond with Elizabeth Lawrence / Elizabeth Lawrence ; edited by Ann L. Armstrong and Lindie Wilson.

p. cm.

Includes index.

ISBN-13: 978-0-8223-3887-1 (cloth : alk. paper)

1. Gardening—Southern States. I. Armstrong, Ann L. II. Wilson, Lindie. III. Title.

SB453.2.S66L379 2007

635.0975—dc22 2006027823